Horace Kallen Confronts America

MODERN JEWISH HISTORY
Henry Feingold, *Series Editor*

SELECT TITLES IN MODERN JEWISH HISTORY

American Jewish Political Culture and the Liberal Persuasion
Henry L. Feingold

Between Persecution and Participation: Biography of a Bookkeeper at J. A. Topf & Söhne
Annegret Schüle and Tobias Sowade; Penny Milbouer, trans.

Einstein's Pacifism and World War I
Virginia Iris Holmes

Jewish Libya: Memory and Identity in Text and Image
Jacques Roumani, David Meghnagi, and Judith Roumani, eds.

Leaving Russia: A Jewish Story
Maxim D. Shrayer

One Step toward Jerusalem: Oral Histories of Orthodox Jews in Stalinist Hungary
Sándor Bacskai; Eva Maria Thury, trans.

"We Are Jews Again": Jewish Activism in the Soviet Union
Yuli Kosharovsky; Stefani Hoffman, trans.; Ann Komaromi, ed.

"What! Still Alive?!": Jewish Survivors in Poland and Israel Remember Homecoming
Monika Rice

For a full list of titles in this series, visit https://press.syr.edu/supressbook-series/modern-jewish-history

Horace KALLEN Confronts America

Jewish Identity, Science, and Secularism

◆ ◆ ◆

Matthew J. Kaufman

Syracuse University Press

Syracuse, New York 13244-5290

First Edition 2019
19 20 21 22 23 24 6 5 4 3 2 1

∞ The paper used in this publication meets the minimum requirements of the American National Standard for Information Sciences—Permanence of Paper for Printed Library Materials, ANSI Z39.48-1992.

For a listing of books published and distributed by Syracuse University Press, visit www.SyracuseUniversityPress.syr.edu.

ISBN: 978-0-8156-3623-6 (hardcover)
978-0-8156-3641-0 (paperback)
978-0-8156-5469-8 (e-book)

Library of Congress Cataloging-in-Publication Data
Names: Kaufman, Matthew J., author
Title: Horace Kallen confronts America : Jewish identity, science, and secularism / Matthew J. Kaufman.
Description: First edition. | Syracuse, New York : Syracuse University Press, 2019. | Series: Modern Jewish history | Includes bibliographical references and index.
Identifiers: LCCN 2019005455 (print) | LCCN 2019006063 (ebook) | ISBN 9780815654698 (E-book) | ISBN 9780815636236 (hardcover : alk. paper) | ISBN 9780815636410 (pbk. : alk. paper)
Subjects: LCSH: Kallen, Horace Meyer, 1882–1974. | Jewish philosophy—20th century. | Philosophy. | Jews—Identity. | Cultural pluralism. | Philosophers—United States—Biography. | United States—Biography. Classification: LCC B945.K284 (ebook) | LCC B945.K284 K38 2019 (print) | DDC 191—dc23
LC record available at https://lccn.loc.gov/2019005455

Manufactured in the United States of America

◆ ◆ ◆

Contents

◆ ◆ ◆

Preface

THE QUESTION of Jewish identity is a complex one. Certainly, Judaism is widely understood to be a religion, but this definition is inadequate. Beyond the fact that the term *religion* itself must first be unpacked, and that the term's development within a Christian context has led to numerous problems with applying the term to other so-called world religions, there is also the fact that many Jews feel connected to Judaism without any feeling for religion. In addition, how Jews relate to Judaism has been, and continues to be, influenced by how non-Jews perceive it. Whether Jews perceive Jewish identity as an expression of religious affirmation or of ethnic affiliation, the conclusion that emerges from the diversity of opinions is that one may only properly speak of Judaisms, rather than a single Judaism.

Although today most American Jews accept and celebrate diverse expressions of Jewish identity, this respect for pluralism was hard-won. Just one century ago, the question of whether or not Jews were a religion, a race, or an ethnicity was hotly contested. This book tells a story about that struggle in the form of an intellectual biography of Horace M. Kallen (1882–1974). It shows how one man's quest for authenticity contributed to a gradual shift in Jewish self-perception in America and how, in turn, his struggle led to America's embrace of Kallen's well-known term *cultural pluralism*. It shows how his struggle helped to change America's self-perception into one that affirms religious and cultural pluralism—a message that seems particularly relevant today.

◆ ◆ ◆

Acknowledgments

I AM GRATEFUL to the Jacob Rader Marcus Center of the American Jewish Archives for the honor of being selected as a Lowenstein-Weiner Fellow, which allowed me to pursue research there. Rabbi Gary P. Zola, executive director; Kevin Proffitt, senior archivist; Dr. Dana Herman, managing editor and academic associate; Elisa Ho, archivist and special projects coordinator; and Nancy Hersh Dowlin, executive assistant, were all tremendously gracious and helpful. Thanks as well to archivist Gunnar Berg at the Archives of the YIVO Institute for Jewish Research for welcoming me there. I am grateful to archivist Jenny Swadosh at the New School Archives and Special Collections for her extraordinary helpfulness and for introducing me to the new Horace Kallen research files collection there. This project originated as my doctoral dissertation at York University, and I would like to thank my dissertation committee—Michael Brown, Mitch Hart, Bernie Lightman, Scott McLaren, Alexandra Rutherford, Victor Shea, and Marlene Shore—for their help. The Midwest Jewish Studies Association gave me the opportunity to work through some of my ideas at conferences. My editor, Deborah Manion, provided invaluable support and guidance. Finally, this book would not have been possible without the love and support of my family, Don and Liz Kaufman and Stephanie Todd.

Horace Kallen Confronts America

◆ ◆ ◆

Introduction

Horace M. Kallen and Authenticity

> Men can do nothing without the make-believe of a beginning . . . No retrospect will take us to the true beginning.
>
> —George Eliot, *Daniel Deronda*

THIS BOOK TRACES the career and thought of the American Jewish philosopher Horace Meyer Kallen (1882–1974), who is best known for having coined the term *cultural pluralism*, a theory of democratic cooperative discourse that affirms the inclusion of different immigrant ethnicities as distinct but equal participants in society. In the form of an intellectual biography, *Horace Kallen Confronts America* describes the heritage of scientific ideas that shaped not only Kallen's thought but that of his entire generation. It elucidates how Kallen's relationships over the course of half a century with other authors, publishers, and editors shaped his influence and legacy in social thought. It follows Kallen's growth from a radically antireligious thinker to a believer in democracy as a religion. It addresses itself to the broad question of how American Jewish identity is fashioned through social contexts and responds to scientific culture.

At the same time, this book develops the particular thesis that Kallen's Jewish identity, as unique and idiosyncratic as it was, exemplifies the modern responsiveness to what Lionel Trilling calls the moral ideal of "authenticity," an ideal in which one discovers within oneself one's own unique and particular way of being. Charles Taylor suggests that the search for authenticity, and the discovery of identity, emerges out of a dialogical process of negotiation with others. He calls it a "discourse of recognition" that takes place "first, in the intimate sphere, where we understand the formation of identity and the self as taking place in a continuing dialogue and struggle with significant others. And then in the public sphere, where a politics of equal recognition has come to play a bigger and bigger role."[1] Kallen grounded his sense of Jewish authenticity in the framework of scientific culture, negotiated it with other thinkers, articulated it with his unique interpretation of (and lifelong fascination with) the biblical book of Job, and displayed it in the public sphere of the press.

Kallen's evolving self-understanding as a Jew is displayed, contested, and refined in the public arena of the American popular and Jewish presses. Over the course of some seven decades, Kallen worked through his relationship to Judaism, the Jewish people, and America in nearly forty books and more than four hundred articles. Writing about Jews and Judaism became a primary way in which Kallen expressed his Jewish identity. As was typical of many among his generation who were the first to be raised in America, Kallen had to struggle with what being American meant and what Jewishness signified in this new setting, and he came to believe that being Jewish and being American are mutually reinforcing identities. Through his struggle, Kallen helped to shape the direction of formative discourses concerning race, ethnicity, modernism, and secularism that affected the entire American Jewish community, discourses that engaged authors, editors, publishers, and readers. Seen in this light, Horace Kallen's writing is a valuable artifact that records how social discourses shape modern American Jewish identity.

Kallen is located at the center of a number of cultural narratives that make a book-length study of his thought particularly relevant. The dawn of the twenty-first century has seen renewed interest in Kallen and in the relationship of cultural pluralism to various understandings of multiculturalism. More recently, interest has arisen in comparing Kallen's cosmopolitanism and Zionism with modern-day discourse concerning Zionism and its relationship to transnationalism.[2]

This book adds a new dimension to exploring Kallen's thought by focusing on him through the disciplinary lens of the history of science, with particular attention paid to the importance that the science of psychology played in shaping Kallen's Jewish identity. Over the course of the first half of the twentieth century, race science, evolutionary theory, psychology, and relativity and quantum mechanics all figured prominently in Kallen's thought. Approaching Kallen from the perspective of the history of science sheds light on how Kallen viewed science as a resource for a values-driven response to life that affirms individuality while also providing a broad warrant for social solidarity.

Kallen's construction of American and Jewish identity emerges from a network of relationships that converge in, and are established through, print culture. By tracing the development of his ideas within the context of a print culture network, this book takes seriously Leslie Howsam's contention that print culture exposes "the connecting tissue between readers and writers and ask[s] questions about relationships."[3] Looking closely at when, where, and why Kallen published as he did allows us to trace a narrative arc of his personal development. It gives shape to the process by which Kallen gained social capital, and situates him within a tangible web of relationships, which, in turn, allows us to evaluate his impact.

Each chapter in this book has its own thesis, but the overall arc of *Horace Kallen Confronts America* charts Kallen's transformation into a *religious* secularist Jew. Taking Kallen seriously as a religious figure is not an obvious tack to take regarding someone so disaffected with organized religion and so clearly an atheist, but it is nevertheless true that he came to see himself as doing theology: "[What] struck me as I came back to these works of my younger days was how much theology I had in fact been writing," Kallen wrote in 1932. "I was not aware of this [before] . . . But there they are today, a redefinition, sketchy, perhaps, and as I see it now, more serious than perhaps need be, of Judaistic dogma in the light of modern trends in science and social life."[4] By investigating Kallen from the perspective of science and religion, this book opens a window onto a possibility of how science and Judaism may be said to relate. Kallen, a lifelong devotee of the Jamesian pragmatist program, would come to apply the scientific method as laid out by the founders of pragmatism, Charles Peirce and William James, to his belief system, to cultural pluralism as a lived experiment, and to democracy as a living faith. *Horace Kallen Confronts America* claims that Kallen's religiosity as a Jew crystallized not through traditional Judaism, but through a different kind of revelation—one arising from his own experience, leading Kallen to espouse a faith in the salvific power of secularism. It was an approach to life that, quite simply, Kallen was willing to bet his life on.[5]

Horace Meyer Kallen

Born into an Orthodox Jewish home in Silesia (Germany) in 1882, Horace Meyer Kallen was the eldest of eight children born to Rabbi Jacob David Kallen and Esther Rebecca (née Glazier). His father, forced by political circumstance to leave Germany, assumed the pulpit of an Orthodox congregation in Boston, and after a few years managed to bring his family to join him in 1887, when Horace was five years old. Rabbi Kallen had his son pursue traditional studies at home and prevented him from attending a secular public school, until a truant officer finally forced the matter. Horace quickly grew estranged from his authoritarian father, feeling intellectually and spiritually confined by his rigid orthodoxy. Although he achieved some reconciliation at his father's deathbed in 1917, Horace remained alienated from his father's religious practice for the remainder of his life.

Kallen rebelled and even briefly ran away from home. During some of his "truancies from the duties of scholarship," he later recalled, Kallen would "go down to the Tea Wharf to see where the tea had been poured," and "up to Bunker Hill to fight that battle for myself." He learned through textbooks to see the Puritans as American heroes. "By the time I reached puberty the heroic America of the textbook legends had gotten woven into the warp and woof of my inward life," Kallen wrote. It was a "consolation for my sorrows, freedom from my disabilities, promise to my hopes."[6]

In many respects, Kallen's story exemplifies the attitude of children of Jewish immigrants during the 1890s, John Higham observes, in that he experienced a "loss of religion and an uncritical enthusiasm for America."[7] Kallen later reflected, "It seemed to me that the identity of every human being with every other was the important thing and that the term 'American' should nullify the meaning of every other term in one's personal make-up. . . . Everything Jewish could be absorbed and dissolved in something quite non-Jewish and identical with the Yankee being as I knew it in Boston."[8]

Kallen entered Harvard on a financial scholarship in 1900, and three years later received his BA magna cum laude. In 1903 Woodrow Wilson, president of Princeton University and future president of the United States, personally hired Kallen to teach English literature at Princeton, marking the first time a Jew had ever been hired there. It quickly became clear, however, that this event did not mark a newly inclusive atmosphere at Princeton. Kallen was dismissed after only two years, once it was discovered that he was a Jew. "Looking back, I see that I underwent in Princeton what among Presbyterians and Baptists and Methodists would be called a conversion," Kallen reflected. "But it was a negative, not a positive, conversion. After two years, the God-fearing authorities refused any longer to harbor me and my Jewish heresies, which they said were debauching the youth."[9] Kallen returned to Harvard in 1906 to pursue graduate studies, but with his idealization of America now in tatters.

The anti-Semitism that Kallen experienced at Princeton, however, was not new to him. It had also affected him growing up in Boston. "Non-Jews were troubling my days and nights because, through no fault of my own, I happened to be different from them. My difference diminished me, shackled me, deprived me of liberty and subjected me to injustice," he remembered. By the time he matriculated to Harvard in 1900, Kallen had come to see his Jewish difference as an unnecessary liability. "I could 'pass,'" he wrote. "What then was the point of not-passing, of suffering the lameness that not-passing entailed?"[10]

Among the influences that pushed Kallen toward a positive association with his Jewish identity were his professors Barrett Wendell and William James. In his sophomore year, Kallen took a course in American literary history with Wendell, who taught him that American political and literary thought were grounded in the teachings of the Hebrew Bible. Wendell persuaded his argumentative student that the Puritan mindset was fundamentally Hebraic. Their confrontation impressed upon Kallen a newfound appreciation for how his Jewish "difference" should be counted as a virtue. Thereafter, Kallen "began consciously and conscientiously to reclaim, and to identify himself with, his Jewish inheritance, Jewish culture, and the Jewish community."[11]

William James, meanwhile, provided Kallen with the philosophical framework to appreciate the intrinsic value of his Jewish difference. James started Kallen "toward a cure" from the "blindness" that prevented him from seeing that difference was a fundamental fact of nature. Kallen came to understand that the statement in the Declaration of Independence that "all men are created equal" did not signify homogeneity. It meant "equal *as different*; it affirms the parity of the different; it recognizes that their equality does not abolish their diverse natures but preserves and liberates them."[12] This became the guiding principle for Kallen's life's work, undergirding his major philosophical contribution to American social and political thought—cultural pluralism.

During his time at Harvard, Kallen became increasingly involved with Zionism. At a Zionist retreat in 1906, Kallen met Solomon Schechter, president of the Jewish Theological Seminary. Schechter exercised an influence on young Kallen as well, encouraging him to view Jewish life as an organic whole. In addition to his growing attachment to the nascent American Zionist movement, Kallen became deeply involved with the second-generation Jewish students at Harvard, with whom he shared in common a secular, cultural interest in Judaism. This group, guided in part by Kallen's vision of Hebraism as a cultural force in Jewish life, eventually grew to become the nationwide Intercollegiate Menorah Association (IMA). Through their influential periodical, the *Menorah Journal*, the IMA promoted a vision of American Jewish identity that was focused on ethnic and humanist, rather than religious, commitments.

These influences laid the groundwork for what Higham describes as Kallen's distinction between inner experience and public life. "The state may intervene in external conditions to promote justice or equality," Higham explains, "but the collective consciousness of each ethnic group must remain free and spontaneous."[13] These influences also informed Kallen's interest in psychology, which he studied at Harvard together with his main area of concentration: philosophy. At a time when the fields of philosophy and psychology had not yet fully separated, Kallen pursued courses that blended psychology and philosophy with Hugo Münsterberg, Edwin B. Holt (with whom he maintained a lifelong close friendship), Josiah Royce, and, in particular, William James. Royce inspired Kallen to try "to understand how the individual inheritance of 'instincts' was related to the presence of a 'group mind' on which loyalty to the descent group seemed to depend," William Toll writes. "The relationship stood somewhere between the hereditary inheritance of physical characteristics and the voluntary affiliation of the Jeffersonian citizen."[14] Toll adds that, from James, Kallen grew interested in exploring connections between the individual personality and the collective consciousness of a descent group.

In 1908 Kallen completed a PhD under James's supervision, thus formalizing his professional credentials as both a philosopher and a psychologist. That Kallen was a philosopher is well-known, but what is less well-recognized is that he also studied functionalist psychology with William James, Hugo Münsterberg, and his lifelong close friend, Edwin B. Holt. Kallen's friend and colleague John Dewey authored what has become widely regarded as the foundational text of functionalism, *The Reflex Arc Concept in Psychology* (1896), and for decades Kallen collaborated with him on works philosophical, psychological, and political.[15] As a functionalist psychologist, Kallen developed an interest in the mind's coordinating function between an organism and its environment. Such study, deeply influenced by evolutionary theory, seemed, at the turn of the twentieth century, to be a promising avenue to better understand the human condition. It would come to shape Kallen's approach to understanding religion and society.

After graduation, Kallen briefly taught logic at Clark University from 1909 to 1910, but then secured a position teaching philosophy and psychology at the University of Wisconsin from 1911 to 1918. Unhappy with the growing attacks on academic freedom during the war years, Kallen quit that job and was recruited by Herbert Croly to join the faculty of the New School for Social Research in New York when it first opened its doors in 1919. Kallen remained there for the rest of his career as a social philosophy professor.

Kallen's intellectual debt to Wendell, James, Santayana, Royce, and others is widely acknowledged. While these points of connection are important, the points of disconnection are equally important. In many respects Kallen was an alienated individual. He was alienated from his parents, from the religious orthodoxy of his father, from mainstream academia, and from hegemonic Anglo-Saxon culture. Kallen's discontent with the status quo resulted in a tendency to take a rather pugilistic stance as he set forth his opinions in a wide variety of journals.[16] Kallen vigorously fought to promote among Jews a greater appreciation for how a scientific and secular worldview supports American Jewish identity, and he discovered in that worldview a potent defense of Jewish difference against white Anglo-Saxon Protestant American cultural hegemonic pretensions.

When in 1919 the economist and sociologist Thorstein Veblen marveled at the disproportionate preeminence of Jews in science, his theory inaugurated a period of speculation concerning this phenomenon that persists to this day. His basic thesis, which continues to have its supporters and its detractors, is that the Jewish experience of social alienation inculcated in Jews a healthy skepticism, a willingness to challenge the status quo that fostered creativity in the sciences. Writing from his academic home at the New School for Social Research, Veblen's attentiveness to the salience of the Jewish experience of alienation may, to some extent, have been sparked because of the example of his friend and fellow social theorist, Horace Kallen, who had recently persuaded Veblen to join him on faculty there.

Kallen's alienation served him as a source of inspiration, spurring him to consider cures for the problem of the alienation of America from her democratic heritage, and of the Jewish community from participation in the fullness of American life. His lifelong commitment to the American Idea as a prescription for the problems of society reveals the essential optimism that guided Kallen's thinking throughout his life. The remove at which Kallen found himself from the Jewish religious mainstream, the academic mainstream, and the American political mainstream afforded him a perspective from which he could urge change.[17]

We will not here seek to interpret Kallen's enthusiasm for science through the lens of the Veblen thesis, however. Our concern is with a question posed by Noah Efron: "Why have the sciences been so remarkably successful among modern Jews?"[18] Kallen is an excellent subject of study for such a question. Race science, psychology, and physics all proved to be particularly significant buttresses for Kallen's personal beliefs and political rhetoric. Although the world of science changed dramatically during his lifetime, Kallen held fast to his faith that the method of science held forth the best promise to understand, change, and secure Jewish life in the religious and political economy of the land.

With this philosophical framework as his guiding principle, Kallen devoted his life to the ambitious program of persuading American Jews to adopt a secular, scientific framework to define Jewish identity, and to persuade America that the vitality of her democracy likewise depended on adopting a secular and scientific framework. In this way, Kallen exemplifies the hope held by Jews during that time that science would pave the way to full and equal social integration. But this general Jewish acclaim for the salvific effect that the sciences would have on their social status did not lead to a programmatic consensus. Far from unifying Americans and Jews behind his rallying call, Kallen constantly engaged in battle with Jews and non-Jews over his ideas.

The conclusion that emerges from those debates is that what truly advanced American and Jewish life during those years was not the success or failure of Kallen's ideas, but the significance attached to the discourses themselves. Kallen's importance as a historical figure is best gauged by the extent to which he helped to further the discourses with which he was engaged. To this end, this book pays close attention to Kallen's footprint in print culture. The debates in which he participated in the public forum of the periodical press helped to develop a wide variety of views concerning the nature of Jewish and American identity. The transformative effect that Kallen had personally experienced through his confrontation with Wendell became for him a model of the necessary precondition to cause transformation in social thought. As Kallen once reflected to a friend, "Free, if necessary, violent discussion, open and thorough airing of views, oxygenation, seem to me essential to salvation."[19]

The Civil Sphere, Religion, and Secularism

The influx of millions of immigrants to the United States in the late nineteenth and the early twentieth centuries spurred a national debate concerning whether and how they might be assimilated. The image of the "melting pot," a metaphor popularized by Israel Zangwill's 1908 play of the same name, became an important symbol in the debate over the impact of immigration. Zangwill did not invent the term, to be sure. It had been around since the earliest years of the republic, but the recent massive immigration increased its currency. At the turn of the twentieth century, its central meaning was that America should be culturally homogeneous. However, among "assimilationists" (referring to those who viewed favorably the prospect of social integration), the proposed method for and projected result of cultural homogenization remained unresolved. Some (predominantly white, Anglo-Saxon, and Protestant) wished "to melt down the immigrants and to then pour the resulting, formless liquid into preexisting cultural and social molds," David Hollinger observes, while others (including assimilated American Jews) believed that the encounters between the different peoples "would act chemically upon each other so that all would be changed, and a new compound would emerge."[20] These two perspectives are expressed, respectively, in Zangwill's two metaphors, the "melting pot" and the "American symphony." Kallen, however, did not accept either of these options. Rather, he argued for the preservation of difference and distinctiveness, with social stability achieved not through homogenization but through cooperation.

Assimilation was an issue that involved many more groups than just Jews, of course, but what made the Jewish case unique was the lack of connection to their nation of origin. Jews who emigrated from Russia, for example, were not considered to be simply Russian. They were viewed as Jews who hailed from Russia. The Jewish case defied easy categorization. If the Jews were not to be identified with a nation-state, then how should these immigrants be classified? As a race? A religion? This was an open question fraught with political implications. As the symbol of the melting pot quickly became the symbol for the nation, the fact that it came from a play by a Jew and about Jews signaled that Jews were perceived as prominent protagonists in the drama of defining what it means to be American. Into this political environment, Kallen injected an alternative view of nationality, or ethnicity, that was radically different. Although it sparked much discussion, Kallen's rhetoric inspired only a limited following. Still, sympathizers included an impressive array of thinkers such as John Dewey, Louis Brandeis, Jane Addams, and, in particular, Randolph Bourne, who was so inspired by Kallen's thinking that it served as the basis for his famous 1916 essay published in the *Atlantic Monthly*, "Trans-National America," in which Bourne argued against the prevailing melting pot ideology in favor of a culturally diverse vision for America.

Kallen argued that American democracy would thrive if it were to foster the independence of its constituent ethno-racial groups, who, encouraged by an unfettered freedom of association, would then harmoniously cooperate in the federative unity of the United States. His rhetoric regarding the problems of America and of Jewish life in America attracted attention from Jewish and non-Jewish sources. The periodical press was the main arena in which these public discourses took place, although Kallen later also wrote books that sparked responses. Kallen first laid out his argument for cultural pluralism in his well-known article entitled "Democracy versus the Melting Pot," published in the *Nation* in 1915. Kallen contended that America was not, and never had been, a homogenous entity. He pointed out that America is made up of a plurality of ethnic groups who share a common set of democratic ideals. Decades later, Kallen's notion of cultural pluralism came to be criticized for its perceived failure to adequately address race and the power differentials that exist between groups, but the consequent postmodernist preference for the term *multiculturalism* does not detract from the fact that Kallen was among the first to articulate the idea that the United States should promote cultural diversity. It seems a lesson particularly fitting to revisit during this time in which we are once again witnessing the resurgence of xenophobia on a massive scale.

Beyond noting cultural pluralism's place in a genealogy of multiculturalism, what makes studying Kallen particularly interesting is the extent to which he grew to ground his thinking in a religious perspective. This places his thinking in a very special relationship with Jeffrey Alexander's groundbreaking work on the civil sphere. Alexander insists the civil sphere, which "relies on solidarity . . . because of our putative commitment to a common secular faith," describes a world of values that partakes of the "transcendental language of sacred values of the good and profane symbols of evil."[21] Civil discourse, in Alexander's view, engages with a religious discourse concerning the sacred and the profane, an implicit binary code that names the civil "pure" and the anti-civil "impure." "It is in terms of symbolic purity and impurity that centrality is defined, that marginal demographic status is made meaningful, and high position understood as deserved or illegitimate," Alexander writes. "Pollution is a threat to any allocative system; its sources must either be kept at bay or transformed by communicative actions, like rituals and social movements, into a pure form."[22] Kallen, joining his voice to that of many other Jews who had long resisted the construction of Jewishness as anti-civil in American and European civil discourse, advocated powerfully for Jewish incorporation into the civil sphere during the first three decades of the twentieth century. This book argues that science provided Kallen with the vocabulary and the authority to make such a case for Jewish civility. By the mid-twentieth century, when the case for Jewish incorporation no longer needed to be made, Kallen shifted his attention to supporting the continued expansion of the civil sphere by defending secularism as a religious faith.[23] For Kallen as for Alexander, civil solidarity "is the real utopia."[24]

The Melting Pot and Orchestration

Shortly before his ninetieth birthday in 1973, Kallen reflected that the loss of our family and friends silences "a note in the orchestration of our selfhood."[25] The metaphor of an orchestra was very significant to Kallen. He used it here in reference to a person's selfhood, but decades earlier Kallen had used it as a way to describe the functioning of a pluralistic society. It was a metaphor, then, with personal and political overtones, the original inspiration for which undoubtedly came from Zangwill's use of it in *The Melting-Pot.* In the play, the protagonist, a musician named David Quixano, composes an "American Symphony" symbolizing the beneficent effect of the American cultural melting pot. Zangwill's "American Symphony" resists the notion that Anglo-Saxon conformity was the true American ideal, and evokes the image of a new America born of the blending of different immigrant groups. Although this idea was popular with some American Jews, it had its critics among those who, like Kallen, felt that its commitment to cultural homogeneity was misguided.

The Reform rabbi Judah Magnes's 1909 critique of *The Melting-Pot*, for example, points out that orchestras are made up of different instruments and sections, playing different parts and notes. He preferred to use the metaphor of the symphony to support the idea of difference and pluralism: "The symphony of America must be written by the various nationalities which keep their individual and characteristic note, and which sound this note in harmony with their sister nationalities."[26] Six years later, Kallen wrote in the same vein that society is like an orchestra composed of "every type of instrument," each with "its specific timbre and tonality." The "instruments" are the ethnic groups, and the "melody" is the spirit and culture of the society. The "harmony and dissonances and discords of them all make the symphony of civilization."[27]

Kallen, like Magnes, used the orchestra metaphor to argue for the preservation of difference and distinctiveness, even as cooperation and harmony are achieved. This fairly describes what Kallen meant by the term *cultural pluralism*, an idea that gradually became normative by the 1950s. The orchestra metaphor proved to be such a lasting and powerful metaphor that, as late as 1951, Bertrand Russell used it to describe how Americans now see themselves: "We conceive society as like an orchestra, in which the different performers have different parts to play and different instruments upon which to perform, and in which cooperation results from a conscious common purpose."[28]

The metaphor of orchestration may aptly be applied to Kallen's biography. Milton Konvitz writes that Kallen orchestrated "a multiplicity of diverse interests," including "adult education, worker education, Jewish education, general education, consumerism, the labor movement, the cooperative movement, Zionism, art and aesthetics, censorship and civil liberties, the philosophy of secular Judaism, the Book of Job, the League of Nations and the United Nations, civil rights, pragmatism, the philosophy of pluralism, the philosophy of individualism, the nature of comedy, the State of Israel, and the whole of Western, especially American, culture and civilization."[29] Kallen's creative struggle to self-orchestrate and to maintain his integrity withal is seen in his exposition of the philosophy of science, in his understanding of humanism and Hebraism, and in the way he understood freedom and democracy. "I do experience a unity," Kallen wrote near the end of his life, "not the structured unity built by the logic of a systematic treatise but the unity of intermittent unification generated by the confluence, next to next, of waves of consciousness."[30] Considering Kallen as a unique musical instrument, as it were, with its own qualities, we are in a better position to appreciate how, metaphorically speaking, historical actors all play in a symphony orchestra with other distinctive instruments, creating new harmonies, dissonances, and discords.

Jewish Identity as a Response to Modernity

Kallen appeared at the juncture of the creation of a new American modernity. He navigated the new realities, conceived, as he argued, as a response to humanism, industrialization, democracy, and science. He articulated a conception of Jewish ethnicity based upon post-Darwinian scientific discourse, and at the same time created space for Jews in a non-Jewish environment. Kallen's evangelizing zeal made him a significant node on a social network that bridged Jewish and non-Jewish America. Markedly distinct from Reform Judaism's vision, his vision of modernity was conceived in a post-Darwinian, urbanized, university-educated, and secular context.

Kallen's construction of Jewish identity and his passionate advocacy for Jewish survival in the modern context, however, may be subjected to the same criticism that has been applied to cultural pluralism—that it is not a theory sufficiently developed to be practically implemented. This is because it is not possible to point to any specific content that bounds Jewish identity in Kallen's thought. Furthermore, beyond his view that Jewish education is the key to continued Jewish survival, Kallen provides no way to guarantee a commitment to Jewish identity. But this lack was, to him, a virtue, because it prevents the restriction of Jewish identity to propositional content, and it allows for maximal diversity of expression. Kallen believed that the continual process of voluntary social affiliation (including affiliation as a Jew) is what creates society, and in a voluntaristic context there are no guarantees. Kallen, in the mold of Putnam's neo-pragmatist religious perspective, did not desire to discover guarantees. He believed that secularism provided the only viable ground for the continued flourishing and diversification of Jewish life. This was the foundation of Kallen's faith. His aim was not to *ensure* that Jewish life would continue but rather to support the conditions that would best *allow* for Jewish flourishing in a pluralistic and interconnected world.

In tracing Kallen's construction of Jewishness, this book's purpose is to show how his Jewish identity motivated him to change the world around him, to engage in particular social relations and print culture relationships, to associate with certain institutions, and to imagine America as he did. Kallen's effort to self-orchestrate had a more ambitious goal than simply to balance particularist and universalist impulses. He fused American democracy, secularism, and

Jewishness into an interconnected whole. Out of these, he fashioned an idiosyncratic religious faith. This, in essence, captures Kallen's path to authenticity.

As a contribution to Jewish studies, this book points to how Jewish identity is continually constructed and modified within a wider social, political, religious, and scientific context. It shows how Jewish identity emerges from out of what Taylor calls a "discourse of recognition." The following chapters highlight select moments in Kallen's life in which he took a position in that discourse. From the xenophobia of the 1910s and the experimental mood of modernism in the 1920s to the fear of totalitarianism in the 1930s and 1940s and the desire to instill religious values in the 1950s, these chapters trace Kallen's evolution as a Jew, an American, and a secularist. They show how he helped to shape the direction of formative discourses concerning race, ethnicity, modernism, and secularism that affected the entire American Jewish community. Through his prolific writing, Kallen carved out a prominent position for himself in the Jewish and non-Jewish worlds of print culture. He drew on the scientific discourses of race and psychology to describe the Jewish condition and the place of religion. He articulated a scientific basis for Jewish participation in American democracy, defending the Jewish community against racial theorists in the public forum of the periodical press, and playing a role in transforming the conception of American democracy into a pluralistic philosophy. Kallen also played a role in bringing sociological and psychological conceptions of religion to the fore in Reform religious discourse. His is the story of a man whose quest to orchestrate different discourses and to self-orchestrate his diverse interests into a unity of purpose and, above all, to defend his integrity, made a lasting impression on his interlocutors. He played an accompaniment for the symphonic harmony, dissonances, and discords of twentieth-century American Jewish life.

• 1 •

Race, Hebraism, and Civility

> Not like the brazen giant of Greek fame,
> With conquering limbs astride from land to land;
> Here at our sea-washed, sunset gates shall stand
> A mighty woman with a torch, whose flame
> Is the imprisoned lightning, and her name
> Mother of Exiles.
>
> —Emma Lazarus, "The New Colossus"

SENATOR LODGE: Do I understand you to deny that the Jews are a race?

MR. WOLF: How?

SENATOR LODGE: Do you deny that the word "Jew" is used to express a race?

MR. WOLF: As the representative of the Union of American Hebrew Congregations[,] . . . [I say that] the Jews are not a race.

SENATOR LODGE: [The *Jewish Encyclopedia* contains] a statement by Joseph Jacobs, B.A., formerly President of the Jewish Historical Society of England. "Anthropologically considered, the Jews are a race of markedly uniform type, due either to unity of race or to similarity of environment." Do you mean to deny . . . that the word "Jew" is a racial term?

MR. WOLF: I have made my statement.[1]

Commissioned by Congress to inquire into the negative effects of immigration generally, the United States Immigration Commission, known as the Dillingham Commission, met from 1907 to 1911. It found that immigration from Southern and Eastern Europe threatened to pollute American culture and society. The aforequoted passage is excerpted from the testimony of Simon Wolf, representing the Reform movement's Union of American Hebrew Congregations, before the joint House-Senate Commission. At the beginning of the twentieth century, the US government seriously investigated how to categorize Jews in order to decide how to treat them under immigration law.

The Dillingham Commission's recommendations to Congress fed into the xenophobic and nativist sentiment of the era, paving the way for a series of restrictive immigration laws over the next decade that affected, among other groups, Jews seeking to immigrate to the United States. The testimony of the Jewish community leaders from the American Jewish Committee and the Union of American Hebrew Congregations gripped the entire Jewish community. The text of this deposition was published in full in the Philadelphia Jewish weekly, the *Jewish Exponent*, and in the American Zionist monthly, the *Maccabaean*. A 1910 editorial in the *Exponent* explained that Jewish communal leaders intended to convince the commission that Jewish immigrants should be designated according to nation of origin, rather than by race.[2] The form the questioning took, however, reframed the issue into an either-or distinction between race and religion. This contributed to the increasing divisiveness within the Jewish community. The political temper was forcing Jews to choose a definite position, affirming either a religious identification with Judaism or a racial one.

At stake was how to frame the case for Jewish incorporation into the civil sphere. Reform Jewish leaders, representing the established and acculturated American Jewish community, generally pursued a strategy of establishing Jewish identity to be strictly concerned with matters of faith. They desired to project an image of Jewish civility by asserting that the only difference separating Jews from Gentiles in America was their preferred place of worship. Jews should be considered to share the same civic values identified with white, Anglo-Saxon Protestants, thus rendering them, in Alexander's terminology, pure. But, as millions of Jews were now arriving in America from Eastern Europe, their significant cultural and linguistic differences destabilized this image. Complicating matters for many (such as those on the Dillingham Commission), was the fact that many Jews were comfortable identifying as Jewish both by religion and by race. Others, like Horace Kallen, rejected religious affiliation altogether and positively embraced an exclusively racial identity as Jews. In this chapter, we shall see that Kallen developed a unique justification for Jewish incorporation that relied on a racialized view of Jewishness. He argued that Jewish civility was guaranteed by the Jewish contribution to world civilization of Hebraism, conceptualized as a racialized cultural construct.

From our twenty-first-century vantage point, to speak of the "Jewish race" smacks of anti-Semitism. But in the early twentieth century, racial science was viewed quite differently. It was a respected science, and its conclusions were widely accepted among both Jews and non-Jews. While some Jews may not have agreed with the assignation of the term *race* to describe themselves, many others could, and did. It was quite common to hear Jews make claims about the Jewish race without any necessarily negative associations attached to that claim.

Although it is true that race in America has always been an issue primarily concerned with skin color, it must nevertheless be pointed out that this was not the only valence of the term. The idea of race encompassed a constellation of perceptions about the character, integrity, and transmission of group identity. The belief that race described the determining nature of one's national origin, culture, psychology, and biology persisted in scientific and popular circles into the third decade of the twentieth century.

Making matters more confusing for the modern reader is the fact that the terms *nationality* and *ethnic group* blurred into *race* as well. In many respects, these terms were little more than synonyms when it came to discussing groups like the Jews, although for those social scientific thinkers who, like the anthropologist Franz Boas and the sociologists associated with the University of Chicago (popularly referred to as the Chicago School), had begun to challenge the assumptions of racial biological determinism, the term *ethnic group* began to serve as a useful contrast with the term *race*. For them, it signified a cultural construct of group identity dissociated from biology.[3] During the time period here under consideration, however, the notion of *ethnicity* was just beginning to take shape, and for social scientific thinkers like Kallen and many anthropologists and psychologists, the idea of *culture* was not yet cleanly separated from biological speculation.

There was no single view on race among Jews. Nor was there any single locus in which the discourse took place. This issue and other matters of importance to the American Jewish community were discussed and debated in the pages of the many different English and Yiddish presses that were available, representing the two main languages of American Jews. There was also a Hebrew press in America, but, unlike other immigrant presses, it came into being not to serve the needs of a public that did not yet read English, but as a consequence of an ideology that people should read Hebrew. The Hebrew press insulated itself from American life.[4]

The Yiddish and English presses, however, were fully engaged with American Jewish life and wrestled more directly with issues relating to life in the new adoptive land. In some ways, the Yiddish press was of primary importance. At the height of their popularity in 1925, Yiddish newspapers enjoyed a circulation of more than a half million readers. Although they served the needs of a Yiddish-speaking community, most readers were in fact fluent in English, and read English-language newspapers regularly. Editors and writers were well aware that the demand for Yiddish papers was due in no small part to the sentimental attachment of the readers to that language, as well as the desire to read news of particular interest to the Jewish community. In contrast to the insular Hebrew press, the Yiddish press sought to hasten the process of Americanization among Jewish immigrants, its writers and editors working to help Jews fit in with American culture and values.[5]

The Yiddish press, however, could not claim to speak for American Jews as a whole. Neither, for that matter, could the English-language Jewish press. They inhabited different worlds of discourse. The Yiddish press served mainly working-class Jewish immigrants from Eastern Europe. The English-language Jewish press served the needs of acculturated, Western European, American-born, middle-class Jews. The readers of the English-language Jewish press, Hasia Diner writes, were "less working-class, less centered in the garment trades, less immigrant, less socialist, and less orthodox." The English-language Jewish press therefore focused its gaze not on the leaders of the immigrant world, but on accomplished Jewish businessmen, lawyers, political figures, and other economically and socially successful American Jews.[6] It was for this press that Kallen wrote.

Locating Kallen in American Racial Discourse

Progressive Era America, Gary Gerstle observes, was preoccupied with making America over into a unified moral community. Americanization and social hygiene (and, later, Prohibition) helped to fashion that national image. Progressive liberal ideology required that ethnic group attachments be dissolved into the American melting pot to release the full potential of that American moral transformation.[7] Two competing discourses—civic nationalism and racial nationalism—framed the national debate about the limits of ethnic civic incorporation. For those of white European descent, the battle for full social and political inclusion was eventually won after some decades, but America continued to enshrine racial inequality. Civic nationalism would continue to exclude nonwhites. Thus, a contradictory impulse emerged that sought to define rigid boundaries of what it means to be American even as the rapid growth of social, demographic, and economic pressures brought with it a push for more inclusivity.[8] In light of this narrative arc of the American twentieth century, it is clear that although Kallen's argument in support of hyphenated Americans (e.g., Irish-American, Italian-American, Jewish-American, etc.) aimed to disrupt racist rhetoric, he nevertheless did not recognize "racial nationalism" for the foundational discourse that it was. "His limitation, like that of most liberals before the 1960s," William Toll writes, "was to see racism as just another form of compensation for individual limitations, rather than as a profound building block of American culture."[9] Kallen was blind to this in part because he had absorbed the racist attitudes of his environment, and in part because his main interest lay in addressing the issues facing immigrant Jews like himself.[10]

Scholars such as John Higham have argued that cultural pluralism was, from the outset, so "encapsulated in white ethnocentrism" that it had to be replaced by the multiculturalism of the latter half of the twentieth century.[11] It did not adequately challenge the powerful narrative of whiteness that had enshrined oppressive power structures from the very origins of the nation. Eric Goldstein argues that the issue of whiteness was particularly pressing during the Progressive Era. As massive immigration, coupled with increased urbanization and industrialization, reshaped the social, economic, and political contours of American life, the US government responded by trying to assess the racial impact of these new immigrants on native white, Anglo-Saxon stock. Because Jews came to represent the sweeping changes in American life, Jews "became a frequently discussed 'racial' figure in American culture," Goldstein observes. "White Americans often tried to obscure Jewish distinctiveness and to understand it within a black-white context." In response, Jews sought to more firmly establish their whiteness, Goldstein argues, and it is in that context that Kallen "relied on the notion that the whiteness of European immigrant groups made them potential contributors to American society rather than a racial threat."[12] "In Kallen's racial schema," David Weinstein writes, "Jews, or at least Ashkenazi Jews, could and should be designated as white."

Narrowly focusing a critical reading of Kallen through the lens of American whiteness discourse alone, however, misses how Kallen sought to establish Jewish civility on the basis of what he held to be a racial connection to Hebraism. His first print articulation regarding Jewish racial identity and its connection to Hebraism appeared in August 1906 in an article entitled "The Ethics of Zionism." Kallen had just left Princeton University, his experience there having disabused him of the notion that he, as a Jew, could "pass" among non-Jews. Kallen's status as "impure" had been impressed upon him and, having now returned to Harvard to pursue graduate studies, he was newly inspired to act to remedy that social assignation. Jewish racial identity took on a new moral imperative for Kallen as he began in earnest to find a way to establish Jewish civility for himself and for all American Jews. By August 1906 Kallen was within months of chairing the first meeting of the Menorah Society, a Jewish student association that launched a movement promoting the ideal of Hebraism as a historical and living Jewish culture, and he had also become even more active in the American Zionist movement.

"The Ethics of Zionism" appeared in the *Maccabaean*, a monthly magazine published by the Federation of American Zionists. The *Maccabaean* was unapologetically propagandistic, but it was also devoted to Jewish culture and literature and featured many articles on Jewish philosophy, art, and history, as well as original literary works.[13] Kallen found the journal to be a suitable home, for it aligned with his political views, Zionist sympathies, and his antipathy toward religious Judaism (particularly Reform). It was also a forum in which Kallen could begin to establish a presence as a spokesman for secular American Jews.

Hebraism and Race

Although "The Ethics of Zionism" is significant because it is where Kallen first linked Hebraism to race, he was not the first to make that link. Matthew Arnold (to whom Kallen explicitly referred in a later publication) had already discussed Hebraism and Hellenism as racialized cultural forces. Arnold's concept of culture, Robert Young writes, was inseparable from race: "*Culture and Anarchy*, the highly influential, virtual founding document of English culture, locates the culture's energy and history as a product of racial difference."[14] Similarly, Miriam Leonard observes that Arnold was deeply influenced by Ernest Renan's racial schema, and "maps his abstract concepts of Hellenism and Hebraism on to the ethnographic categories of 'Indo-European' and 'Semite.'" Of critical importance to understand Kallen's writings on the subject is an appreciation of the psychological dimension in Arnold's construction of the terms. Hellenism and Hebraism, Greeks and Jews, had, for Arnold, "become descriptions of internal psychological predispositions."[15] We shall see that Kallen believed that such psychological predispositions were physically inherited. Lewis Fried describes how the apposition of Hebraism and Hellenism was a central concern to the Menorah Society (later, the Intercollegiate Menorah Association) and its *Menorah Journal*, and notes Kallen's role in placing Hebraism at the center of its mission from the time of its inception in 1906.[16] For Kallen, resituating Hebraism was essential to the project of establishing Jewish civility.

In "The Ethics of Zionism," Kallen imagined Hebraism to have been successfully transmitted in pure form only among the Jews due to their putative racial purity. Jews, he wrote, were "purer than most European races." The relative purity of the Jewish race seemed to Kallen to ensure the unalloyed transmission of pure Hebraism. As Kallen saw it, Hebraism had become polluted in its reception and transmission among Gentiles.[17] The notion of Jewish racial purity was the subject of much debate among anthropologists at the time. Believing that skull shapes and sizes were the most reliable indicator of race (craniometry was the anthropological racial gold standard at that time), the debates about whether or not Jews constituted a pure race were concerned mainly with whether or not Jewish skulls had changed shape over time. The argument went something like this: if Jewish skulls had always remained unchanged, then that would be evidence of the lack of interracial mixing, and, hence, a confirmation of Jewish racial purity.

The anthropological assumptions were inherently flawed, of course, and the entire pseudoscience of craniometry would fall out of favor within a decade or so, in large part thanks to the work of Franz Boas, the founder of cultural anthropology. In 1906, though, it was still considered to be a valid science. One of Kallen's Harvard professors, William Z. Ripley, author of the influential *The Races of Europe* and considered the foremost American race scientist of his day, had earlier argued that the typical Jewish skull shape had changed over time, becoming brachycephalic (roundheaded), a type associated with Asian races. This led him to conclude that Jews had either departed from their original dolichocephalic (longheaded) shape, a type associated with Semites (a formerly linguistic category that had become transformed into a racial one), or they were descended from an original Asian pattern. Ripley opted for the first explanation. This, to him, was proof that "the boasted purity of descent of the Jews is, then, a myth."[18]

Kallen confidently presented his own interpretation of the relevant findings of anthropology, but he was no anthropologist. His assertions do not so much reflect a definite scientific pedigree as they do his absorption of a hodgepodge of racial ideas. Still, it was perfectly defensible for Kallen to claim as he did that the brachycephalic Jewish skull type is original and has remained unchanged (Ripley's less preferred explanation). "The fact is that the Jewish race is of Asiatic, probably of Turanian, and not Afro-Semitic origin," he asserted. Kallen took to task Ripley and Maurice Fishberg, a well-regarded Jewish physician and anthropologist, for their arguments against Jewish racial purity, calling Ripley's view "a prejudice" and denigrating Fishberg as "unseeing." Unlike them, however, Kallen cited no particular studies to support his point of view, although he did name two other thinkers on the Jewish racial question whom he believed were in agreement with his racial views.[19]

Kallen's central aim, as mentioned earlier, was to lay claim to Jewish civility. As he saw it, arguing that Jews were racially relatively pure, and of Asiatic origin, helped to make the case. Kallen's position represents a creative inversion of the anti-Semitic racial gaze. The seeds to challenge the perception of Jewish incivility lay in asserting Jewish origins at the boundaries of Europe and Asia, in the Caucasus, the purported origin of the Caucasian race. His mention of Jewish Turanian origins is a reference to the so-called Khazar-origin theory of how Jews became white (and roundheaded).[20] In this regard, Goldstein's observation that Kallen sought to make Jews white is quite correct.[21] But what would have been even more compelling for Kallen is that his racial claim meant, by implication, that Hebraism had not been grafted into Western civilization from a foreign (Afro-Semitic) race, but derived from a people who originally hailed from the same region of the world from which, it was commonly supposed, had emerged the European races. Jews, in other words, were not only white, they were also psychically and culturally linked in situ to the progress of Western civilization.

From today's vantage point, any arguments for racial purity are morally problematic. They have contributed historically to claims of racial hierarchy and superiority, and have been linked to a politics of violence and oppression. Kallen may fairly be criticized for his participation in such an ethically dubious discourse. He accepted the existence of the racial categories, and, implicitly, the notion of racial hierarchy, even as he sought to reverse the anti-Semitic implications. But this was not uniquely Kallen's problem. As Sander Gilman observes, while it may have been theoretically possible for Jewish thinkers engaged with the racial question to develop a resistance strategy against anti-Semitic racial and psychological tropes by rejecting the entire field of discourse, this is not in practice what happened. Jewish thinkers generally accepted the established discursive boundaries, working through them even as they sought to counter anti-Semitic views.[22] Kallen's views thus hint at the very difficult situation in which Jews found themselves. Jewish civility had to be established through a reinterpretation of received categories. It is arguably implicit in Kallen's thought that the proper place for Jews in the racial hierarchy was at the top. However, Kallen would have felt this line of thinking to be a perversion of his intent. Kallen explicitly rejected notions of racial hierarchy and superiority. His oeuvre is indisputably a testimony to his lifelong commitment to the fundamental worth and equality of all people and all ethnicities. From the very beginning, Kallen insisted that an ethno-racial group's moral claim to incorporation in the social fabric was linked to its commitment to democratic ideals and cooperation with other groups. As he was fond of saying, he had come to understand that the proclamation in the Declaration of Independence that "all men are created equal" affirms "the parity of the different."[23]

Kallen's interest in the anthropological origins of the Jewish race was fleeting, and he did not revisit the subject in any of his future writings. No doubt this was due in part to the rapid changes taking place in the field. Here, it simply served his purpose to establish an historical chain and a framework of logical consistency for resituating Jews and Hebraism. Even here, however, Kallen's primary focus was not on Jewish physiognomy, but on the Jewish psyche, which achieved expression as Hebraism. That psyche, Kallen maintained, was indelibly marked by a moral insight of "recognition of the inner value of the human drama" and a desire to foster justice in the world. That moral insight constituted, for Kallen, the "psychical character-mark of the Jewish race."[24]

Kallen's central argument was that Jewish life was justified not only by physical survival (that is, on evolutionary grounds) but also by its moral contribution to world civilization. "By these two facts, his vigorous, biological, organic endowment and his definite moral efficacy," Kallen asserted, "the Jew fulfills the condition we set upon which a race can ethically assert its right to maintain its self-hood." Jewish civility was guaranteed by establishing Hebraism as a pure racial and cultural psychological predisposition that was fully in accord with modernity. Indeed, it served as a vital source of strength against the despair that would otherwise follow upon realizing nature's true indifference to the human condition.[25]

Zionism, Civility, and the Jewish Psyche

Kallen assumed the validity, as did many psychologists and social scientists at the turn of the twentieth century, of the notion of inherited racial psychic patterns. He appealed to ethnology and history to claim that the "psychical character-mark of the Jewish race" rested in its unique "moral consciousness." The idea of an inherited racial psyche had been popularized almost a half century earlier by the German Jewish ethnopsychologists Moritz Lazarus and Heymann Steinthal, whose theory of *Völkerpsychologie* ("folk psychology") influenced social scientific thinkers across Europe and in the United States. Although they established this field to justify a Jewish ethnic presence in Germany, the field did not stay rooted there for long. Notable thinkers who absorbed Lazarus and Steinthal's idea of a distinctive group psychology include Sigmund Freud, and, most notably, Wilhelm Wundt, with whom *Völkerpsychologie* is primarily associated because of his monumental *Elemente der Völkerpsychologie* (1912). In America, Lazarus and Steinthal's ideas influenced Franz Boas, the Chicago sociologist William Isaac Thomas, and the psychologists G. Stanley Hall and James Mark Baldwin.[26] William James also studied with Steinthal (although he would come to criticize his work). Lazarus and Steinthal's attempt to trace the mental and ethical self-consciousness, the unifying psychological essence, of a *Volk* (i.e., a people or nation), and to ascertain how the *Volk* affects the mental development of individuals born into it, was absorbed and transformed in the hands of these various thinkers. It was seen to support diametrically opposed views, from those who, like Kallen and Freud, believed that group psychology was based in physical inheritance, to those who, like Boas and Thomas, rejected notions of physical racial inheritance.

For Kallen, the notion of an inherited racial psyche gave him the vocabulary both to articulate a racial claim that was fundamentally egalitarian and democratic, and to stake out his vision for American Zionism. "It is this spiritual self-hood, expressing a vigorous natural life and the moral law in social organization, art and letters, functioning in the family of nations as an indispensable force, that constitutes, by virtue of its effect on human civilization and progress, by virtue of its physical integrity and spiritual splendor, the Jew's moral right to live," Kallen asserted. "It is in this self-hood, so understood, that we posit the ethic of Zionism."[27] Kallen's "ethic of Zionism" rested upon the positive contributions that Jews would make to the whole of human civilization and progress. Jewish national life was morally justified by this virtue. What Kallen calls the "ethic of Zionism" was, more baldly, the very *raison d'être* for him for Jewish survival. He predicated the justification for Jewish group survival on its social "moral" value—meaning, its ongoing cooperation with other nations and its continuing contribution to the larger project of human civilization and progress.

Kallen's claim is a striking reversal of the anti-Semitic attribution assigned to Jews of an inherent Jewish psychopathology. This was a trend which John Efron notes was particularly strong in Germany, where psychiatry diagnosed the Jewish psyche as mentally ill. Jewish psychiatric literature, he observes, developed various resistance strategies against this trend to argue that Jews were psychologically healthy. These crystallized in the form of "nationalist psychiatry," written from a Zionist perspective. Efron cites the example of a Viennese neurologist's description of the Jewish psyche as having a "high ethical predisposition to sacrifice their political, social, and economic interests to profound ideas and convictions."[28] A different response was offered by Leon Pinsker, a physician and prominent Zionist activist. He diagnosed anti-Semites as mentally ill. It is they who suffered from a psychopathology, not the Jews. Thus, Pinsker preferred to use the term *Judeophobia* instead of *anti-Semitism* because of its clear connection to a psychological condition. In Pinsker's view, there was no use in trying to fight such a condition—Jews and Gentiles simply could not live together.[29] Kallen's response to this anti-Semitic climate was unique in its own right, especially insofar as he was committed to a cooperative ethic. Jewish difference would not only be a mark of pride, but would also be a motive force in the cooperative pursuit of justice and equality in the national and international arenas.

Kallen was influenced by the philosopher Herbert Spencer's idea that morality was the product of the evolution of human sociality. Darwin also gestured toward this idea, but in the American context it was Spencer whose influence in this regard was particularly significant. Spencer had made a profound impact on the American intellectual landscape during the last quarter of the nineteenth century. Thanks to his American disciples, John Fiske and Edward Youmans, Spencer's ideas were communicated to a large American readership, but Kallen's exposure to Spencerian ideas about the mind, culture, and society was mediated through his professors at Harvard, William James and Josiah Royce, and his friend and colleague John Dewey, a group that has been dubbed the "reforming Spencerians."[30] Kallen absorbed, and reframed in a Jewish modality, Spencer's view of morality as "not the root but the fruit of civilization," as one popularizer of Spencer summed it up, and as part of what Kallen and others came to see as a positive social evolutionary trend toward peaceful internationalism.[31]

Kallen also absorbed Spencer's view of the evolutionary primacy of the group over the individual. "The simple fact which emerges from the ethnological and sociological study of mankind is the fact that the group and not the individual is the fighting unit," he wrote. "It is the race and not the man who, in the greater account of human destiny, struggles, survives or dies."[32] This was an important rhetorical strategy in an America weaned on tales of rugged individualism and desirous that individuals should shed their ancestral cultural heritage. For Kallen, this Spencerian evolutionary principle validated the survival of distinct ethnic groups.

Kallen's view of the social group as the "fighting unit" for survival, and not the individual, reflects a perspective close to that articulated by the psychologist James Mark Baldwin just three years later.[33] Their shared view in this regard came not from a personal connection between them, but from a common source of intellectual legacies, including *Völkerpsychologie* and Herbert Spencer's organicist understanding of society. Tracing the similarity of their views is particularly useful here because Baldwin's notion of organic selection, conceptualized as a supplement to natural selection, helps to highlight how Kallen's notion of a heritable racial psyche similarly transcended biology but remained framed by it.[34]

Biology, Baldwin wrote in 1909, deals with organs and material living beings. "The social matter is not the same," he wrote. "It is not merely vital, but something more. It is mental. This is shown by any analysis of a social situation. Social 'fitness' is not measured by physical characters, but by mental and moral characters."[35] The fact that social "matter" is psychical rather than physical gives, for Baldwin, "a sort of selection and survival which is quite different from that recognized in the strictly biological sciences."

> We find that the utility to be subserved is one of conscious coöperation [*sic*] and union among individuals; and the unit whose selection is to secure this utility must have the corresponding characters. This unit is not the individual, but *a group of individuals who show in common their gregarious or social nature in actual exercise*; each is selected in company with certain others, who survive with him and for the same reason. Thus the selective unit, considered from the external or social point of view, is *a group of individuals*, greater or smaller as the utility subserved may require; and from the point

of view of the subjective or psychic process it implies the mental attitude which brings the individual into useful coöperation [*sic*].[36]

For both Baldwin and Kallen, then, the social unit was the operative selection unit, and its survival value could be assessed primarily through its "mental and moral characters," and in its commitment to cooperation.

For Baldwin, however, the principle of cooperation extended only to individuals within the same social unit; he saw competition as the operative rule for struggle and survival between social units. In this regard, Kallen's view was markedly different, for he believed in "the prophetic ideal of internationalism as a democratic and cooperative federation of nationalities."[37] Cooperation, not competition, was, in Kallen's view, of the greatest utility for the survival of the human race and the progress of civilization.

Just as Jacobs had argued that Jews had always been a part of European civilization, and had "earned their right to continue to work for the European culture that they have helped to develop," so, too, Kallen on more than one occasion claimed that the right of the Jewish race to survive was established by its continuing contribution to world civilization.[38] Thus, for example, Kallen wrote in 1910: "The Jews, in the degree that they are a differentiated and distinct human group, on whatever basis, racial or sectarian, are morally entitled to life only if that difference is elementally and by its very nature contributory to the values of culture and civilization. . . . To demonstrate their ethical right to be is to demonstrate . . . that the real effect of the Jews is a positive and constructive effect, that by remaining their unaltered selves, by perfecting their nature and distinctive group functions they must contribute to the welfare of nations and serve international comity."[39]

What Kallen calls a moral right to life is an argument for social integration. Already in these early articles, Kallen makes a case for Jewish incorporation into national and international life that is predicated not on Jewish sameness but on Jewish difference. The Jewish "vision of the world" and its "expression of life" as Hebraism, Kallen explained, "has been continuous and unbroken for the Jews and honestly efficacious for Western civilization."[40]

The Jewish Press Gives Kallen a Boost

Kallen's visibility in the Jewish community began to increase after 1906, not only because of his involvement with the Menorah Society and his association with the American Zionist movement but also because of his growing presence in the Jewish periodical press. This development proved to be a crucial contribution to Kallen's accumulation of social capital, as his views began to be debated in widening circles of the American Jewish community. This becomes particularly evident following Kallen's appearance in the largest nationally circulated Jewish journal in the United States, the *American Hebrew and Jewish Messenger*. The *American Hebrew* began publication in 1871, and by the turn of the twentieth century it had absorbed the *Jewish Messenger* and three other periodicals, rapidly establishing itself as the foremost Jewish newspaper in the United States. It was the original home of American Jewish literati, featuring Emma Lazarus among the leading literary figures that it introduced. The *Jewish Encyclopedia* noted that "nearly all the prominent Jewish writers and communal workers in the United States have been contributors to its pages."[41]

Kallen's views concerning the nature and implications of Jewish group solidarity had, until 1910, engaged only a relatively limited audience. The spokesmen for the Reform movement, which was the unofficial Jewish "establishment" of the day, enjoyed the greatest prestige, and they were quite vocal about promoting their religious vision of Judaism. But in 1910, following the Reform rabbis' annual convention at which they adopted the official credo of "universal Judaism," Kallen launched an incendiary attack on the leadership of the Reform movement, sparking a sustained debate in the pages of the *American Hebrew* concerning the essential foundations of Jewish identity, and catapulting him to prominence.

Kallen began by attacking the notion of *universal Judaism*, a phrase that Reform rabbis felt captured their belief in a universal moral God and implied their duty to spread that monotheistic message to the world. The *American Hebrew* trumpeted Kallen's attack by placing "The Value of Universal Judaism" as the lead article of their January 14, 1910, issue. Kallen dismissed the idea of universal Judaism as a meaningless contradiction, posing as both universal and particularistic at the same time. He accused the Reform rabbis of "intellectual deficiency." He suggested that the phrase's popularity was entirely driven by emotional appeal. Arguably, Kallen's own vision of Hebraism as a contributory force for world civilization constituted a "universal secularism" with its own implicit call for missionary service. Although he essentially transposed Reform Judaism's religious ethical mission ideal in a secular key, Kallen had no tolerance for the idea in a religious context. He lambasted both the idea of universal Judaism and the connected idea of a "mission of Israel," opining that it had "imperial" implications, was intolerant of difference, and was based on egotism while insidiously posing as altruism. In the final analysis, "they aim fundamentally at their own aggrandizement alone."[42] Not surprisingly, this provoked a response.

The *American Hebrew* published a letter to the editor by the Reform rabbi and future president of the Central Conference of American Rabbis, Max Raisin, in its February 11, 1910, issue. First, Raisin defended the term *universal Judaism* as expressing "the highest and broadest possible conception of the God-idea." Judaism's God-idea, Raisin insisted, was superior to that held by both Christianity and Islam. In no uncertain terms, Raisin claimed that Judaism is "*the only true faith*." Raisin then sought to marginalize Kallen personally, resorting to an ad hominem argument. "Mr. Kallen," he wrote, "denies having anything in common with the Jews and the Judaism of our day."[43] Raisin all but declared Kallen an apostate. The vehemence with which he denunciated Kallen is all the more remarkable considering the fact that Raisin was part of a vocal minority of Reform rabbis who identified positively with Zionism. Raisin, however, like Reform rabbis generally, embraced an exclusively religious definition of Judaism, and he could not countenance Kallen's attack on that.

A particularly lengthy and strident response to Kallen was expressed in a sermon by the prominent Reform rabbi Samuel Schulman, and reprinted in the *American Hebrew* on February 25, 1910. The Reform Conference, Schulman wrote, "proclaimed joyously and boldly the universal message of Judaism that it is a religion, rational and ethical, and applicable to mankind." But this joyous message "got a conceited sneer from a College instructor who boasts of his indifference to either Orthodox, Conservative or Reform Judaism, and presumably, to any Judaism, and who is a type of 'some intellectuals' who would have us commit ourselves to a mere racialism or Zionism." Such a person should be ignored, Schulman asserted: "He is of the type of the intellectuals who care nothing about the Jewish religion, who for all we know are perhaps not even Theists, but who are Zionists and who want to see the Jewish race perpetuated. If you ask them why, you may get an answer such as this gentleman gave me in conversation, 'I'm a Zionist for "biological reasons."' I might make fun of this term but I will not. What it means is, that the Jews should continue to live as a race, though he deny everything Israel has stood for in history." Finally, Schulman compared Kallen, whom he called "the Jewish indifferentist," to "the Christian anti-Semite," because both see "the characteristic things of Judaism in the *particular*, in rites, racial or tribal customs, which he tells us we have no reason to be proud of."[44]

Schulman, like Raisin, did not hesitate to resort to ad hominem arguments to discredit Kallen. Kallen did not allow that to pass unchallenged: "Now, both Messrs. Schulman and Raisin imagine that the cogency of a discussion or the truth of a proposition is identical with the nature of its source," he retorted in "Judaism, Hebraism, and Zionism." "Hence their method is essentially an attempt to refute my argument by very courteous animadversions upon my person, my traits, and my incidental private beliefs, of which they are completely ignorant." Kallen argued that Hebraism, better than Judaism, reflected the life of the Jews "as a *well-defined ethnic group*." He also articulated for the first time a connection between his cultural conception of Hebraism and his national and moral conception of Zionism. The Jewish spirit which is Hebraism, Kallen wrote, is "a flower whose roots are race and whose soil is nationality. Zionism is the one ethical solution to the Jewish problem because . . . that unique note which is designated in Hebraism will assume a more sustained, a clearer and truer tone in the concert of human cultures, and will genuinely enrich the harmony of civilization."[45] For Schulman and for Raisin, this was a debate between Reform and Zionist Jews. Kallen, however, considered far more than Zionism to be at stake. He was involved in a debate that went to the heart of what it meant to be a Jew and what it meant to be an American. The stridency of the confrontation points to the underlying political tensions concerning the contested suitability of Jews to be incorporated into the American civil sphere. Their conflict was fueled by the pressures brought to bear by Congress's insistence on definitively categorizing what Jews are.

Kallen had personally become a locus for the debate over Jewish identity. It was a debate that took place in the public square of modernity—the popular press. Particularly striking is the fact that both Schulman and Raisin had established positions of authority within the Jewish community. Both were prominent rabbis, and their authority flowed from their positions as communal leaders. Kallen, however, had no comparable standing. The *American Hebrew* played an important role in changing that. Kallen was neither a rabbi nor a leader within an established Jewish community. He was affiliated Jewishly by virtue of his activity in the Zionist movement and his involvement with the Menorah Society, but otherwise Kallen had no mainstream affiliation. He was not an unknown, as is clear from the fact that Schulman and Raisin saw Kallen as representative of American Zionism. On balance, however, Kallen could not be said to have as much Jewish social capital as Schulman and Raisin, who, when they spoke, enjoyed the implicit supporting presence of established Reform Jewish communities. Kallen's social capital was essentially academic in nature. The *American Hebrew* said as much when it listed Kallen in its "Persons Talked about" section of its August 4, 1911, issue because of his faculty appointment to the University of Wisconsin.[46] And yet, the journal made the exchange between Kallen on the one side, and Schulman and Raisin on the other, a debate between equals. By headlining both Schulman's and Kallen's articles, both voices were considered to be on an equal footing in this Jewish public square, and were strong enough to sustain a debate that extended from January through June 1910. Jacobs, as editor of the *American Hebrew* and as someone sympathetic to Kallen's ideas, which so closely followed his own, was aware of the power of the prominent rabbis. Jacobs set out to promote Kallen's social capital.

Among the printed press's novel interventions in the public sphere is that it placed people with different social standing onto the same plane of discourse. The presentation format communicated to readers that all three of these writers had equal authority to speak. The periodical press offered Kallen a unique opportunity to occupy a prominent place within the public sphere of the Jewish community in the only way possible for him, since he was otherwise unconnected to mainstream organized Jewish life. This exchange in the *American Hebrew* offers a striking instance of the role of an editor in boosting Kallen's social capital.

The Scientific Vindication of the Hebraic Worldview

Kallen felt particularly provoked by the type of leadership exercised by the Reform rabbinate, and he attacked it time and again in various articles.[47] It is not that Kallen specifically wanted to counterpose Zionism to Reform, but he did wish to promote a secularized philosophical alternative to a religious definition of Judaism. In the *American Hebrew*'s September 17, 1909, edition, at the urging of his friend Jacobs, Kallen published the earliest and perhaps the most important expression of his philosophical point of view, "Hebraism and Current Tendencies in Philosophy." Kallen considered it important enough to include as the lead article in a book that he published more than two decades later, *Judaism at Bay*.[48]

Kallen described *Hebraism* (the term he preferred over *Judaism*) as the application of philosophical Darwinism. Whereas Hellenism sees the world as "static and structural," Kallen asserted, Hebraism embraces change and flux. Its worldview is "dynamic and functional." The essence of the Greek metaphysical vision, Kallen wrote, is "structure, harmony, order immutable, eternal." The Hebraic metaphysical vision, on the other hand, is "flux, mutation, imminence, disorder."

This difference in worldview extended to views of the operations of science. "Scientific Hellenism," Kallen explained, which understood "the object of science as eternal and immutable substance, as forms, genera, species, varieties, existing eternally in their Aristotelian classifications," had been delivered a "death blow" by Darwin. The Hebraic worldview, Kallen believed, was vindicated by Darwin. To embrace Darwinian thinking is "to espouse the flux, to allow for genuine freedom and chance in the world, to insist on the concrete instance rather than on the general law—in a word, to give an overwhelming scientific background to the Hebraic as against the Hellenic visions of the nature of reality."[49]

It is unlikely that Kallen actually read Darwin. "The crux of Darwinism," he wrote, inaccurately, "lies in the two principles of 'spontaneous generation' and the 'survival of the fit.'" Darwin, however, did not at all advance a hypothesis concerning spontaneous generation. From our current perspective, Darwinian natural selection seemed to be contradicted by Hugo de Vries's theory that genetic mutations play a role in evolution, because it supported the idea of abrupt and sudden evolutionary changes (saltation), whereas Darwin had maintained that only gradual change occurs in nature (a maxim known as *natura non facit saltum*). This apparent contradiction was only later resolved with the modern evolutionary synthesis. However, it is nevertheless also true that in the early years of the twentieth century, not everyone saw a contradiction. "The latest fashion in evolutionary biology," Kallen wrote, "De Vries['s] doctrine of 'mutations,' does not challenge them [i.e., spontaneous generation and survival of the fittest], it only asserts them less modestly than they assert themselves."[50] Darwin and de Vries, Kallen believed, espoused complementary evolutionary models. This view was not Kallen's alone; nor was it even his original idea. He had learned it from William James, who believed "spontaneous variation" to be one of Darwin's key concepts.[51] Kallen's interest in Darwinism, like James's, appears primarily to have been psychological and philosophical in nature. For Kallen, Darwinism articulated the conditions for a new era of pride in the modern relevance, and, indeed, the triumph of the Jewish worldview. This was not a religious vindication supported by divinely revealed truth, but a thoroughly secular one supported by a scientifically revealed truth.

That Kallen chose to publish his views in the *American Hebrew* also reflects his lifelong pragmatic approach to science and philosophy. He criticized the academic life of philosophy as "a ceremonial liturgy of professionals as artificial and detached from the realities of the daily life as bridge or chess." Kallen's philosophical and scientific interests were "crossed by direct participation," as he put it, in the "political and economic movements of the land, especially those aiming at the protection and growth of freedom."[52] Thus, "Hebraism and Current Tendencies in Philosophy" announced Kallen's presence in print culture as one of what Andrew Jewett calls the "scientific democrats" of Progressive Era America. For scientific democrats like Kallen and the philosopher John Dewey, science was a resource for fostering and guiding social change, and they sought to influence public opinion accordingly. Jewett argues that Dewey, for example, "stood for the expectation that science and morality would fuse in a unified, post-Christian, and intrinsically democratic public culture."[53] Kallen believed in the need to spark in his readers an awareness of the scientifically validated foundations of Jewish thought and culture, and to appreciate that culture was more fundamental than religion, economics, or the state, in the life of the people. Kallen hoped that the influence he would exert through promoting his ideas in the popular press would initiate a Jewish cultural renaissance.

Race Science and the American Jewish Press

A visual scan of articles carried by the *American Hebrew* in the decade leading up to the start of World War I shows that it published more on race science than did the *American Israelite*, a leading organ for the Reform movement, and the *Jewish Exponent* combined. No doubt this had much to do with the fact that Jacobs was its editor. Interest in the issue of race was spurred by both the United States Immigration Commission's inquiries into the issue and by the meeting of the Universal Races Congress in London in 1911.

Kallen's particular view on race was not considered uniquely authoritative; the *American Hebrew* had published an opposing view in 1906, which presented Maurice Fishberg's challenge to the idea of a pure Jewish race.[54] From about the time Jacobs became editor, however, there was a marked tendency by the magazine to favor the voices of those who did believe in the reality of a Jewish race. This distinguished the *American Hebrew* from the *American Israelite*, which displayed considerably more indecisiveness on the issue. Thus, for example, the *American Israelite* carried an article in 1912 that rehearsed the German Jewish anthropologist Ignaz Zollschan's views, asserting that he had provided "incontrovertible facts" to combat race prejudice (Zollschan's view was that Jews are roundheaded and racially pure); and it carried a contradictory article the following year that referred to Fishberg as "an authority on Jewish anthropology" who rejected the idea of a pure Jewish race.[55] The *American Hebrew* was more consistent in its presentation of racial science.

The first Universal Races Congress garnered international attention for the spotlight that it shone upon racism. In August 1911 the *American Hebrew* carried an article reprinted from the *Jewish Review of London*, which purported to summarize "from an unbiassed [*sic*] stand-point," the variety of views regarding the position of the Jewish people among the world's races.[56] In October of that same year, the *American Hebrew* published an editorial, "Race and Environment," which observed that the issue of whether racial characteristics were determined by heredity or by environment was still undetermined: "Perhaps one of these days science will come to the conclusion that both factors are equally necessary and efficacious. Carlyle put what is probably the truth in his usual vigorous way, when he declared that a cabbage can never produce a rose, but that circumstances will determine whether it is a good or a bad cabbage."[57] Considering the mechanism of transmission to be an open question, but not questioning the fact of transmission itself, suggests that the issue of whether or not the Jews were a race had already been settled. For the *American Hebrew*, Jews were to be considered a race.

From 1911 to 1914 the *American Hebrew* carried a number of articles (some being reprints of articles first printed in England) that showcased, in particular, the views of Jewish anthropologists such as Joseph Jacobs, Redcliffe Salaman, and Ignaz Zollschan, all of whom continued to promote the notion of a Jewish racial identity.[58] Significantly, the English and German provenance of these racial views shows the importance that European racial discourse played not only for Kallen, but also for a broad-based Jewish audience. The American school of Boasian anthropology had not, at this point, exercised a determining influence on Jewish American views. The development of these racial views, however, left open the question of the implications of the Jewish racial presence on American soil.

The Jewish Psyche and the American Mind

In an address before the Jewish Publication Society's (JPS) twenty-sixth annual meeting in 1914, which marked the significant occasion of the appearance of a Jewish English-language translation of the Bible, Kallen made the startling claim that the Puritans were descendants of English Jews. Thus, he believed that a Jewish psychological heritage has been a factor in American life since the time the Puritans first arrived.

Kallen had originally learned to connect his Jewish heritage with Puritan values from the literary scholar Barrett Wendell. As Kallen recalled it in 1962, "Largely, it was his [Wendell's] appraisal of the Hebraic tradition in the formation and development of the American Idea, as Theodore Parker called it, that opened my eyes to how the Jewish difference had signified as a releasing and strengthening influence in the past and what it might continue to signify, not in the American scene alone, but wherever it was unsuppressed and free to grow."[59] In 1914, however, Kallen not only perceived an affinity between Hebraic and American values, he also believed quite literally that history revealed a biological connection between Puritans and Jews. The *Jewish Exponent* carried the text of Kallen's address, in which he said that the lineage of the Calvinist Puritans who settled in New England could be traced back to converted Jews in Lincolnshire.[60] Moreover, because Judaism and Calvinism both accept God's providence and both lay claim to being God's elect, Kallen claimed that Calvinism was best described as "a sort of de-Judaized expression of Judaism." These "facts" led Kallen to make his claim regarding the Puritans' Hebraic psychic inheritance. "The coincidence in temper is more than a mere accident," he said. "Cultures are racial just as human groups are racial, and psychological heredity is just as capable of characterization in history as is physical heredity and is much more easily to be characterized than physical heredity." The Puritans' Hebraic psychic heritage determined their attitude toward government, he asserted, and the "Hebraic stamp" was "set upon the whole of cultured America."[61]

The image is arresting. Kallen here appears to base his claim for Jewish civility not simply on the basis of being classified as white, or because Jews have served (and continue to serve) a signal role in the cause of world civilization. Rather, Jews were to be considered civil on the grounds of their racial psyche, a psyche shared with the Puritan founders. If the Puritans were racially Jewish, this would render impotent any imputations of Jews being uncivil in the American context. Their incorporation by the core group should be natural and automatic, because they are related.

Kallen's racial claim was immediately attacked by some as absurd. Indeed, his speech sparked an editorial in the *American Hebrew* that appeared on the very same day that his address was printed in the *Jewish Exponent*:

> Any view that attempts to connect actual theories of life with heredity is almost obviously at variance with the facts of the latter science. One cannot imagine that definite views about fate, free will and other metaphysical entities can be carried over from parent to child in the chromosomes of the germ-plasm, which are the only things physically common to the two. . . . Puritanism is a product of the Jewish spirit not of the Jewish race, and the affinity between Americanism and "Hebraism"—as Dr. Kallen calls it—is not due to identity of race but to common ideals which both Jews and Puritans have derived from the same source, the Book of Books.[62]

The anonymous author reacted against his racial identification of Jews with Puritans, and argued that the affinity was due to ideals rather than to biology. The author viewed Kallen's claim as an objectionable instance of the current vogue of connecting biology to culture. Even as the editorial rejected Kallen's peculiar racial assertion, however, it reaffirmed that there exists an essential connection between Jews and Puritans. This notion resonated deeply with a generation of American Jews who wished to establish belonging in American culture, and who resisted the racist nativism that had begun to exercise a profound influence upon the nation from even before World War I.

Not everyone would have dismissed Kallen's racial view as patently absurd, however. In the 1910s it was commonly believed that racially distinct psychic personalities existed, and indeed such ideas had entered popular and psychological discourse as a way to define racial difference, particularly Jewish racial difference. The existence of a Jewish type of mind was assumed by both Jewish and non-Jewish social scientists and psychologists in fin de siècle science.

A growing number of psychological thinkers began to claim that enduring psychological traits, rather than physiological ones, best defined racial difference. Representative of this type of thinking is a 1916 article that appeared in the *Monist.* The author, a psychologist, claimed that "psychic personality" is "the most potent, determining factor for each and every race," and is "by far the best guide for distinguishing one race from the other; and while physical characters fail, being as they are subject to environment, physiological, and other changes, it persists in spite of all outward changes." The Jewish race, the author argued, serves as a particularly good example of the persistence of racial "psychic personality." The article was reprinted in the *American Israelite* in October 1916.[63] A Jewish readership was thus exposed to this alternative racial construction, one that was very much aligned with Kallen's view.

Kallen's view of a Jewish psychic personality soon led him to develop a claim that was intended to support the continued mental health and well-being of that group personality, but which is perhaps jarring to our ears. There is a positive need, Kallen believed, to practice Jewish eugenics. Kallen proposed that Jewish racial purity should be preserved through endogamy, in order to promote Jewish racial hygiene. It is difficult for the modern reader to hear such a statement without experiencing a horrified shudder. The memory of the monstrous Nazi implementation of Aryan eugenics is, for us, all too vivid. But in the 1910s the horrific potential of eugenics was not part of American consciousness, and, moreover, eugenics was a respectable form of science which came to play an important role in American social and political discourse.[64] It figured prominently in the debates concerning the large-scale immigration taking place, and stoked fears over racial dilution and pollution.

Although Jewish thinkers like Kallen opposed eugenics-based arguments that were used to support an immigration quota, they were also responsive to the fact that racial hygiene was a widespread concern among both Europeans and Americans. A number of Jewish thinkers, in fact, extolled the virtues of Jewish sexual hygiene in light of this larger social concern. Jewish advocates of eugenics sought to demonstrate that Judaism had always been as concerned with racial health as contemporary Europeans and Americans.[65] It was practically an indicator of Jewish self-respect for thinkers such as Kallen to make an argument for Jewish eugenics.

Kallen had been concerned about the consequences of intermarriage between a Jew and a Gentile from at least 1908.[66] The first printed articulation of his concern appeared in his 1910 article "Judaism, Hebraism and Zionism," published in the *American Hebrew*: "For the present I can only register my conviction of this fact, *in which lies the negative reason of the moral inevitability of Zionism. This reason, also, I can merely indicate. It is the fact that—popular opinion to the contrary notwithstanding—the crossing of Jews with Gentiles is eugenically undesirable. The progeny is not so good as either parent of pure stock. There is considerable reason to believe that in the long run, crossing means deterioration.*"[67] At this stage in his thinking, Kallen perceived intermarriage to be a threat to Jewish racial integrity. He accepted the postulate of eugenics—that is, that miscegenation would result in diminished survival capacity.

In context, it should be noted, this assertion follows on the heels of Kallen's thesis that concerns the continued "cultural efficacy" of the Jews, or, their ability to continue to contribute to the progress of civilization: "For the purposes of cultural efficacy it is not necessary that the Jews shall be a *pure* race; it is necessary that they shall be a *prepotent* race."[68] *Prepotency* was not Kallen's own idiosyncratic word. It had been used by Jacobs in his studies of heritable traits. As Jacobs explained in the *American Hebrew* in 1911, the term *prepotency* was a throwback to pre-Mendelian biology: "We used to speak of 'prepotency' then where the Mendelians speak of dominance, and of 'atavism' where they refer to recessives."[69] Kallen's concern with Jewish eugenics, then, was tied to his concern for the preservation of a dominant Jewish heritable trait, the desirability and suitability of which is demonstrated by the purported Jewish racial cosmopolitan commitment to justice and equality for all.

Kallen was hardly unique among Jews in his opposition to intermarriage on eugenic grounds. The Bloch Publishing Company, for example, was among those who brought the issue of intermarriage to the Jewish reading public. In 1916 it published a pamphlet containing a paper by an influential Reform rabbi, Max Reichler, on Jewish eugenics that was read before the New York Board of Jewish Ministers. Reichler argued that the rabbinic sages had intuited the wisdom of eugenicists and made marriage laws accordingly. He accepted eugenics as a valid science, and sought only to establish a prior Jewish intuition about it. Reichler interpreted Jewish marriage laws to teach a kind of sexual hygiene, asserting that "a number of precautions in sexual relations were prescribed in order to prevent the birth of defectives." Like Kallen, Reichler's notion of Jewish sexual hygiene took into account that, as he put it, "both physical and psychical qualities were inherited." Reichler concluded that a rabbinic interdiction against intermarriage had been established "to preserve and improve the inborn, wholesome qualities of the Jewish race."[70] Reichler's essay was cited approvingly by Maurice Fishberg.[71] The notion of a Jewish psychophysical inheritance and the importance of Jewish eugenics had a receptive Jewish audience.

American Jewish readers of the *American Hebrew* in 1910 also learned that the effects of intermarriage on Jewish group integrity were the subject of scientific inquiry. They read that the Anglo-Jewish biologist Redcliffe Salaman, who applied Mendelian genetics to Darwinian theory, "believed that the Jews were a pure race."[72] In fact, Salaman argued that the Jews were, in Mendelian terms, a "recessive" type. The evidence for this, Salaman felt, was only strengthened by Francis Galton's experiments and the composite portraits that he had done in collaboration with Joseph Jacobs in 1885.[73]

As editor for the *American Hebrew*, Jacobs solicited his readers' assistance in accumulating statistical data for an anthropological study. He had proposed a test of whether Mendelism applied to intermarriages between Jews and Gentiles by looking at the offspring of the intermarried children of intermarried parents. Jacobs wished to determine if, following the Mendelian rule of genetics, three-fourths of those children would resemble the dominant Gentile parent and one-fourth would resemble the recessive Jew. Jacobs appealed to his readers to alert him to any such cases of a double intermarriage in order to help resolve the "oft-vexed question of the purity of the Jewish race." He signaled to them the social significance of this investigation: "Many Jews are only kept faithful to their Jewish connections by the conviction of their being of the same race with their fellow Jews. This conviction may help to tide them over the present era of transition but, if broken down by anthropology, may cause them to fall entirely away from Jewish communion. What seems at first a merely biological problem may thus have far reaching spiritual results."[74] The findings of anthropologists, Jacobs seemed to believe, could influence the future marriage pattern of Jews and so affect the Jewish future. Significantly, Jacobs sought to enfranchise his readers in the scientific process of investigation.

Kallen's racial views thus not only reflected the views of important Jewish scientific thinkers like Jacobs and Salaman but would also have had a receptive audience among Jewish readers. The latter were exposed to the same set of racial ideas and assumptions upon which Kallen drew. Kallen's racial assertion was not an original scientific insight, nor was it merely his idiosyncratic belief. Kallen's novel contribution to the question of Jewish identity in the material discussed thus far is therefore not discovered in his scientific claims but rather in his interpretation that a specific racial claim both supported secular Jewish identity and justified Jewish incorporation into the civil sphere.

By the 1930s, as the influence of cultural anthropology continued to grow, and as the specter of Nazi racial science loomed threateningly on the horizon, Kallen's views had completely changed. Franz Boas specifically sought Kallen's help to "expose the falsity of the racial theories" of Nazi propaganda. To that end, Boas wrote to Kallen, proposing "a thorough scientific investigation of alleged racial characteristics," the results of which were to be popularized "as rapidly as possible." The very next day, Kallen responded that he fully supported Boas's proposed educational enterprise to expose the "fantasy of the Nazis about race."[75] This later collaboration between Boas and Kallen nevertheless has a certain thread of continuity with Kallen's earlier views. Ultimately, Jewish race scientists all anchored their views in what John Efron terms "a hopeful and redemptive liberal humanism."[76] Jewish racial theory had none of the associations of hierarchical dominance that was characteristic of non-Jewish racial science. For Kallen, during these early years of his development, as we have seen, race science bolstered his case for Jewish incorporation and supported his cosmopolitan outlook.

Competing for Social Capital

American politics in the 1900s and 1910s helped to polarize American Jews into ideological camps. One camp, represented by the Reform movement, insisted on prioritizing a religious definition for Judaism. Another camp, represented in the main by Zionists, identified with a racialized view of Judaism, and attempted to negotiate the murky ground between culture, psychology, and biology. At issue were the conditions for Jewish belonging in America. Kallen's perspective was unique, as he argued that Hebraic psychophysical inheritance offered a moral justification for Jewish existence, and that this inheritance was also shared with the Puritan founders of America. Kallen's point of view was not so idiosyncratic, however, that it failed to find any traction in American Jewish discourse. The periodical press carried his ideas into the public domain, and it also provided a forum in which extended debate concerning them took place.

Kallen's growing presence in Jewish print culture established him not only as a vocal participant in an ongoing racial discourse but also as someone who was able to appropriate scientific discourse and reframe it in the popular mind such that it articulated a secular redemptive vision for Jews and for America. Kallen attempted to lay the groundwork for a liberal humanism designed to ensure Jewish health and survival even as he sought to integrate Hebraism into the fabric of American ideals. The Jewish press, in turn, helped to boost Kallen's authority in the public square of American Jewish discourse.

A racialized cultural conception of Hebraism and Hellenism was, for Kallen, central to the discourse concerning Jewish civility. Hebraism was the key to a contributory discourse in which the Jewish psychical character mark is vindicated by post-Darwinian reality and by its cosmopolitan cultural efficacy. Hebraism was the cultural expression of a heritable Jewish psyche and justified Jewish identity on a secular and scientific basis. Jewish group integrity was necessary to maintain in order to be assured of the purity and continued transmission of Hebraism. Finding political expression as Zionism, Hebraism's central aim was to further the progress of civilization. Kallen maintained that Hebraism's central teaching is to affirm the value of human life and the pursuit of righteousness, and that this suffused the Puritan worldview and thus served as a basis for American values. For Kallen, this shared racial inheritance linked Jews to American universal values even as it simultaneously reinforced ethnic particularism.

· 2 ·

Transnational Social Psychology and Nationality/Ethnicity

> There is no place for . . . hyphenated Americans.
>
> —Louis Brandeis, "What Loyalty Demands" (1905)

> To be good Americans, we must be better Jews, and to be better Jews, we must become Zionists.
>
> —Louis Brandeis, "Americanism and Zionism" (1914)

HEBRAISM, for Kallen, transcended the religion of Judaism. It signified the "total biography of the Jewish soul," embracing not only religion but also history, language, and culture.[1] We have seen how Kallen retooled Matthew Arnold's transhistorical Hellenism and Hebraism in the service of his own secularized vision of Judaism's compatibility with the modern scientific zeitgeist. He had argued that, just as Darwin's challenge to the idea of the fixity of species meant seeing the world as existing in a state of flux, so, too, Hebraism allowed for chance and freedom in the world. Humanity had begun to perceive the world for what it is, Kallen contended, rather than to impose an idea of what it ought to be. This modern worldview was, to Kallen, fundamentally Hebraic; it was imprinted on the psyche of the Jew as a way of relating to the world.

Hebraism served a dual function for Kallen. It was both particularistic and universal. It laid claim to an essential Jewish identity, rooted in the heritable matrix of the ethnic psyche in a manner reminiscent of Baldwin's supra-biological "organic selection." At the same time, it affirmed the special and unique contribution of the Jewish people to world civilization. In Kallen's view, Hebraism offered the world the gift of a moral insight in the form of its commitment to righteousness and its recognition of the value of human life even in the face of indifferent nature.

Jakob Egholm Feldt characterizes Kallen's view as a Jewish cosmopolitanism. It is a cosmopolitanism that resists the universalist pretentions of Enlightenment-based cosmopolitanism by insisting on the contributory role of minority groups. "Despite his blatant Eurocentrism and synonymous use of the West and civilisation as concepts often meaning the world, Kallen's thought nevertheless invokes many of the same themes as minoritarian modernity and postcolonial cosmopolitanism," Egholm Feldt writes. "*Avant la lettre*, Kallen's 'Jewish cosmopolitanism' insisted that true cosmopolitanism must be pragmatic, postcolonial, and experimental."[2] In this sense, Kallen's thought aligns well with that of the Chicago School of Sociology and fellow pragmatists who all resisted discourses of universalism.

But Kallen's racial construction of Jewish identity distinguishes him, and distances him, from John Dewey and his cosmopolitan allies. Although Kallen was, like Dewey, a functionalist psychologist, his application of functionalism to race psychology was unique. The functionalist approach to psychology grounded Kallen's claim for an inherited Jewish psyche that is especially attuned to Hebraism, understood as an adaptive cultural and spiritual force particularly well-suited for the modern zeitgeist. From the functionalist point of view, Kallen would have understood psychophysical inheritance to constitute a conditioned mental instinct defined by a functional role. That role would be to contribute to the overall coordination between an individual's thought and behavior and the social environment in which he or she lives. When properly calibrated with the group's cultural consciousness (i.e., Hebraism), the individual's coordination efforts are maximized to their full potential, leading to the healthiest possible expression of living. This feature of his thinking allows us to resituate Kallen within an ongoing discourse concerning the nature and limits of ethnicity. We shall see that, in a different *avant la lettre* capacity,

Kallen's construction of Jewish identity anticipates constructions of ethnicity that were advanced only beginning in the late twentieth century.[3]

The primary institutional venue through which Kallen promoted his notion of Hebraism was through the Intercollegiate Menorah Association, the university-based Jewish cultural movement that he helped to found in 1906 while a graduate student at Harvard. This chapter traces Kallen's growing social capital through his engagement with the IMA and its publication, the *Menorah Journal*, during the 1910s. In the course of his involvement with the Menorah Association, Kallen developed his ideas concerning Jewish identity and the place of the Jews in America in the context of contemporary racial discourse. He developed a secular conception of Jewish identity rooted in *nationality*, or, in today's parlance, *ethnicity* (the term *ethnicity* did not appear in print until 1941). It was through the IMA and the *Menorah Journal* that Kallen introduced his ideas concerning Jewish nationality, and the *Menorah Journal* devoted significant attention to the subject subsequent to that. The Menorah movement and the *Menorah Journal* were instrumental in shaping the notion of Jewish ethnicity.[4]

As Daniel Greene has shown, Kallen, and with him the Menorah Association, attempted to stimulate a Jewish cultural renaissance on American soil, and advocated making a place for a hyphenated Jewish-American identity, arguing that it was possible to harmonize and affirm Jewish nationality with American citizenship.[5] In this chapter, we shall see that Kallen's notion of Jewish nationality/ethnicity grew out of his engagement with a transnational social psychological discourse, brought to the fore by the advent of World War I.

The Harvard Menorah Society was the first of what would become a nationwide series of Menorah chapters, organized as the IMA, devoted to furthering Jewish cultural life. Thanks in large part to Kallen's missionizing energy, new Menorah Society chapters were quickly established on other American campuses. Kallen organized a number of Menorah societies from Columbus, Ohio, in the Midwest to Berkeley, California, on the West Coast. In January 1913 the

Menorah Society chapters banded together to form the Intercollegiate Menorah Association and became the most influential Jewish organization on American campuses. The IMA enjoyed the endorsement and support of prominent Jewish leaders, including Louis Brandeis, Joseph Jacobs, Judah Magnes, Cyrus Adler, Kaufmann Kohler, Stephen Wise, and Solomon Schechter. By 1919, there were nearly eighty campus chapters.[6]

The significance of the IMA in American Jewish life goes far beyond its institutional status as a society established for Jewish university students. Daniel Greene traces the immense contributions to cultural pluralism made by the circle of intellectuals associated with the IMA in his excellent study of that organization. He discusses its grand aim to revitalize Jewish culture and to change America in the process. Horace Kallen is central to their story. He was, Greene writes, "the group's intellectual guide for . . . fifty years."[7] Kallen's Hebraism formed the core of the group's ideals from the beginning. It "provided them with a way to express themselves as Jewish without limiting that self-conception to what they viewed as their ancestors' anti-modern worldview," Greene explains. "The notion that Hebraism represented the modern infused all aspects of the Menorah Association's early history. Indeed, Hebraism defined what group members often called "the Menorah idea."[8]

That idea was secular, and not religious. At the IMA's third annual convention in 1914, Kallen spoke about the distinction he saw between Hebraism and Judaism. Judaism "stands exclusively for a religion," he said, "for that partial expression of the Jewish genius which is religious." Hebraism, on the other hand, stands "not for that particular expression of the Jewish mind, religion, but for all that has appeared in Jewish history, both religious and secular." It is the "flower and fruit of the *whole* of Jewish life. Its root is the ethnic nationality of the Jewish people."[9] As Kallen and the IMA understood it, Hebraism, not Judaism, was fundamental to Jewish ethnic consciousness.

Kallen envisioned the Menorah Association bringing "the separate Jewish classes together in terms of a common ideal," and serving as the source for "the revitalization of Jewish idealism among Jews who are to be the leaders of the next generation."[10] In 1962, reflecting upon the beginnings of the movement, Kallen recalled that it appeared to him an "expression of a new mood and a new outlook in America's overall Jewish scene." He explained:

> Wittingly or unwittingly, the Society was conceived and organized with the end-in-view of liberating the Jewish student from his feelings of inferiority as a Jew and the escapist compensations which he brought to college from his community. It was designed therefore to bring Jews of all derivations and persuasions together as Jews, in order that they might become aware of every one of the diverse expressions of vision and action which Jewish history records and Jewish culture embodies. It was designed to bring about an orchestration of the diversities, a consensus about the totality of the Jewish heritage worthy to be nourished, sustained, and transmitted to future generations. Existing modes of association would not do; the Zionist mode was too limited, since so many were either indifferent or antagonistic to the Zionist design, while the Judaist was too narrow. A national Reform religious organization had proposed a unit at Harvard which could further alienate and segregate Jewish students from one another. It was felt that every Jew, whatever his affiliations, should be able to join a society of Jews without reservation, and that its aims should be such as non-Jews could share. Such were the feelings that shaped the matrix of the Menorah Idea and eventuated in the formation of the Harvard Menorah Society.[11]

Kallen's extensive use of the passive voice in this passage to describe the Menorah Society conceals that he was in fact the active agent behind its conception, organization, and design. His desire to orchestrate the diversities of Jewish expression "shaped the matrix," as Kallen put it, of the "Menorah Idea." The Menorah Idea, in essence, was to shape American and Jewish perception of Jews such that Jews would be considered civil, and thus deserving of full incorporation into society as a culturally distinct group, in a manner evocative of what Jeffrey Alexander lauds as the multicultural mode. "With multiculturalism, there emerges the possibility that out-group qualities can be purified—that they can, in fact, become objects not only of tolerance but of respect and even desire," Alexander writes. "As the multicultural mode of incorporation becomes more than merely a theoretical possibility, the language of incorporation changes from integration to diversity. But the siren song of difference can attract only if it represents a variation on the chords of civil society."[12] In the context of the early 1900s, such a worldview was largely disparaged by a society that dismissed the idea that American identity could be hyphenated with an ethnic identifier.

Claiming space as a "hyphenated American" was controversial. Presidents Theodore Roosevelt and Woodrow Wilson both unequivocally rejected the idea that Americans might couple their American identity together with their national or cultural origins. For Roosevelt and Wilson, calling oneself Jewish-American, Irish-American, or German-American, for example, called into question whether or not that individual was truly an American. Moreover, the idea of a hyphenated identity suggested to them the possibility that one's true allegiance might lie with a nation other than America. Wilson and Roosevelt, as a biographer of Roosevelt puts it, "together unleashed an anti-hyphen movement."[13] Affirming hyphenation as a positive principle was a serious challenge to mainstream American sentiment, which trumpeted 100 percent Americanism. Kallen occupied a prominent position in the discourse concerning hyphenation beginning in 1915, when he affirmed the necessity of a hyphenated Jewish-American identity in both the Jewish and non-Jewish press.

Hebraism as Mission

Kallen's notion that Hebraism is the cultural expression of the Jewish racial psyche formed the kernel of his construction of Jewish identity as nationality. In a toast that he gave at the second annual Menorah Society convention dinner in 1913, Kallen was adamant that the term *race* should communicate something urgent, necessary, and more important than religion. The notion of purely voluntary association was the essence of religion. For Kallen, the involuntary association of race presented the stronger link to his heritage. Kallen's claim for an inborn psychic racial inheritance allowed him to minimize the importance of religious belief in his construction of Jewish identity. "Jews change their religion; I am myself an adherent of no religion, but I should resent harshly a statement that I am therefore no Jew," he said. "And I think that even Mr. Schiff, who denies that he is a member of a Jewish race and insists that he is a member of a religious sect, called Jews, will find it very much harder to change his grandfather than to change his religion."[14] Race was fundamental; religion was only one of the "external forms of associative unity."

But religion, as a voluntary form of "associative unity," was not a compelling expression of Jewish culture, according to Kallen, and, in fact, risked leading to the petrification of a living culture. Near the beginning of his speech, which shortly followed an address by the Reform movement's Hebrew Union College president Kaufmann Kohler, Kallen made it clear that he rejected Reform Judaism's universalism, seeing it as a fossilized thing, not as an active producer of culture. He attacked the Reform idea of a "mission of Israel," characterizing it as "a barbarous and egotistical doctrine." The continued existence of a mission depended, Kallen claimed, upon its nonfulfillment, and posited a condition under which Jews alone could "be noble and godly," whereas the rest of mankind was required to remain "ignoble and wicked."[15] To Kallen, Reform Judaism's idea of a mission to promote monotheism was arrogant, considering that it was Christianity that had been most active historically in spreading that doctrine; it served only the social interests of the Reform movement's wealthy elite. Kallen felt, moreover, that Reform's embrace of the universal brotherhood of man ignored the realities of particular ethnic distinctiveness.[16]

Kallen's opposition to the idea of a religious mission extended to the connected idea of the Jews as a "chosen people." That belief, Kallen argued, was a compensatory dogma, serving to make palatable the Jews' difficult lived reality under oppression and anti-Semitism. Kallen had no patience for such metaphysics; he insisted on the data of sociologists and anthropologists to describe Jews. He believed that the facts showed that Jews had certain inborn characteristics: "A special bias, an inherited *psyche*, makes us respond to it [Hebraism] more readily, makes us the natural conservers and developers of the Hebraic vision." Jews, in other words, were psychologically predisposed to Hebraism.

We have seen how, in 1914, Kallen had used the notion of Jewish psychophysical inheritance to claim the Jewish origins of the Puritans, seeking to establish Jewish belonging in America through that association. Here, he relied on the idea of Jewish psychophysical inheritance to make a different claim. He sought to establish the priority of Jewish secular and cultural identity over a religious one. This explained and justified the urgency Kallen felt to create a venue for a Jewish cultural renaissance. It made the mission of the Menorah Association, guided by the "comprehensive humanism" of Hebraism, more vital than any existing religious program.[17]

The IMA's "privilege and duty," Kallen insisted, was "to *advance* Hebraic culture and ideals."[18] His notion of Hebraism as the expression of Jewish psychophysical heredity, coupled with the notion of noblesse oblige (which Kallen enthusiastically embraced), functioned, ironically, as a secular version of the chosenness dogma that he so vehemently rejected. He replaced a religious concept of chosenness with a secular one. As Greene observes, where Mordecai Kaplan, the founder of Reconstructionist Judaism, replaced "chosenness" with "vocation," Kallen replaced it with "Hebraism."[19] Instead of spreading the theological doctrine of monotheism, Kallen wished to spread a secular doctrine of Hebraic culture and ideals.

Although in its early years the Menorah movement entertained debates at its conventions regarding whether or not religion should be a part of its mission, Kallen's secular vision nevertheless remained at the core of that mission. Its shared mission with the *Menorah Journal* incorporated Kallen's humanistic message: "For conceived as it is and nurtured as it must continue to be in the spirit that gave birth to the Menorah idea, the *Menorah Journal* is under compulsion . . . to deepen the consciousness of *noblesse oblige*[,] . . . dedicated first and foremost to the fostering of the Jewish 'humanities' and the furthering of their influence as a spur to human service."[20] The *Menorah*

Journal, however, made no reference to a Jewish psychic inheritance. That aspect of Kallen's thought did not become central to the movement's self-understanding, although the *Menorah Journal* did publish articles that accepted the notion of a racially inherited psyche. Two figures whose writings appeared there are especially noteworthy in this regard—Granville Stanley Hall, president of Clark University and the founder of the American Psychological Association, and Charles William Eliot, president emeritus of Harvard University. Through Hall and Eliot, the *Menorah Journal* exposed its Jewish readers to leading scientific and academic authorities who, like Kallen, understood race to describe the supra-biological condition of the psychological and ethical self-expression of the group.

The *Menorah Journal* and Psychic Inheritance

The *Menorah Journal* was the voice of the Menorah movement, but it was far more than a house organ. It was known as one of the better literary quarterlies in the country and it enjoyed a national circulation and prestige beyond the bounds of college campuses. It featured regular contributions from leading Jewish intellectuals and important Gentile thinkers.[21] "There has been something of the Menorah idea, and, in fact, some of the *Menorah* writers in every Jewish journal of intellectual aspirations that has appeared since the late 1930's," Robert Alter writes.[22] Daniel Greene refers to the *Menorah Journal* as the "leading journal of Jewish opinion in the English language" in its day.[23]

A distinguishing layout feature of the *Menorah Journal* was that each article featured a photograph of the author and a facsimile of the author's signature, and included a biographical sketch of the author, including, where applicable, the author's scholarly credentials, or their status as a university student, and their connection to the Menorah Association. The print layout thus flagged the *Menorah Journal*'s rootedness in the university context, its desire to establish itself as an intellectual journal, and, finally, its role in promoting the Menorah movement itself (the latter was also naturally reinforced by its regular reports on the happenings of the Menorah Association).

G. Stanley Hall's "Yankee and Jew" appeared in the *Menorah Journal*'s April 1915 issue. Hall was introduced as president of Clark University, "a leading authority on education and psychology, and author of a number of important books, notably *Adolescence* (2 vols. 1904)." It advertised Hall's engagement with the IMA by noting that he had originally delivered "Yankee and Jew" as a speech to the Clark Menorah Society. In "Yankee and Jew" Hall remarked on the commonalities that he observed between Yankees (i.e., Puritan Anglo-Saxons) and Jews. These commonalities stem, Hall argued, from ideals Jews share with Jesus. Hall sought to draw attention to the psychological affinity between his construction of Jesus and his perception of Jews. "Such of us psychologists as have recently been interested in the psychological aspect of Jesus' life and work understand, as had never been understood before, how purely Jewish he was. . . . According to many conceptions the chief trait of Jesus was a strong and deep enthusiasm for the loftiest things in life," Hall wrote. "His soul was unconquerable by misfortune and disaster, like that of the Jewish race itself." Jesus was, therefore, "an extremely representative man of your race."[24] Hall thus expressed the idea that psychology holds the key to understanding racial identity.

Hall derived from this psychological insight the lesson that the "enthusiasm for the loftiest things in life" shared by Jews and Gentiles should lead to tolerance for difference: "We must neither of us abandon our birthright. We must be the very best Puritan Anglo-Saxons we possibly can, and you must be the best Jews possible, for out of these component elements American citizenship is made up. This country stands for the dropping of old prejudices, such as those that are inflaming Europe now with war. If we can satisfy each other's ideals and meet half way the thing is done, and the melting pot which America stands for has got in its work. I want the Menorah Society to feel that it is in the van of this movement."[25] Hall here suggested that the American melting pot need not imply the obliteration of ethnic and racial distinctiveness. Sharing values and committing to "satisfy each other's ideals" suffices for the melting pot to have "got in its work." Puritan Anglo-Saxons and Jews should each strive to be the best representatives of their respective race that they could be. Such differences as there are would be relatively inconsequential, since each race makes the same commitment to American citizenship. Hall thus posited Jewishness not as a faith-based identity, but as a racial one, rooted in the psyche and expressed as ideals. This led him to affirm the principle of hyphenated citizenship on a racial footing.

Similarly, Charles William Eliot spoke about Jewish ideals in racial terms. His article titled "The Potency of the Jewish Race" occupied the front page of the *Menorah Journal*'s June 1915 issue. The journal introduced Eliot as president emeritus of Harvard University, and stressed that he was "revered . . . by all Americans as a great leader of thought and opinion." It highlighted Eliot's connection to the Menorah movement, noting that he had welcomed its initial organization in 1906 and had facilitated its subsequent growth. Preparing this article for the *Menorah Journal*, it suggested, was a demonstration of Eliot's "continued sympathy with the Menorah aims and his interest in the *Menorah Journal*." Eliot shared with Hall the view that races may be judged by their inherited ideals. "The Jewish race," he wrote, "affords the strongest instance of the influence on a human stock of lofty ideals." This is because "in all generations and in all their various environments they have exhibited, and still exhibit, a remarkable racial tenacity and vigor." The Jewish race's continued tenacity and vigor are due, Eliot averred, "to the rare strength and significance of its ideals."[26]

If the Jewish race is to pass "the test of liberty," Eliot wrote, "it will get over its apparent tendency of the moment towards materialism and reliance on the power of money, hold fast to its social and artistic idealism, and press steadily towards its intellectual and religious ideals."[27] As uncomfortably as Eliot's remark sits with us today, it was, at the time, a relatively enlightened stance to take. Although Eliot granted legitimacy to the anti-Semitic slander of Jewish materialism, his statement undermined the claims of racial theorists who identified this as an essential Jewish racial characteristic. For Eliot, it marked only an "apparent tendency of the moment." The essential characteristics of the Jewish race are positive, he insisted, discovered in their social, artistic, intellectual, and religious ideals.

Psychological perspectives provided an alternative racial construction that proved attractive to progressive, cosmopolitan pluralists like Kallen, Hall, and Eliot. In anthropological circles, however, the scientific integrity of the term *race* was coming under more and more fire. Here, too, as we shall now see, the *Menorah Journal* offered readers insight into this aspect of the ongoing debates concerning Jewish racial identity.

Race and Religion: Enter Anthropology

The IMA and the *Menorah Journal* entertained a broad variety of opinions concerning the nature of Jewish identity, including religious and anthropological views that were opposed to Kallen's. Kaufmann Kohler, for example, had said at the Menorah Association's third annual convention, "We must insist that the Jewish race, the Jewish people or nation, if you want to call it so, can form only the body; Judaism, the Jewish religion, is the soul. And we will always stand not merely for the body, not merely for the material side, not merely for race, which is the lowest kind of life, but for the spirit, the soul of Judaism, and that is its religious truth."[28] Kohler's intolerance for Kallen's perspective quickly turned personal. He barred Kallen from speaking at Hebrew Union College in 1915 because he was an atheistic Zionist. Embarrassed, Hebrew Union College's Literary Society sent Kallen a formal apology, but it took many decades for the rift to heal.[29] Reform religious leaders were not the only ones, however, to take issue with Kallen's racial construction of Jewish identity. He also faced the opposition of American anthropologists such as Alfred Kroeber and Maurice Fishberg. These anthropologists tended to locate religion at the core of Jewish identity, a perspective that was incompatible with Kallen's conception of Hebraism. The *Menorah Journal* functioned as a prominent public platform where these different points of view were aired.

Kroeber published "Are the Jews a Race?" in the *Menorah Journal* in December 1917. He too accepted the then-prevalent common wisdom that inheritable racial features might be mental as well as physical. Kroeber offered up as examples the rather unsavory descriptions of "the Negro" as "unstable" and "emotional," and "the Mongolian and the American Indian" as mentally "slow." He maintained that there is a distinction to be made, however, between acquired and inherited mental characteristics: "What human minds acquire, they receive from education, from environment. What human minds inherit from their race is instinctive and unalterable." This distinction would, for Kroeber, prove crucial to his argument. He drew upon the same set of scientific assumptions as did Kallen, but Kroeber's interpretation of that data led him to draw the opposite conclusion. Jews, Kroeber insisted, are not a race. With regard to anatomy, Kroeber rejected the idea that Jews bore any distinctive traits. With regard to physiognomy, such as facial expressions, he granted that there are Jewish traits, but that these traits were the result of having a common religion, education, and habits of life. With regard to mentality, Kroeber granted that there is such a thing as a "'typical Jew' in character and temperament, but he is the product of social conditions, not of heredity and race."[30]

"If, then, the Jew is not a race, what is he?" Kroeber asked. "For over two thousand years, he has not formed a nation in the political sense." Kroeber concluded that the only thing common to all Jews, both past and present, was their faith: "The Jew, then, is a group, a caste, in the better sense of the word, held together by religion."[31] Kroeber concluded that the Jews were, at root, a religion, and not a race. Whereas Kallen maintained that Jews inherited "a natural capacity for Hebraism, not an acquired one," Kroeber believed that Jewish character and temperament were socially conditioned.[32] For Kroeber, as for the Reform movement, Jewish identity is, at root, religious, and not racial.

The *Menorah Journal*'s articles provoked discussion beyond its own pages. A critical response to Kroeber's article appeared on the lead page of the December 1917 issue of the Zionist weekly, the *American Jewish Chronicle*. The *Chronicle* editorial took issue with Kroeber's assertion that the Jews are not a race and are bound only by religion. Taking up almost four columns of space, it chastised the *Menorah Journal* for promoting the "errors" of anthropologists to the reading public: "The racial theoretician of the *Menorah Journal* repeats the error of many other anthropologists who are too materialistically orientated to apply the same methods to human races which are applied to animal races. It is altogether wrong to consider the question of the human race from a purely physiological point of view. That is more veterinary physiology than race theory. A. L. Kroever [*sic*] as well as the *Menorah Journal* should know that race is not a physiological notion only, for if it were, the word race would have to be cut out from our vocabulary."[33] For this author, the definition of *race* should not be limited to the physiological parameters defined by Kroeber. Race also describes people linked by propinquity and the sharing of ideals: "If a group of human beings have lived under the same conditions for thousands of years, if they have clung together all the time, and if they have been dominated by certain definite principles and have cherished the same ideals, they are a race, whether they are all long-headed or not and whether the hair of all of them is black or blond." This author appears to have shared the same view of race as Hall and Eliot.

The editorial concluded by noting that Kroeber's claim was a tired rehearsal of the position of Reform rabbis everywhere, little more than a platitude: "Nor is the assertion of A. L. Kroever [*sic*] that the Jews, not being a race, are held together by religion new. This he can hear every Saturday or Sunday from every reformed rabbi here and abroad."[34] The author here identified—and rejected—an important consequence of Kroeber's thesis, which is that it suggested a possible alignment of his anthropology with the ideological position of the Reform movement.

The author's heated rebuttal to Kroeber, however much he may have misread him, serves as a pointed reminder of how emotionally charged was the issue of a Jewish race among Jewish readers. This author's impassioned defense of the notion of a Jewish race leaves unclarified what to modern ears must sound like a fuzzy ambiguity concerning the nature and limits of race. But the widespread acceptance of the idea that nonphysiological mental and emotional racial markers exist gave the author the latitude to refute the "veterinary physiology" of those who would deny the Jews a racial identity.

Fishberg made much the same argument as Kroeber in "Assimilation: A Statement of Facts by a Scientist," published in the *Menorah Journal* in February 1920. Billed by the *Menorah Journal* as "an authority on the anthropology and the pathology of the Jews," Fishberg attacked the "pseudo-scientists known as race theorists." He offered for general consumption some of the conclusions that he had drawn from his 1911 study, *The Jews: A Study of Race and Environment*: "I have shown in my book, 'The Jews,' that from the standpoint of race purity the Jews do not materially differ from other groups of white people in civilized countries. Anthropologists have agreed that, when carefully examined, there are discovered among the modern Jews various racial elements and that it is not purity of ethnic strain that characterizes the Jew, but community of religious belief."[35] What bound Jews together was not racial purity, Fishberg maintained, but religious community. For him, this meant that the barriers between Jews and other whites in America were not insurmountable, biologically speaking, and that, therefore, assimilation was possible: "There are, consequently, no more racial obstacles to assimilation of the Jews among white peoples than there are to the assimilation of the Germans in America." Assimilation, Fishberg explained, occurs "when the language, religion, customs and habits of the population are or become homogeneous."[36]

Fishberg stressed that religion was at the core of Jewish identity. In his view, the main source of resistance to assimilation lay in the religious character of Judaism. Positioning himself as representing the received wisdom of the consensus of sociologists, Fishberg wrote, "It is the opinion of sociologists that certain Jewish religious rites, ordinances, and rituals have been more effective in preventing assimilation of the Sons of Jacob than all the Christian and Mohammedan laws which have been ordained against their coalescence with the general population during the entire period of their dispersal among the nations." The consensus, as Fishberg understood it, was that assimilation in the past had been prevented because of fidelity to Jewish religion, and not because of racial determinism. Fishberg's rejection of the idea of Jewish racial purity may not have been as definitive a rejection of the very category of race as applied to Jews as Kroeber had articulated, but it nevertheless left open the possibility that, absent the suasion of religious authority that had proved so effective in the past, or the social segregation suggested by political Zionism, which, Fishberg opined, "might prove to be the only preservative of Judaism which has thus far been suggested," American Jewish group consciousness would eventually erode.[37]

Although there is no record of a direct response from Kallen to either Kroeber or Fishberg, it is nevertheless clear that Kallen could not countenance such a conclusion. He refused to accept the suggestion that assimilation could only be countered by either religious fidelity or social segregation. The very idea of cultural homogenization ran counter to Kallen's philosophy of cultural pluralism. His vision of Jewish participation in American life as a secular identity required the support of the conceptual framework of Jewish nationality, which, in Kallen's view, existed prior to a Jewish religious identity.

The birth of Jewish group consciousness, Kallen believed, was marked not by monotheism but by an ethical attitude. Kallen expressed his views in a letter written to Judge Julian Mack in 1915. He insisted that the historic and primary Jewish contribution to the world was not monotheism but an ethical attitude: "That the Jews have contributed monotheism to the world is a legend, not a fact. The ancient world was about as monotheistic as it is now when the Jews entered it, and the importance of monotheism is derived from interpretations by religionists, not interpretations by historians and sociologists. It is rather an ethical attitude to which an incidental monotheism was accessory that the Jews have contributed to the world."[38] For Kallen, the ethical attitude, or Hebraism, was primary, not religious belief. "Religion is less than life, and as life becomes more and more secularized, the religion of the Jews becomes less and less of the life of the Jews. I use the word Hebraism, consequently, to designate the whole of that life, of which Judaism is a part," Kallen explained to Mack. "This is justified by history also—for Judaism appears toward the end of the history of the ancient Jews; it is post-prophetic, and it goes on from the time of its appearance with other *secular* expressions of the spirit of the Jewish nation. These are not Judaism, but Jewish, and such usage gives us the word Hebraism for the whole."[39] In light of the growing trend toward secularism that he saw all around him, Kallen believed that as Jews became less religious but were no less Jews, the truth of his proposition had become self-evident. *Hebraism*, not *Judaism*, was a term better suited to designate the whole of Jewish life, a life that included "*secular* expressions of the spirit of the Jewish nation." To Kallen, the racially tepid conclusions of anthropologists like Kroeber and Fishberg offered no path forward to the revitalization of Jewish cultural life in America. Kallen expressed his notion of Jewish nationality, resting on a foundation of racial identification, as a vision for the flowering of the secular expressions of the Jewish spirit in the context of an ethnically distinct group living in a democratic, multiethnic state, and, considered internationally, in the context of Israel contributing as a nation to the welfare of all nations.

Zionism, for Kallen, did not imply the political or social isolation of Israel. As he told both Jewish and non-Jewish reading audiences, it represented "first and foremost the Jewish programme of international service through national self-realization." Citing the nineteenth-century Italian revolutionary Giuseppe Mazzini, Kallen wrote that Zionism would lead to the fulfillment, "in Mazzini's words, [of] the Jews' 'special function in the European work of civilization.' . . . To the nations of the world it [Zionism] reasserted the prophetic ideal of internationalism as a democratic and cooperative federation of nationalities."[40] For Kallen, then, Jewish "national self-realization" was inextricably linked to international service. Far from being isolationist, Zionism represented for Kallen a commitment to the ideal of "internationalism," a progressive narrative that ran counter to the prevailing isolationist nationalism of the World War I era.

If Fishberg were right, that isolation alone would preserve Judaism, then Kallen's vision of Zionism as internationalism would not prevent its eventual dissolution. For Kallen during the 1910s and into the 1920s, only the notion of Jewish nationality, understood to signify primarily the lived expression of the psychophysical inheritance of the Jewish people, provided the necessary assurance that Jewish life would thrive. Thus, Kallen faced a battle on two fronts. He opposed not only the Reform religious leaders (who, at the time, spoke for American Jews generally) who insisted on a religious definition of Judaism, but also the scientific views of American anthropologists like Kroeber and Fishberg. Indeed, the logic of their position only lent credence to the religionist perspective.

The *Menorah Journal*'s receptivity to publishing the articles of scientists underscores how much they, like the academics and other literary intellectuals also regularly featured in the *Menorah Journal*, were perceived to be leading cultural authorities. Their contributions furthered the *Menorah Journal*'s stated mission of nurturing a Jewish cultural renaissance. It also highlights the fact that, as intimately connected as Kallen was to the Menorah Society as a whole and to the *Menorah Journal*'s editor, Henry Hurwitz, in particular, the journal did not simply promote Kallen's perspective. Hurwitz, chancellor of the IMA as well as editor in chief of the journal from its founding in 1915 until his death in 1961, published Kallen's views together with those of people who differed with him. Although Kallen did not speak for the journal, his views were nevertheless put into active circulation by it, and thereby became an important part of the public discourse concerning the nature of Jewish identity.[41]

Locating Kallen in Zionist Racial Discourse

There is a significant record of Zionist thinkers who shared Kallen's belief in an inherited Jewish psyche. For example, in 1913 "The Jewish Racial Problem" appeared in the Viennese Zionist newspaper founded by Theodor Herzl, *Die Welt*. It summarized the views of the well-known anthropologist and Zionist activist Ignaz Zollschan, whose popular *Das Rassenproblem* was already in its third edition. The author explains "what actually ought to be understood by the notion of racial talent . . . : namely, not an inborn, eternally immutable trait, but an inherited disposition to cultural achievement that emerges through either an extended or a brief cultural process. And it does not appear open to question that we belong, from this point of view, to those peoples that are eminently well suited for culture."[42] Zollschan's belief in "an inherited disposition to cultural achievement" maps precisely onto Kallen's point of view.

Kallen explicitly relied on Zollschan's anthropology during the 1910s, because, as Efron explains, it "contained sharp strictures against those who were misguided enough to think that cultural assimilation altered the biological facts of race."[43] Thus, Kallen wrote in 1918, "Where you find a certain definite continuity in a social unit, traceable through history, a continuity of mental type, a continuity of physical type, together with continuity of social function, and psychological activity, there you have what for the purposes of history constitutes a race. From that point of view, it need not be argued, the Jews are as Dr. Zollschan shows, a race and one of the purest of races."[44] For Zollschan, as for Kallen, the essential features of the Jewish race were cultural and psychological. Moreover, the Jewish psyche, although inherited, was also plastic and subject to environmental influence. Kallen never specified how the racial psyche was transmitted, but Zollschan did. It is possible that Kallen accepted Zollschan's belief in an inherited mneme that determined psychic instincts, but, as a functionalist psychologist, he would not have focused on the physiology of mental structures.[45]

Identifying exactly when Kallen abandoned these racial views is hard to pinpoint, but it is certain that he had ceased to make any such references by the 1930s. Regardless, his change of mind does not represent the terminus ad quem of Jewish thinkers who believed in an inherited Jewish psyche. In fact, we find a number of instances of Jewish thinkers who espoused this point of view on into the 1930s. For example, in 1927 Chaim Zhitlowsky, a prominent advocate of diaspora nationalism, wrote that understanding "'racial Jewishness'—or, better: Jewishness by descent, psychophysical Jewishness" is "significant not only for us but for the entire civilized world—it is important for the history of culture to discover what each nationalist race has achieved and produced among the cultural treasures of humanity. This is necessary in order to clarify the fundamental role of biology in human progress."[46] René Hirschler, the chief rabbi of Strasbourg and the Bas-Rhin department until his murder by the Nazis, recorded in

1929 his Jungian-inspired belief in the persistence of a collective Jewish consciousness.[47] Additionally, Sigmund Freud's 1939 *Moses and Monotheism* put forth the view "that Jewishness is constituted by the biological inheritance of an archaic memory that Jewish people are inexorably compelled to transmit to future generations, whether consciously or unconsciously."[48] To be sure, Freud's thought is unique in its own right, and his psychoanalysis and theories of the unconscious have little bearing on Kallen's psychological perspective, but this only underscores how the idea of an inherited Jewish psyche was powerful enough to be received in different psychological discourses. The persistence of such references up until the Shoah points to the power of the romantic notion of Jewishness as an innate, biologically transmitted, spiritual-cultural force.

The Urgency of the Moment

Social psychological discourse assumed an increasingly urgent importance in the context of World War I. Kallen's commitment to cultural pluralism and Zionism was shaped not only by the American context but was also intimately intertwined with a transnational nationalist discourse. This transnational discourse, Noam Pianko argues, fundamentally shaped a stream of Zionist discourse, pioneered by Ahad Ha'am and Simon Dubnow, that was not limited to the nation-state paradigm of nationalism. Together with Judah Magnes and Sir Alfred Zimmern, among others, Pianko counts Kallen with these cosmopolitan Zionists, framing him as a "nationalist" rather than a "pluralist" in order to unpin him from being considered only within a uniquely American discourse of difference. In "Democracy versus the Melting Pot," Pianko points out, Kallen uses conceptual vocabulary such as *commonwealth*, *nationality*, and *federation of nationalities* to describe how he viewed the ideal cooperation of ethnic groups in a democratic national framework. These terms, Pianko explains, carried "very specific connotations . . . regarding the ethical and practical need to contest the spread of self-determination as the principle of nationalism."[49] This view thus links Kallen to the British internationalists of the World War I era who, like his friend Sir Alfred

Zimmern, a Zionist and a leading internationalist associated with the Round Table, were suspicious of the mainstream nation-state paradigm of nationalism. They envisioned a new postwar era of increased social interaction and economic cooperation among a "federation of nationalities."

Understanding the implications of race and psychology for the nation, Glenda Sluga argues, was the most important issue in defining the ideology of the 1919 Paris Peace Conference. Even before World War I, links between British and American intellectuals around the topic of nationality and race were already being established.[50] What these thinkers generally shared in common was the belief that race undergirded nationality but was not precisely identical with it. The relationship of race to nationality for them may be compared to the movement from unconsciousness (instinct) to consciousness (will). Although the term *race* had proved flexible enough in the hands of thinkers like Kallen to accommodate the tension between consent and descent in relation to ethnic identity, the term *nationality* provided a new and compelling way to describe a balance between these poles.

Kallen's crispest articulation of how nationality bridges descent and consent appeared in 1918, in a book that he wrote in support of President Woodrow Wilson's postwar reconstruction agenda, *The Structure of Lasting Peace*. "Nationality falls between race and other more external forms of associative unity," Kallen explained. "That racial quality underlies it and is near to it, must be granted, but it is false that racial quality is identical with it."[51] As Kallen here framed it, race describes a psychological foundation, but this carries no greater significance than that it serves as the fertile soil from which the group life grows, expressed as nationality. Thus, race marks Jewish life; however, Jewish life is lived not as race, but as nationality. This better aligned Kallen's views with those of the internationalists, but this subtle shift did not really represent a new perspective for him. This view was compatible with Kallen's strong claim that Jewish persons, and all other such ethnic groups, are "facts in nature."[52] Race and nationality, considered together from the functionalist point of view, describe the organic unity of the ethnic group's coordination with its environment. As we have seen, Jewish racial thinkers (and Kallen in particular) had long understood the Jewish "race" in terms that are virtually indistinguishable from this now-preferred term, *nationality*. However, this vocabulary had the advantage of highlighting the salience of group consciousness and will, and in the context of the postwar reconstruction it had much more political traction.

Kallen interacted with a number of prominent internationalists who understood nationality in the way he articulated it in 1918. In some cases, he even helped to promote their ideas. Pianko notes, for example, that Kallen connected Zimmern to the *Menorah Journal*, bringing that readership into contact with his ideas.[53] For Zimmern, nationality functioned as a kind of instinct, an "intimate subjective" and "psychological sentiment" that, now shocked into conscious awareness by the war, functioned as a source of resistance against moral and spiritual decline.[54] A rival group of British internationalists, the Union for Democratic Control (UDC), counted among its members Kallen's friends Israel Zangwill and Norman Angell. Although Kallen criticized Zangwill's views in "Democracy versus the Melting Pot," he maintained collegial ties with him. Sluga observes that Zangwill, representative of the views of the UDC, held that nationality "was a manifestation of unconscious and irrational forces such as herd instinct, gregariousness, or the crowd mind," with "psychological theories of the 'subconscious'" throwing "lurid light upon ancient mythologies."[55] Angell, for his part, believed that "nationality is a very precious manifestation of the instincts by which alone men can become socially conscious and act in some corporate capacity."[56] Angell occupied a significant moment in Kallen's biography. He resigned from his position as professor of philosophy and psychology at the University of Wisconsin over issues of academic freedom, his outrage sparked in part because Angell was forbidden from speaking on campus "because of his seemingly pacifist views."[57] Zimmern, Zangwill, and Angell, all representative British internationalists, crossed paths in significant ways with Kallen during this time.

Kallen's psychological assumptions were not precisely the same as theirs. He rejected the notion of an unconscious primitive irrationality undergirding nationality, a view reinforced by the psychoanalytic school of Jung and Freud. Nevertheless, all shared in common a view of nationality as based upon a racial psyche that functions below the conscious level, and, brought to consciousness, seeks to find self-expression. Kallen's psychologized notion of race and nationality was thus embedded in a broadly received and deeply rooted transatlantic discourse.

Daniel Deronda

Kallen's construction of nationality as the natural expression of Jewish psychophysical inheritance was quite likely inspired by George Eliot's *Daniel Deronda*. From the time of its publication in 1876, it rapidly became an international sensation among Jewish readers, including in England, Germany, Poland, France, and the United States, and was perceived by them to have articulated a powerful justification for Jewish life. For her part, Eliot (Mary Anne Evans's nom de plume) was pleased with the positive reception of her effort "to bring an 'ennobling' Judaism to the consciousness of Christians and Jews."[58] Eliot's romanticism exercised a profound influence on the development of the Zionist movement, in which Kallen played an active role. *Daniel Deronda* figured in the thought of early European Zionist leaders like Theodor Herzl and A. D. Gordon. Nahum Sokolow, former secretary general of the World Zionist Congress, later reflected that Eliot paved the way for Zionism. Her romanticism made an impression on the prominent American Zionists Judah Magnes and Louis Lipsky, and on the poet Emma Lazarus.[59] Kallen, an architect of American Zionism, would almost certainly have read the novel as well.[60] He was also a literary critic, served as a professor of English literature at Princeton University from 1903 to 1905, and was well-versed in Victorian arts and letters. Eliot, who was intimate with Herbert Spencer, was profoundly influenced by his social and psychological views. Spencer's views on psychology and heredity are very much on display in *Daniel Deronda*. A close reading reveals a marked resonance linking Kallen's and Eliot's views concerning inheritance. Eliot's romanticized view of identity, which Kallen embraced, resisted the common Victorian anti-Semitic view of a deficient racial Jewish heritage.

Daniel Deronda suggests that Jews pass along a moral inheritance that is linked to memory, a Spencerian notion that bears more than a passing resemblance to Kallen's articulation of Hebraism. The character of Daniel Deronda is a man of evident moral and spiritual superiority who is inexorably drawn to his Jewish ancestral ties by an innate drive. For much of the novel, Deronda is unaware that he was born a Jew, but he becomes drawn by a mysterious compulsion to the prophetic figure of Mordecai. Responding to Deronda's evocation of Mazzini, whom he cites as an example of one whose national consciousness stirred "memories and hopes" and inspired "arduous action," Mordecai pronounces that the "heritage of Israel is beating in the pulses of millions; it lives in their veins as a power without understanding," transmitted as "the inborn half of memory." There is an inherited Jewish psyche, Mordecai claims. He continues: "Let the reason of Israel disclose itself in a great outward deed, and let there be another great migration, another choosing of Israel to be a nationality whose members may still stretch to the ends of the earth, even as the sons of England and Germany, whom enterprise carries afar, but who still have a national hearth and a tribunal of national opinion. . . . Who says that the history and literature of our race are dead? Are they not as the living history and literature of Greece and Rome, which have inspired revolutions, enkindled the thought of Europe, and made the unrighteous powers tremble?"[61] The parallel between Mordecai's declaration and Kallen's expression of Jewish nationality, linked to Hebraism and Zionism, is striking.

Kallen explicitly identified psychophysical inheritance with memory in 1918:

> Individuality of living things counts, and is itself social. I have been accustomed to phrase this fact in the formula that, . . . although you can change almost any connection which you establish with your environment, . . . you cannot change your grandfathers. Now this melodramatic way of phrasing the fact of heredity implies simply,

> that human individuality, that, indeed, the individuality of any living thing is a special kind of social fact. And, as a social fact, the individuality of any living thing cannot be detached from a social setting in time, even if it can be detached from a social setting in space.[62]

Not being able to "change your grandfathers" was thus a "melodramatic way" to communicate that only an individual's "social setting in time" is fixed, and nothing else. Consistent with the Spencerian organicist view of society, Kallen believed that the individual's life is marked by association with both the "natural" and inherited ethnic group and with external and voluntary modes of association. The ethnic group defines one's social setting in time; and external, or "artificial," groups "like states, churches, professions, castes," define one's social setting in space.[63] For Kallen, individuality, and the freedom of will that is associated with it, are real. The individual makes his or her own choices regarding any number of voluntary forms of social affiliation. At the same time, Kallen asserted, the individual is not a blank slate, and is marked by a psychological relationship to one's history. In this fashion, ethnic identity emerges balanced between consent and descent.

Deronda's Jewish identity consists of no particular beliefs or practices, but he is a hero, a cultured and civilized man, whose "inborn half of memory" draws him to learn about his grandfather and impels Deronda, at the end of the novel, to turn toward the east in a dramatic nod to nascent political Zionism, symbol of the future hope not only of Jews but also of international comity. So, too, Kallen believed that Jews were naturally drawn to their psychic cultural inheritance. He underscored this idea with his oft-cited claim (also found in his toast discussed earlier) that whatever else the immigrant changes, "he cannot change his grandfather."[64] This inheritance, Kallen maintained, found natural and healthy expression through Hebraism and Zionism.

Kallen's self-admitted "melodramatic" fashion of describing Jewish inheritance notably identifies Jewish inheritance not with the mother, as per Jewish law, but with the grandfather. Kallen's idiosyncratic turn of phrase likely found its inspiration from this novel. Reflecting upon the possible influence of *Daniel Deronda* offers a possible explanation for Kallen's idiosyncratic turn of phrase. Deronda, who had grown up without any knowledge of his parentage or his Jewish heritage, becomes reunited with his mother. When pressed to explain why she had hidden his heritage from him, she justifies herself by explaining that she had secured for him the social status of an English gentleman. Angered by Deronda's rebuke that she had no right to choose his birthright for him, his mother retorts, "I chose for you what I would have chosen for myself. How could I know that you would have the spirit of my father in you? How could I know that you would love what I hated?—if you really love to be a Jew."[65] Deronda's reclamation of his Jewish heritage occurs despite his mother's violent opposition. The spirit of his grandfather had awakened within him.

Deronda's spiritual stirring is animated by an innate impulse as well as by a voluntary commitment. Deronda tells his mother, "No wonder if such facts come to reveal themselves in spite of concealments. The effects prepared by generations are likely to triumph over a contrivance which would bend them all to the satisfaction of self. Your will was strong, but my grandfather's trust which you accepted and did not fulfill—what you call his yoke—is the expression of something stronger, with deeper, farther-spreading roots, knit into the foundations of sacredness for all men. . . . That stronger Something has determined that I shall be all the more the grandson whom also you willed to annihilate."[66] Deronda here expresses what Kallen later takes to be scientific fact—that Jewish ethnic consciousness inevitably resurfaces and asserts itself despite all efforts to repress it. When his mother challenges him by asking if he would make himself into a Jew just like his grandfather, Deronda replies, "That is impossible. The effect of my education can never be done away with. The Christian sympathies in which my mind was reared can never die out of me . . . But I consider it my duty—it is the impulse of my feeling—to identify myself, as far as possible, with my hereditary people, and if I can see any work to be done for them that I can give my soul and hand to, I shall choose to do it."[67] Deronda's racial psychophysical inheritance marks him; it serves him as a foundation. But he has also been marked by his education and upbringing. Deronda cannot simply replicate his grandfather's Judaism. He must choose his own way. Recovering his Jewish inheritance and committing himself to the nationalist yearnings of the Jewish people becomes the only way for Deronda to fully integrate all the various influences in his life. Deronda exemplifies how an integrated personality successfully coordinates consent with descent.

In his quest to learn more about his heritage, Deronda seeks out a friend of his grandfather, the banker Joseph Kalonymos.[68] He thanks Kalonymos for saving him from remaining ignorant of his parentage and for taking care of the chest his grandfather had left in trust to him: "The moment wrought strongly on Deronda's imaginative susceptibility: in the presence of one linked still in zealous friendship with the grandfather whose hope had yearned toward him when he was unborn, and who, though dead, was yet to speak with him in those written memorials which, says Milton, 'contain a potency of life in them to be as active as that soul whose progeny they are,' he seemed to himself to be touching the electric chain of his own ancestry." Kalonymos then presents Deronda with his grandfather's chest, thus restoring to Deronda his heritage. Finally, Deronda declares, "I shall call myself a Jew."[69] When Kallen declared that one cannot change one's grandfather, surely he had Deronda in mind.

Deronda's reclamation of his heritage would have resonated for Kallen, since he had only come to reclaim his Jewish heritage as a young man at Harvard. Deronda confesses to Mordecai, "It is through your inspiration that I have discerned what may be my life's task. It is you who have given shape to what, I believe, was an inherited yearning—the effect of brooding, passionate thoughts in many ancestors—thoughts that seem to have been intensely present in my grandfather."[70] Just as Deronda was profoundly affected by his relationship with Mordecai, so too was Kallen deeply influenced by his teachers. We have seen that Barrett Wendell and William James played seminal roles in awakening within him what he, like Deronda, experienced as an "inherited yearning."

Deronda's connection to his Jewish heritage is rooted not in religious affiliation, but, like Kallen, in psychophysical inheritance. He, like Kallen, uses musical metaphors to describe that inheritance. Deronda speaks of ancestral life, or the "habit of their inherited frames," as an unplayed musical instrument that awaits the right touch to give music; so too, Kallen likens ethnic groups to musical instruments that contribute their unique timbre and tonality to the symphony of American civilization. Deronda, like Kallen, harkens back to a primordial ethnicity that unites all Jews. He allows him to imagine for himself a leadership role "in spite of heresy." So too, Kallen imagined a leadership role for himself despite being publicly called out as a heretic by Reform rabbis. One could easily imagine Kallen adding the same caveat as does Deronda: "But I will not say that I shall profess to believe exactly as my fathers have believed."[71] The interlinked nature of culture and race was a self-evident proposition for Kallen. The idea of an inborn core of Hebraism was the product of the force of a half-century's absorption of English, philo-Semitic, racial discourse. It stands as a testimony to how Spencer's evolutionary views of psychology served as fertile soil for romantic nationalism and for imagining ethnicity.

Nationality/Ethnicity

Kallen's "Nationality and the Hyphenated American" appeared in the *Menorah Journal*'s April 1915 issue, the same issue in which Hall's article was published. Its appearance paved the way for him to circulate his ideas concerning Jewish identity as nationality/ethnicity. The *Menorah Journal* introduced Kallen by documenting his scholarly credentials. It noted especially Kallen's contributions to philosophical and general periodicals, and that he was the author of the recently published *William James and Henri Bergson* (1914). The *Menorah Journal* also highlighted Kallen's connection to the Menorah movement, as "one of the founders of the Harvard Menorah Society," who "has rendered signal service, both by tongue and pen, to the Menorah movement." Kallen's focus in "Nationality and the Hyphenated American" was on the American national stage. Writing in the shadow of World War I, Kallen, a pacifist, was acutely attuned to the growing urgency of nationalist rhetoric. He argued that the Jews are a nation, and advocated the desirability of conceiving of America as a commonwealth of nationalities. He believed that the very viability of democracy depended upon recognizing and validating this pluralist vision.[72]

Distinguishing between nation and nationality, Kallen explained that nations were fundamentally composed of nationalities. "Nationality is not nationhood, although it is the most important constituent of nationhood," Kallen explained. "Many nationalities may compose a nation (such is the case of the British, Russian, Austro-Hungarian and Turkish Empires, of the Swiss Republic, of our own Union), and then the relation between the nationalities will determine the strength or the weakness of the nation."[73]

Kallen's claim constituted not only a claim for Jewish identity but also an argument against understanding American identity to mean being white, Anglo-Saxon, and Protestant, and against envisioning America as composed fundamentally of individual citizens. The logic of assimilation in the melting pot of America was based upon these premises. It had inspired an extensive campaign to assimilate newcomers through Americanization programs. These were vigorously promoted, championed by myriad institutions, including the Reform Jewish establishment. By 1918 there were over one hundred organizations involved in the Americanization of Jewish immigrants. Kallen, however, replaced the notion that individuals constituted the basic building blocks of the nation with the idea that ethnic groups were the basic building blocks: "Political freedom in America has tended to generate self-expression of each national group, and our country is to-day, broadly speaking, a great coöperative [*sic*] commonwealth of nationalities, British, French, German, Slavic, Jewish, each freely developing, in so far as it is self-conscious, its national genius, its language, literature and art in its own characteristic way as its best contribution to the civilization of America as a whole, realizing in this way the ideal of the democracy of nationalities, of international comity and coöperation [*sic*] which our prophets were the first to formulate."[74] The strength of the nation, Kallen argued, depended on the relations in America between these constituent group units, not on the successful homogenization of the population.

Homogenization of the nation through compulsion, Kallen wrote, was the antithesis of democracy. Citing the example of Austria-Hungary, he asserted that the "direct occasion of the great war" was due to the fact that the government there, "instead of being a democracy, has in the long run been directed toward the control and exploitation of many nationalities by one or two. . . . In Austria-Hungary, nationality, having been exploited and suppressed, has been the enemy and destroyer of nationhood." In Switzerland, by way of contrast, "nationhood, being democratic, is the safeguard and insurance of nationality." Supporting the free cooperation of nationalities in America, Kallen continued, best expressed American democratic ideals, ideals that were inspired by the Hebraic influence. "In this country," he wrote, "the whole spirit of those institutions which constitute American nationhood makes for the liberation and harmonious coöperation [*sic*] of nationalities. This spirit is also a part of the Hebraic spirit, . . . the spirit that literally inspired the democracy of our America." Jews immigrated to America, Kallen claimed, precisely because they were "moved to undertake their great American adventure by the ideal of nationality. . . . They sought freedom to be themselves, to realize their national genius in their own individual way."[75]

The Jewish need to seek freedom "to be themselves" and to "realize their national genius" was rooted, Kallen believed, in that inheritable quality called nationality, which inevitably exerted a claim upon every individual. Thus, Kallen wrote, nationality "is a force much deeper and more radical, distinctly more primitive and original, than anything else in the structure of society. It hyphenates English and Germans and Austrians and Russians and Turks no less than it hyphenates Americans, and, in the failure of the external sociopolitical organization of Europe to give it free play, it is the chief, almost the only, cause of the present unendurable European tragedy."[76] Nationality, for Kallen, thus exhibits features of what is called the perennialist view of ethnicity, which posits a timeless essence to ethnicity. Nationality, in this view, is an inherited component of identity that exists prior to any identification with an external sociopolitical organization (i.e., a nation).

At the same time, however, Kallen acknowledged that modernity has fundamentally transformed the consciousness of nationality. This aspect of his thought resembles the contrasting modernist view of ethnicity, which approaches ethnicity in the vein of Benedict Anderson, who describes the sociopolitical imaginary of the modern nation-state and the modern invention of imagined national connectedness.[77] Kallen did not believe that nationality was invented by modernity, however, but he did maintain that it had experienced an awakening in the nineteenth century, when people understood for the first time the "entire significance" of nationality. Only then did it come "to full consciousness in fact and idea. . . . Its great voice is the Italian thinker and patriot, Mazzini." Quoting Mazzini, Kallen explained that his paean to nationality helped to rekindle hope in international democracy: "They seek to elaborate and express their idea, to contribute their stone also to the great pyramid of history. . . . In principle, nationality ought to be . . . the recognized symbol of association; the assertion of the individuality of a human group called by its geographical position, its traditions and its language, to fulfill a special function in the European work of civilization."[78] As Kallen understood it, modernity awakened within nationalities an awareness regarding their potential to advance the cause of democracy and of civilization.

In sum, nationality was, for Kallen, a natural feature deeply rooted in the premodern past, but modernity had effected a change in nationalities by awakening within them an awareness of their potential to advance the cause of civilization. In its broad contours (absent the biological assumptions), Kallen's thought anticipates the balance between the perennialist and modernist views proposed more recently by the theoretician of ethnicity Anthony Smith. Although Smith agrees with Anderson that nationalism as an ideology and the nation-state as a political norm are quite modern, he qualifies that by understanding these in light of their relative continuity or discontinuity with collective cultural units and sentiments of previous eras. Smith strikes a similar balanced stance in his interpretation of ethnicity, observing that ethnicity exhibits features of both schools of thought. For Smith, "the 'core' of ethnicity . . . resides in the quartet of 'myths, memories, values and symbols' and in the characteristic forms or styles and genres of certain historical configurations of populations." Modern nations, Smith believes, are built upon this preexisting form that he calls *ethnie* (the French derivative from the Greek term *ethnos*). Smith's position is that while nationalism may be a modern creation, the clusters of populations that make up the nation nevertheless created it out of preexisting relational bonds consisting of cognitive elements, cultural practices and mores, and common sentiments and attitudes.[79]

Ethnic consciousness, Smith argues, experienced a transformation coextensive with the rise of nationalism. Ethnic groups not only provided the raw material for the rise of nationalism and the creation of the modern nation-state, but they themselves were transformed and politicized in the transition to modernity. "The pressures for ethnie to move towards nationhood (but not necessarily independent statehood) are extremely powerful," Smith writes. "In practice, this meant a triple movement: from isolation to activism, from quietism to mobilization and from culture to politics."[80] The constitutive importance of ethnic groups to the modern nation-state, Smith contends, is discovered in their triple movement to activism, mobilization, and politics. Ethnic groups thus do not simply exist as static entities within the national body; they interact dynamically with and shape the modern nation-state. In this dynamic sense, too, Kallen's notion of nationality resonates with Smith's.

Kallen's view led him to posit an ethical obligation for Jewish nationality: "Our duty to America, inspired by the Hebraic tradition,—our service to the world, in whatever occupation,—both these are conditioned, in so far as we are Jews, upon the conservation of Jewish nationality. That is the potent reality in each of us, our selfhood, and service is the giving of the living self. Let us so serve mankind; as Jews, aware of our great heritage, through it and in it strong to live and labor for mankind's good."[81] Nurturing and supporting the growth and development of Jewish nationality, or the Jewish group personality, would, in turn, support the growth and development of a stronger, healthier American nation. Kallen thus laid the foundation for an understanding of Jewish ethnicity that exists in a symbiotic relationship with the modern democratic nation-state.

Justice Louis Brandeis

Like Kallen, Louis Brandeis's views were shaped by the transnational discourse concerning nationality. In particular, Kallen's article exercised a palpable influence on him. In April 1915, the same month that Kallen's article on nationality appeared in the *Menorah Journal*, Brandeis delivered an address entitled "The Jewish Problem: How to Solve It" (subsequently published as a pamphlet by the American Zionist movement) at the Reform rabbis' annual conference.[82] Brandeis's speech follows Kallen's writing so closely in concept, word choice, and structure, that it is clear that he had thoroughly absorbed Kallen's views.

Brandeis's ideological position regarding Zionism had earlier been shaped by his contact with Kallen.[83] In 1905 Brandeis had rejected Zionism and the idea that America could tolerate "habits of living or of thought which tend to keep alive difference of origin," but by 1914 he had come to support the idea that one could be both a Zionist and an American. "To be good Americans, we must be better Jews," Brandeis proclaimed, "and to be better Jews, we must become Zionists."[84] Kallen gave Brandeis the intellectual justification necessary to change his point of view. He helped Brandeis find a way to make Zionism compatible with American patriotism. Brandeis's view of Zionism was predicated on Kallen's premise that nationality was the cornerstone of Jewish identity, and that a proper understanding of nationality involved appreciating both its heritable characteristics as well as its modern significance.

Brandeis's "The Jewish Problem: How to Solve It" echoes Kallen's claims about nationality. "The difference between a nation and a nationality is clear; but it is not always observed," Brandeis said. "Likeness between members is the essence of nationality; but the members of a nation may be different. A nation may be composed of many nationalities, as some of the most successful nations are." Brandeis, then, like Kallen, distinguished between nations and nationalities, and stressed that successful nations are composed of nationalities. Like Kallen, Brandeis also affirmed the idea that the unity of nationality is not a mere modern sociopolitical construct but is "a fact of nature." "The movements of the last century have proved that whole peoples have individuality no less marked than that of the single person," Brandeis asserted, adding that "the individuality of a people is irrepressible." He repeated Kallen's claim that the cause of World War I lay in the attempt to suppress and homogenize nationalities: "The false doctrine that nation and nationality must be made co-extensive is the cause of some of our greatest tragedies. It is, in large part, the cause also of the present war. It has led . . . to cruel, futile attempts at enforced assimilation."[85]

Brandeis, moreover, asserting the modern significance of nationality, also cited Mazzini and quoted from the same passage as did Kallen. He claimed, like Kallen, that the newly awakened consciousness of nationality not only inspired within people the desire for freedom for full development, but it also provided the framework to support the flowering of democracy and advance the cause of civilization: "The new nationalism proclaims that each race or people, like each individual, has a right and duty to develop, and that only through such differentiated development will high civilization be attained," Brandeis said. "Not until these principles of nationalism, like those of democracy are generally accepted, will liberty be fully attained, and minorities be secure in their rights." American democracy and civilization stood to gain by recognizing and supporting the nationalities that comprise the nation. Furthermore, he asserted, Jewish nationality, in particular, resonates with American ideals, echoing Kallen's claim that the Hebraic spirit undergirds American values: "Our [Jewish] teaching of brotherhood and righteousness has, under the name of democracy and social justice, become the twentieth century striving of America and of western Europe. Our conception of law is embodied in the American constitutions which proclaim this to be a 'government of laws and not of men.'" Therefore, Brandeis proclaimed, "Let us make clear to the world that we [Jews] too are a nationality clamoring for equal rights, to life and to self-expression."[86]

Brandeis's speech was fundamentally shaped by Kallen's "Nationality and the Hyphenated American." Remarkably, Brandeis did not acknowledge Kallen's influence. Why this is so can only remain a cause of conjecture. Perhaps Brandeis knew that in order to persuade a room full of Reform rabbis of his position, it would be best not to invoke Kallen's name. Whatever the reason for his omission, the fact remains that Kallen's construction of Jewish identity as nationality entered into wide circulation and became an important part of American Jewish discourse.

This is not to suggest that Brandeis's support inaugurated a sea change in American Jewish self-perception. In fact, opposition to this construction of Jewish identity remained strong, in no small part because Brandeis and Kallen insisted on linking Jewish nationality to Zionism. For example, in 1916 the *Outlook*, a weekly progressive magazine of opinion, dedicated its January 5th issue to the subject of political Zionism. It juxtaposed two competing perspectives. First appeared an article by Brandeis ("Palestine and the Jewish Democracy"), in which he repeated his earlier claims regarding Zionism.[87] The second article, by the Reform rabbi Samuel Schulman, rejected that position: "We do not desire the creation of a new nationality within the American people," Schulman wrote. "America is a democracy that deals directly with the individual, irrespective of his racial descent or religious profession. America is not organized on the basis of race, but on great moral ideas. Therefore, American nationality has no room within itself for the cultivation of an alien national consciousness on the part of any group."[88] Schulman did not distinguish between nation and nationality, and therefore perceived Zionism in America to represent the threatening idea of divided national loyalties. Furthermore, America, in Schulman's estimation, was composed of individuals, not nationalities. America, Schulman asserted, "deals directly with the individual," not with racial or religious groups. The *Outlook*'s editors expressed their agreement with Schulman's position in opposition to Brandeis.[89] The meaning of American Jewish identity was still being contested. The idea of ethnicity had not yet won the day.

The Chicago School

The Chicago School's original nucleus included John Dewey, George Herbert Mead, James Hayden Tufts, James Rowland Angell, and Edward Scribner Ames. They shared with Kallen an aversion to the Americanization vogue in American politics. They were "vociferously tolerant," Fred Matthews observes. Hostile to "biological racism" and committed to the notion of the "malleability of personality," Matthews writes, "the Chicago sociologists argued against the exclusionism and forced-assimilation programs of the years during and after World War One."[90] They were, in a sense, allies with Kallen against the threat posed by nativists and even against the liberal progressives who denied the validity of a hyphenated American identity.

The Chicago School shared with Kallen the view that the significant basic unit in society was the cultural group—a fundamentally important step toward validating the presence of distinct ethnic groups within the national body. As it had with Kallen, Spencer's organicist notion of society influenced them. The Chicago School "asserted the historical, logical, and therefore ethical, primacy of society to the individual," Matthews writes. "The isolated individual was an abstraction; in reality, the irreducible unit was the individual embedded in a network of relationships and statuses—fathers, sons, masters, workers, burghers, peasants."[91] The Chicago School's understanding of culture, however, was markedly different from Kallen's. It was derived from the American school of anthropology (including, especially, Franz Boas, Alfred Kroeber, and Edward Sapir), who rejected the postulate of fixed racial characteristics in connection with the ethnic group.[92] These pioneering social scientists contributed to the understanding that ethnicity should be understood as a nonracial social category, a conceptual shift that finally separated culture from nature.

This conceptual shift was founded on the principle of the malleability of personality, derived from the functionalist school of psychology represented by James and Dewey.[93] Thus, they stressed the plasticity of ethnicity. The Chicago social scientists validated the ethnic experience, but they did not endeavor to establish a programmatic resistance to assimilation. On the other hand, neither did they believe that assimilation required adopting the beliefs, ideas, and customs of native-born Americans. What theorists like Robert Park meant by the term *assimilation* is *integration*, Chad Goldberg explains. Reflecting on one of the foundational texts of that school of thought, Goldberg writes, "A careful reading of *Old World Traits* suggests that its authors did not primarily conceive assimilation as a means of preserving an existing Anglo-Saxon culture or promoting conformity to it, but rather as a means for organizing a democratic public."[94] In this respect, Kallen's aims aligned well with the Chicago School.

Even more striking, Kallen shared with the Chicago School a particular interest in Jewish integration. Goldberg shows that, for the Chicago School, the Jewish group served as a paradigm for their discussions concerning minority ethnic incorporation into society. They saw the New York Jewish community's kehillah as an exemplar of how Jewish communal life reinvented itself in the American urban environment, demonstrating its ability to flexibly adapt to the needs of Jewish immigrants and to modern conditions. The Chicago School suggested that America could learn from its example on a larger scale. Kallen and the Chicago School were allies in their opposition to the universalistic cosmopolitanism that was the intellectual inheritance of the Enlightenment, and in their opposition to constructions of Jewishness as clannish and a polluter of the civil sphere. Together, they promoted the image of Jews as civil, and as valued contributors to society.

Nevertheless, Kallen's construction of ethnicity was roundly criticized by some progressive thinkers. Isaac Berkson, a student of John Dewey, disputed Kallen's claim that ethnicity describes an inheritance that inevitably exerts itself in the psyche of the individual. This claim is what separated Kallen, at this stage in his thinking, from other Jewish American architects of ethnicity. Berkson developed his "community theory" of ethnicity as the thesis of his doctoral dissertation, which was later published as *Theories of Americanization*.[95] Shortly before its publication, Berkson presented his thesis to *Menorah Journal* readers in an article entitled "A Community Theory of American Life: The Problem of Adjustment in the Light of Jewish Experience."[96] That Berkson presented his argument in the *Menorah Journal* indicates his desire that his thesis be read as part of the intra-Jewish discourse concerning the terms of Jewish group life in America.

An editor's note in the *Menorah Journal* summarizing Berkson's article preceded it. It reads: "In his forthcoming book on 'Theories of Americanization' (to be published by Teachers College, Columbia University), Mr. Berkson seeks to define a position for ethnic minorities in American democracy. Following a condemnation of various programs for this adjustment of minority groups, such as 'Americanization,' the 'Melting Pot,' and the 'Federation of Nationalities,' he elaborates in a suggestive chapter from which the ensuing essay is a selection, a 'community' theory as illustrated by American Jewish life."[97] Providing a summary of the article was an unusual editorial step—the *Menorah Journal* usually provided biographies, not synopses. Hurwitz, it would seem, was intrigued by Berkson's ideas. The introduction went on to make special note of Berkson's connection to the Menorah movement as a founder of the Menorah Society of City College of New York and its second president. It was typical for the *Menorah Journal* to make special note of its contributing authors' connections to the Menorah movement, and the inclusion of that information here suggests that Berkson's theory of American Jewish ethnicity was considered as a contribution to the movement, furthering the aim of the Menorah Association to promote the advancement of Jewish culture.

Berkson dismissed Kallen's idea of democracy functioning as a federation of nationalities, focusing particularly upon Kallen's formulation that one cannot change one's grandfather:

> In the "federation of nationalities" theory, which is pivoted on the identity of race, the argument is primarily that "we cannot change our grandfathers." The community theory, on the other hand, makes the history of the group, its esthetic, cultural, and religious inheritance, its national self-consciousness, the basic factor. This change of emphasis from race to culture brings with it a whole series

> of implications, arising from the fact that culture is not inherited but must be acquired through some educational process. The difference is crucial. A community of culture possible of demonstration becomes the ground for perpetuating the group, rather than an identity of race, questionable in fact and dubious in significance.[98]

Berkson removed heredity entirely from consideration. As he saw it, group cohesion was maintained not by racial determinism but by persuading its members of the value of its cultural and spiritual aspirations: "The perpetuation of the ethnos in a democratic land must rest on the clear consciousness of the worth of the ethnic heritage."[99] Ethnic groups were, in other words, cultural groups, constituted as contingent and voluntary affiliations of people.

Berkson expanded on his views concerning nationality as ethnicity in *Theories of Americanization.* The "Cultural Zionists," who, he said, identify the Jewish people with their cultural and spiritual aspirations, come "very close to the view that nationality is essentially a psychological force." Defining a nation as "a race which possesses its own language, customs, culture and enough self-consciousness to preserve them," Berkson suggested that "this definition of nationality in cultural terms gives the clue to the solution of our problem of harmonizing two nationalities dwelling side by side. . . . It reveals a way of retaining loyalty both to the cultural life of the ethnic group and to the life of the total group in all its aspects. . . . Two cultures have possibilities of harmonization which two political or economic independences would never have."[100] Nationality, Berkson made clear, referred not to a psychologically inherited force, but to the cultural life of the ethnic group. This, for Berkson, solved the problem of justifying Jewish nationality within the American nation.

Berkson essentially reformulated and expanded upon the position that his teacher Dewey had earlier presented to *Menorah Journal* readers in "The Principle of Nationality." Dewey had also cautioned against a racialized understanding of nationality: "The concept of a nation of one race and one blood has mainly been invented after the event to account for certain unclear ideas of nationality, rather than to state the presence of a physiological fact." Rather, Dewey believed that nationality signified "the cultural fact that people live together in [a] community of intellectual life and moral emotions, of sentimental ideas and common practices, based upon common traditions and hopes." Such a "community of tradition, ideas and beliefs, or moral outlook upon the problems of life," Dewey wrote, "which is perpetuated and more or less fixed by language and literature, creates a body of people somehow distinctly united by very strong ties and bonds."[101] So, too, Berkson could affirm the idea of Jewish nationality insofar as it was understood to be a cultural construct separate from racial heredity and from political and territorial ambitions.

Berkson, summarizing the advantages that his "community" theory had over both the "Americanization" and "Federation of Nationalities" theories, highlighted the constructed nature of culture and the contingency of ethnic affiliation: "The 'Community' theory . . . leaves all the forces working; they are to decide what the future is to be. Both the 'Americanization' and 'Federation of Nationalities' theories presume too much to 'fix' conditions; the one would make the citizen conform to the nature of a mythical Anglo-Saxon, and the other to harmonize with the soul assumed to reside in the ethnos." Berkson, on the other hand, desired "that all forces be given a just opportunity to exert their influence." Thereupon, if "the ethnic group perpetuates itself, only then does it become justified to the reason. On the other hand, if the ethnic group finally disintegrates, the 'Community' theory really resolves itself into the 'Melting Pot' theory, accomplishing the fusion without the evils of hasty assimilation."[102] Berkson believed that theories aimed at fixing conditions for ethnic groups were misguided. He preferred a laissez-faire attitude. People were, and should be, free to choose their affiliations.

Kallen rebutted Berkson's views in *Culture and Democracy in the United States.*[103] Berkson's "community theory" of ethnicity, Kallen contended, was inadequate because it did not recognize what he perceived to be the enduring, stable, and persistent nature of ethnicity:

> The adaptability of life is wonderful, and communities, like persons, suffer much and surrender more, only to save their souls alive. . . . In one way or another, that inward half of his being, the "methods of valuation," the group patternings, the consuetudinous rhythms and symbols of custom and speech that are his heritage, the springs of his character, will color and direct his response. This inward half necessarily and automatically behaves in such a way as to maintain itself and grow, and if it is prevented from doing so directly, openly, in free interplay with its social *milieu*—then, necessarily and automatically, it will do so obliquely, hiddenly, in conflict with its *milieu*. The *milieu* may exterminate it, but the *milieu* will not assimilate it.[104]

The salient point for Kallen is that ethnicity will naturally and of necessity find expression in the life of the individuals who form it. As happens with Daniel Deronda, the "inward half" that is the individual's ethnic heritage will inevitably assert its claim. If the social environment is inimitable to that "group patterning," then it will seek to adapt and find oblique expression. There were limits to the malleability of individual and group personality.

Revisiting Kallen's Model of Ethnicity

Kallen's entry into the realm of public discourse regarding Jewish ethnicity is marked by the 1915 publication of "Nationality and the Hyphenated American" in the *Menorah Journal.* The journal was uniquely positioned to entertain the issues that he raised precisely because it had no stake in the various Jewish movements or political trends. It had no religious or Zionist affiliation, and, moreover, it enjoyed national circulation and a broad readership that included Jewish and non-Jewish intellectuals, Jewish university students, and Jewish communal leaders. The *Menorah Journal* quickly became the premier forum to discuss the developing consciousness of Jewish ethnicity. Kallen had helped to fashion the Menorah movement's mission, and he believed it would lead the way to a Jewish cultural renaissance. This cultural renaissance movement, as Kallen envisioned it, merely continued the project that "Hebraism" had begun. Considering his involvement with the Menorah movement, it seems only natural that Kallen would choose the *Menorah Journal* as a venue to promote his vision of Jewish nationality to a Jewish audience for consideration and debate.

Kallen's ideas were embedded in a transnational social psychological discourse, the roots of which extended back into the last half of the nineteenth century. Kallen's notion of nationality was shaped not only by his engagement with other Zionist thinkers and British internationalists but also obliquely through the influence of nineteenth-century theories of the mind that fed into romantic notions of Jewish belonging. Kallen helped to further the discursive development of notions of Jewish ethnicity not only through his influence on receptive thinkers such as Justice Louis Brandeis but also through his role as a foil for social theorists like Isaac Berkson.

In the context of an emerging world in which nationalities began to receive international legal recognition based in part on the perception of the primordial roots of their natural solidarity, Kallen sought to establish the natural solidarity of Jewish belonging by attaching his racial views to the concept of nationality. As he framed it, however, the primordialist, racial dimension of ethnic belonging serves only as the foundation of personality. It functions as a collective memory, an imprinted pattern that marks one's life without determining it. At the same time, Kallen's conception of nationality/ethnicity embraced the possibility of adaptation to modern conditions. In this regard, he found support from fellow pluralists and progressive scientific thinkers, including sociologists associated with the Chicago School, and anthropologists like Alfred Kroeber and Maurice Fishberg. They all stood opposed to the racial determinism that supported the views of politically influential racist scientists like Madison Grant, author of *The Passing of the Great Race* (1916).[105] Their ideas, however, could not provide the assurance that Kallen sought of the durability of the bonds that had held Jews together. Kallen's view of psychophysical inheritance placed him in a unique position of opposition not only to racist eugenicists but also to the Chicago School and cultural anthropologists. Jewish psychophysical inheritance made a supra-biological claim for Jewish identity, rooted in a Spencerian evolutionary model of mind, that simultaneously allowed for freedom of will and individuality conjoined with the continued growth and evolution of Jewish culture.

Kallen thus charted a different path toward ethnicity by conceptualizing group belonging as balanced between the poles of consent and descent. The romanticized notion in *Daniel Deronda* of nationality as the natural expression of ethnic psychophysical inheritance aptly captures Kallen's construction. Eliot's novel likely influenced Kallen as an idealized exemplar of how consent and descent both contribute to configuring the personality. The practical function of this construction of ethnicity is that it challenged the then-prevailing notion that American identity was fashioned from ethnically disembedded individuals, a conceptual consequence of Enlightenment-based universalism. Kallen insisted on the impossibility of the individual remaining unaffected by ethnic affiliation. Although by the 1930s he would cease to hold by the racial views outlined in this chapter, he would continue to maintain his commitment to the idea that the individual and the ethnic group are co-constituted personalities.

There are significant ways in which Kallen's theory of ethnicity finds resonance today. His views prefigure contemporary theory like that suggested by Anthony Smith and John Hutchinson, for example, who emphasize the ethnic characteristics of the modern nation, and argue, as had Kallen, that the fundamental building block of nations is ethnic groups. Kallen's belief in the indestructibility of the ethnic group bears some conceptual relationship to what Smith calls the persistence of *ethnie*. Smith and Hutchinson find, furthermore, that ethnic groups are not simply residual subnational groupings. Ethnicities, rather, dynamically interact with and shape the modern nation-state, exercising an "important regulatory principle" in politics, as Hutchinson puts it, "concerned with questions of the moral content and boundaries of a collectivity over which power is exercised."[106] Kallen, similarly, had argued that Berkson's static model of ethnicity and his laissez-faire attitude were inadequate. He believed that American Jews had, through Zionism, an active role to play in American politics and a moral obligation to shape the direction of American democracy. The conceptual connections that may be drawn to contemporary theorists suggest that Kallen's voice in the discourse continues to this day. He figures among those who find ethnicity to describe a group identity at once modern in invention and premodern in origin. The transnational social psychology discourse out of which Kallen developed his notion of Jewish ethnicity contributed to shifts in Jewish self-perception in America, and charted a path toward the legitimization of a hyphenated Jewish-American identity.

• 3 •

Darwinism and Democracy

He drew a circle that shut me out—
Heretic, rebel, a thing to flout.
But Love and I had the wit to win:
We drew a circle that took him in!
—Edwin Markham, "Outwitted"

NOW CONSIDERED A CLASSIC in the literature on the invention of ethnicity in America, Kallen's "Democracy versus the Melting Pot" appeared in the *Nation* in 1915.[1] Much has been written concerning Kallen's notion of ethnicity and its relationship to cultural pluralism and Jewish identity.[2] Little attention has been paid, however, to how Kallen deployed evolutionary theory in that article to dismantle the arguments of his opponents, which is surprising considering that it was critical that he succeed in doing so in order to establish scientific support for his vision of the positive function of ethnic participation in American democracy. This chapter closely examines Kallen's use of evolutionary sociology and considers the place of "Democracy versus the Melting Pot" in its print culture context.[3]

Cultivating a Public

Kallen's transition from a pragmatist philosopher to a writer and social commentator may be said to have begun in earnest with the publication

This chapter is slightly modified from Kaufman, "Horace M. Kallen's Use of Evolutionary Theory in Support of American Jews and Democracy."

of "Democracy versus the Melting Pot." That essay, in which Kallen set forth for the first time the basic parameters for cultural pluralism, responded to a provocative anti-immigration book entitled *The Old World in the New* (1914), written by Kallen's colleague at the University of Wisconsin, Edward Alsworth Ross.[4] Ross, a pioneering sociologist who has left behind a complicated and contradictory legacy of progressive social reform ideals coupled with scientific racism, undertook to analyze the specific physical, mental, and moral racial traits of Celtic Irish, German, Scandinavian, Italian, Slavic, Eastern European Hebrew, and other "lesser" immigrant groups.[5] Ross determined that the massive influx of immigrants was having a deleterious effect on native, white American racial stock. Ross's ideas regarding dysgenic racial selection were rendered timely by the unprecedented waves of millions of immigrants that had been admitted to the United States over the previous two decades. He warned not only of the disastrous economic, political, and social effects that unrestricted immigration would cause but also of the physical and moral degradation that would take place because of the intermingling of these races with the American pioneering breed. America, Ross concluded, was committing race suicide.

Kallen acknowledged that Ross's opinions were widely shared. "Mr. Ross is no voice crying in a wilderness," he wrote. "He simply utters aloud and in his own peculiar manner what is felt and spoken wherever Americans of British ancestry congregate thoughtfully."[6] Kallen's perception of popular attitudes was quite correct. The specter of race suicide had been raised by no less prominent a figure than President Theodore Roosevelt as early as 1907, and the American Immigration Act of 1924 (also known as the Johnson-Reed Act), which severely curtailed immigration, was passed "to preserve the ideal of U.S. homogeneity."[7] Progressive Era America began to assert state regulatory powers over race-related issues, including marriage, fertility, and immigrant population.[8] This was the racially charged climate of anti-immigration sentiment into which Kallen fired a salvo against Ross.

"Democracy versus the Melting Pot" marks a significant moment in American social thought. In it, Kallen set forth the basic parameters of cultural pluralism (although he did not employ that term there). In order for his ideas to gain traction, Kallen knew he would have to take steps to cultivate a receptive audience. There were three distinct strategies that Kallen employed to do this. First, Kallen sent his writing to select public intellectuals who, he hoped, would use their influence to propagate his views. This proved to be an effective strategy; thus, for example, Dewey responded positively to Kallen's article: "I quite agree with your orchestra idea, but upon condition we really get a symphony and not a lot of different instruments playing simultaneously. I never did care for the melting pot metaphor, but genuine assimilation *to one another*—not to Anglo-saxondom—seems to be essential to an America. That each cultural section should maintain its distinctive literary and artistic traditions seems to be most desirable, but in order that it might have the more to contribute to others."[9] Dewey's approval was conditional, but at the same time it reassured Kallen of the approval of one of America's most important philosophers. The essayist and public intellectual Randolph Bourne acknowledged his indebtedness to Kallen for his thesis in "Trans-National America," published in the *Atlantic Monthly*, and again in "The Jew and Trans-National America," published in the *Menorah Journal*. Kallen's friend and mentor, the Harvard psychologist Edwin B. Holt, thanked him for sending his articles and reflected on his hopeful ending: "Your articles in the *Nation* are very profound and interesting. I wish that 'the dominant classes in America' shall 'want such a society.' But I have misgivings. I stake no hopes on anything good com[ing] out of us for many generations yet." Kallen was also pleased to learn, as he noted in a letter to Henry Hurwitz, that his article had attracted the notice of the president of the United States: "Democracy *vs.* Melting Pot seems to [have] created [a] stir. I'm told even [President] Wilson has mentioned it."[10]

Second, Kallen was very active on the lecture circuit. He addressed Jewish students on university campuses across America, intent on promoting the Menorah movement and building the Zionist movement. His cross-country touring schedule was grueling, and ended up invaliding him for a time. In a one-week period alone, January

27–February 3 (his first article in the *Nation* appeared just two weeks later, on February 18), Kallen delivered no fewer than nine different addresses to students in California, and attended a half-dozen other meetings. Among the topics Kallen spoke on was "Democracy versus the Melting Pot," which he delivered in San Francisco on January 29, 1915.[11]

Third, Kallen engaged with a reading public. In two consecutive issues of the *Nation*—an intellectual weekly magazine of opinion published then as a weekly supplement to the daily *New York Evening Post*—Kallen sought to cultivate a receptive climate of public opinion among its liberal intellectual readership. The *Nation* typically covered a wide range of topics, from current events to literature, science, and philosophy. Its subscription numbers were, by its own admission, rather small, but the *Nation* prided itself on its disproportionate influence and its educational appeal: "Those whom it taught and inspired were all the time going out to teach and inspire others," read an editorial on the occasion of the *Nation*'s semicentennial in 1915. "In the colleges it was a power with the choicer natures; on more than one farm it was a college to awakening intelligences denied a college education."[12]

Under the editorial leadership of Paul Elmer More, the *Nation* was only moderately supportive of Progressive Era reformers. It would become ideologically committed to a Progressive agenda for social change only after 1918, when Garrison Villard took over as editor. It was Herbert Croly's newly created *New Republic* (founded in 1914) that assumed a role as the primary voice of Progressivism during World War I. Still, More, possibly encouraged by their mutual Harvard connection, proved to be receptive to publishing Kallen's politically radical article. For his part, Kallen saw an opportunity to make his voice heard in a well-established journal where he could try to create a new climate of public opinion. Whereas the *Nation* appealed to a liberal readership, Ross's readers were of a different ilk. Ross's book, published by the Century Company, was a compilation work of essays that he had contributed over the course of a year to the conservative monthly *Century Magazine*. Thus, although Kallen's article responded to Ross, their different publishing venues shows that Kallen and Ross addressed different reading publics. Kallen did not try to convince a public already swayed to Ross's point of view; he attempted to foster an alternative body of public opinion.

Even though the *Nation* afforded Kallen a substantial twenty-four columns of space over the course of two issues, there was little response to his article in the popular press. The Jewish press appears to have taken the most interest in him. The first review for Jewish readers appeared in the *American Israelite*, the print organ for the Reform movement. Its editors were delighted with the prominent public forum Kallen had been accorded. To them, Kallen had arrived as an able defender of the Jews against the racist, eugenics-driven ideology of scientists like Ross: "Prof. Edward A. Ross, whose unjust attacks on the Jews the *Israelite* refuted in its issue of September 30, found a very able opponent in Dr. Horace M. Kallen," read an editorial following the appearance of Kallen's first installment. "It is a source of gratification that a paper of the standing of the New York *Nation* allows to Dr. Kallen's argument thirteen columns of space. . . . We are glad that the championship of the Jewish immigrant is in such able hands and receives the advantage of such a prominent public forum."[13]

The editorial, however, carefully qualified its approbation of Kallen: "We may be pardoned for the suggestion that Jews, more than anybody else, should welcome men of such brilliant attainments as Brandeis and Kallen, and gladly extend to them the freedom of expounding their views which is granted to them before a larger public, though these men may differ with the views held by the majority of Jews on the religious interpretation of our cause."[14] The editorial thus intimated that the ideological divide separating Kallen (who propounded a secular, racial identification with Judaism) from Reform Judaism (which insisted that Judaism was an exclusively voluntary, faith-based identity), would normally preclude the *Israelite*'s receptivity to him, but there was a pressing need to provide a united front against anti-Semites.

Two weeks later, the *Israelite* published a second editorial on Kallen's article. The *Israelite*'s continuing interest in Kallen indicates that he had provoked an ongoing discussion among its readers. This second editorial was largely a reprint of one that had appeared a week earlier in the preeminent English-language Jewish periodical, the nondenominational *American Hebrew and Jewish Messenger.* There, the editorial caption noted Kallen's "striking article" as a response to "the views of those who consider that all ethnic, racial and religious divergencies of the immigrants into America will be obliterated by 'Americanism.'"[15]

In contrast to the *Israelite*, which had printed its editorial in a visually nondescript manner, as one among many different editorials on various topics of current interest, the *American Hebrew* visually spotlighted Kallen's article among its other editorials. It placed a special, double-lined box on the page with the title "Democracy versus the Melting Pot" in bold and enlarged print, occupying the horizontal space of two columns. A separate editorial was carried in that same issue of the *American Hebrew* that focused attention on Kallen's sociological thesis:

> In short, Prof. Kallen would have the United States, instead of playing "Yankee Doodle" on a penny whistle, conduct a grand concerto in which all the elements of the nation can contribute their share. The picture is a pleasing one, but we fancy that Prof. Kallen rather underrates the influence of American surroundings on even the newer immigration and exaggerates the permanent effect of ethnic diversity. . . . But there can be no doubt that his thesis is true of the new immigration for the next generation or so, and his careful analysis of the sociological consequences deserves widespread attention. . . . It is signally appropriate that so careful a study should come from a son of the "new immigration."[16]

The *American Hebrew* thus also registered qualified support for Kallen. Its reservation, however, was not ideological, but sociological. It suggested that the social forces of assimilation would eventually erode the boundaries of ethnic diversity. Kallen's thesis, the *American Hebrew* opined, was therefore valid only "for the next generation or so." At this stage in Kallen's career, the record from the English-language

Jewish press shows that, with respect to his acceptance as a social critic and politically active public intellectual, Kallen had begun to acquire social capital within the Jewish community. His Jewish readers appreciated his contribution to the debates of the day, but his thesis was not uncritically accepted.

The editorials in the two different Jewish periodicals were, in effect, engaged with two different discourses that were in simultaneous circulation in the Jewish community. A defensive discourse had developed as a response to anti-Semitism, but another discourse had also emerged in which Jews positively embraced certain racial constructions of Jewish identity.[17] Whereas the *American Israelite* was interested in Kallen's article as a response to anti-Semitism, the *American Hebrew* engaged with a discourse concerning the constitution of Jewish identity, and evaluated Kallen's views on ethnicity accordingly. Discussions concerning the viability of ethnicity in the face of the forces of assimilation emerged from a desire to understand the enduring foundation of Jewish identity. With the replication of parts of Kallen's article in both periodicals, his essay had become the subject of a conversation extending over several weeks at least, and it was a conversation that Kallen sought to see continued when he reintroduced his essay into circulation a decade later in *Culture and Democracy in the United States* (1924).[18]

The Social Application of Natural Selection

Kallen first presented his mature thesis to the first joint meeting of the American and Western Philosophical Associations, held at the University of Chicago in December 1914.[19] In his address, entitled "Democracy and the Melting Pot," Kallen identified three phases through which the meaning of *democracy* had passed in modern times. The first phase was the idea of basic equality for all, together with the creation of the concept of the individual. The second phase characterized the present age (the 1910s), and was illustrated by current Progressive Party politics. Attention was fixed upon society, rather than the individual. Democracy "insists that government is an instrument aiming at the welfare of the governed and that the machinery of government must . . . be easily abandonable when it proves inefficacious. But it tends in practice toward the suppression of individualities, the centralization of power, and the hypostasis of instruments." Democracy in this stage, Kallen wrote, "is instrumental and corrective, not intrinsic in its significance." The growth of industry and communications, together with the pressures of assimilation, Kallen opined, had led to the illusory belief that America is a melting pot, or "the womb of a newer and happier race."[20]

The reality, Kallen asserted, is that the United States is far from homogenous. Urban and rural populations were geographically, industrially, and socially stratified, and American ethnic groups retained their "distinct physical and cultural heredity" and tended not to intermarry, Kallen claimed. Americanization, in fact, amounts to little more than superficial imitation. Consciousness of this reality, Kallen argued, may lead to the development of a new, third phase in the meaning of democracy, which "may lead to a restoration of its intrinsicality." This new phase would understand that the United States "is, in fact, *states*, a federation of politically and ethnically diversified peoples, who as they become more prosperous become more self-conscious and nationalistic. All in all, this is as it should be. . . . The freedom of self-development implied in the Declaration is now conceived as the freedom of a *social* self, this self is at its broadest efficacy ethnic."[21] Thus, as Kallen conceived it, democracy should be understood as a cooperative federation of nationalities.

In Kallen's view, then, the melting pot is a natural consequence of what he identified as the second stage of democracy, in which attention shifts from the individual to society as a whole. It is an intermediate stage on the way to the final stage of democracy, which finally recognizes that American society needs to affirm not only individual freedoms but freedom of the social self, the self that is expressed through ethnicity, or nationality. "Democracy versus the Melting Pot," however, contained no reference to gradual developments in conceptions of democracy. There he presented a bluntly provocative rhetoric, a binary opposition between democracy and its antithesis, the melting pot. Significantly, the title of Kallen's presentation before the

American and Western Philosophical Associations had been "Democracy *and* the Melting Pot," not *versus* (emphasis added). The wording change signals Kallen's intent to simplify and polemicize his message for a popular audience. In "Democracy versus the Melting Pot," readers would not discover a continuum of development, and, moreover, were told that the terms were opposed in intent. From the very title, "Democracy versus the Melting Pot," readers were asked to make the simple choice between right and wrong.

Democracy's "intrinsicality," as Kallen developed the idea in "Democracy versus the Melting Pot," derived from evolutionary discourse, which had become the driver for socioeconomic and political theories. Both Kallen and Ross accepted the notion that racial and cultural traits were inseparable from each other and were heritable, but a close examination of their divergent claims shows that they had different underlying assumptions. Ross emphasized competition in society, citing the "modern competitive order," whereas Kallen highlighted the value of cooperation.[22]

Ross began *The Old World in the New* by highlighting the defining role of the struggle for existence: "When you empty a barrel of fish fry into a new stream there is a sudden sharpening of their struggle for existence. So, when people submit themselves to totally strange conditions of life, Death whets his scythe, and those who survive are a new kind of 'fittest.'" In Ross's construction of America, pioneers were a noble and hardy stock, whose value and mettle were proved by prevailing against hostile environmental forces. The "sifting of the wilderness" resulted in improved American stock "fiber" that was passed on to their descendants. "It is such selection that explains in part the extraordinary blooming of the colonies after the cruel initial period was over."[23] Ross's evaluation of each immigrant group was, in essence, an assessment of their relative ability to contribute to the survival worthiness of the American stock, and each group was found wanting. Based on his racial analysis, Ross then drew pessimistic conclusions concerning the economic, political, and social effects of immigration, and ended with the warning that the mixing of "American blood" with "immigrant blood" would result in dysgenic selection.

Ross identified specific heritable mental, behavioral, and physical characteristics that attached to various immigrant groups—the Celtic Irish, Germans, Scandinavians, Italians, Slavs, Eastern European Hebrews, and other so-called lesser immigrant groups. Ross's inclusion of Eastern European Jews in this listing reveals his belief that Jews were primarily an ethno-racial, rather than a faith-based, group. In this regard, Kallen and Ross shared the same basic assumption, since Kallen also viewed the Jews as, first and foremost, an ethno-racial group. Ross, however, was particularly focused on the provenance of Eastern Europe because of the larger question of the assimilability of these new immigrants: "It is too soon yet to foretell whether or not this vast and growing body of Jews from eastern Europe is to melt and disappear in the American population just as numbers of Portuguese, Dutch, English, and French Jews in our early days became blent with the rest of the people."[24]

Ross described these immigrant Jews in stereotypical terms: "None can beat the Jew at a bargain, for through all the intricacies of commerce he can scent his profit." He identified "intellectuality," a "combinative imagination," and "abstractness" as specifically Hebrew racial traits, and added, "The Jew has little feeling for the particular. He cares little for pets." These oddly specific traits were, Ross believed, objective facts. He believed that American upper-crust society's discriminatory practices against Jews were a natural reaction to their racially determined objectionable behaviors: "In New York the [race] line is drawn against the Jews in hotels, resorts, clubs, and private schools, and constantly this line hardens and extends. They cry 'Bigotry' but bigotry has little or nothing to do with it. What is disliked in the Jews is not their religion but certain ways and manners." Although Ross found discrimination against immigrant Jews to be understandable, he nevertheless objected to the "cruel prejudice" of "all lump condemnations," and opined that America could absorb "thirty or forty thousand Hebrews from eastern Europe" per year, "without any marked growth of race prejudice." Beyond that number, Ross warned, "there will be trouble." Ross concluded by holding open the possibility that America, "the strongest solvent Jewish separatism has ever encountered," could work its melting pot magic and, through mixed marriages, "end the Jews as a distinctive ethnic strain." Aside from one passing comment imputing "race prejudice" to Ross, Kallen did not directly address Ross's anti-Semitic calumnies, possibly because he desired his article to be read as a call for social change and not merely as a defense of Jews.[25]

Kallen attacked Ross's claim of American racial homogeneity and challenged his conclusion that, were the immigration of Eastern European Jews sufficiently curtailed, the "distinctive ethnic strain" of Jews would likely dissolve in the melting pot of America. Ross's focus on the natural and heritable physical, mental, and behavioral characteristics of races placed these groups squarely in the natural world, subject to the driving force of competitive selection. Kallen, although he acknowledged the role of competitive natural selection in the natural world, believed more fundamentally in the affirmation of diversity implied by natural selection and in the importance that cooperation plays in evolution. In this respect, Kallen approached Darwin's views in *Descent of Man* (1871) concerning the importance of social instinct and sympathy, an idea already advanced in Spencer's evolutionary theory of mind.[26]

The Harvard philosopher Ralph Barton Perry's *The Moral Economy* (1909) made a significant impression on Kallen.[27] His review of Perry's book, published in the *Boston Transcript* in 1909, focuses on how Perry's view of morality, rooted in the Jamesian pragmatist school of thought, was derived from the evolutionary view that morality is at root a natural social instinct and part of the evolutionary process. Morality, understood as a process rather than a concrete set of ideas, and characterized by coordinated group cooperation, had the effect of bringing different, even competing, interests together in a cooperative fashion. Kallen was particularly interested in the connection Perry drew between the moral economy and the proper functioning of democracy.[28] Perry likely gave Kallen the conceptual framework to connect ethics and democracy to his program of cultural pluralism, founded upon a platform of philosophical pragmatism and a post-Darwinian worldview. Cooperative morality, expressed as federative democracy, was, for Kallen, a natural extension and consequence of life because it ultimately supported the further growth and diversification of life. Survival, Kallen wrote in more than one place, is not enough, and, as we have seen, he had asserted as early as 1906 that a group's existence had to be morally justified.[29] Judgment concerning the adequate moral justification for survival hinged upon the extent to which the survival of one contributed to the continued flourishing of diversity. In this light, cooperation, rather than competition, ultimately supported the natural process of life's continual diversification.

Kallen's primary interest in Darwinism lay in what he perceived to be its philosophical application. For him, natural selection's social significance rested in what it teaches rather than in what it does. From the basic observation that diversity is a fundamental fact of nature and that cooperation and interdependency facilitate further diversification, a social principle of cooperative morality expressed in federative democracy followed. Kallen called this idea "philosophical Darwinism." It validated the contributions made by distinct ethno-racial groups to society, and, moreover, justified Jewish group survival. As we have seen, throughout the decade prior to publishing "Democracy versus the Melting Pot," Kallen developed the idea that the "Hebraic" worldview had discovered its scientific affirmation in the post-Darwinian world. That worldview, Kallen believed, contrasted with the premodern "Hellenic" worldview by affirming diversity and flux, and embracing the reality of contingency and change. Kallen argued that Judaism was fundamentally compatible with modernity because of its "naturalism" and "moralism," terms that refer to what he took to be Judaism's empiricism, its self-awareness as an ever-evolving entity, and its view of morality as rooted in the natural order and not given over to otherworldly salvation.[30]

Furthermore, Kallen argued, Zionism was the paradigmatic political expression of the Hebraic spirit in the modern world because, in the spirit of *The Moral Economy*, it sought to embody the moral point of view. The Jews would demonstrate their ethical right to exist by demonstrating that, by its very nature, Zionism is "contributory to the values of culture and civilization," and that "by remaining their unaltered selves, by perfecting their natural and distinctive group functions [Jews] must contribute to the welfare of nations and serve international comity."[31] Whereas Ross saw competition in the natural order and feared the dysgenic influence of groups like the Jews on Americans like him, Kallen saw social cooperation as fundamental, and testified that the Jewish example demonstrates that nurturing the full freedom of the social self ultimately contributes to the flowering of democracy and the harmony of civilization.

Evolution and Rhetoric

To strengthen his argument, Kallen first had to dismantle the scientific premises supporting Ross's claims. Ross worried that native-born white American stock would be driven to extinction as a result of interracial marriage. Two drivers of Darwinian evolution—population pressure and sexual selection—would destroy the American Anglo-Saxon stock and replace it with a new and inferior hybrid American race. Kallen discredited Ross's argument from natural selection on several fronts. First, he argued that there was no such thing as biological American stock. Second, Kallen dismissed the alarms raised by Ross concerning population pressure, which, in the natural world, helps to drive natural selection. Finally, Kallen addressed the issue of sexual selection, which drove the hopes of Americanizers who looked forward to the creation of a new American race, and drove the fears of nativists who feared the weakening of American stock. Kallen concluded that both groups were misguided, and that their attachment to the ideal of the melting pot had blinded them to the heterogeneous reality of America. Instead, Kallen urged the recognition of the emergence of a new democratic order of a cooperative federation of *nationalities* (or, in today's parlance, *ethno-racial groups*), joined together by their common commitment to American ideals. The strength of Kallen's rhetoric rested upon the cultural authority of evolutionary discourse, and, specifically, in his ability to wrest the discourse of natural selection from the cause of nativists like Ross.

Kallen attacked Ross's claim that the core and essential American identity is rooted in Anglo-Saxon racial homogeneity, ostensibly threatened by the immigrant invasion. He wrote that Ross presumed that only Americans of British descent like himself were native white American stock, but that history shows that America grew out of a plurality of nationalities, each imbued with like-mindedness and self-consciousness, and each of which had long ago become American: "Frenchmen and Germans, in Louisiana and in Pennsylvania, regarded themselves as the cultural peers of the British, and because of their own common ancestry, their like-mindedness and self-consciousness, they have retained a large measure of their individuality and spiritual autonomy to this day, after generations of unrestricted and mobile contact and a century of political union with the dominant British populations."[32] American civilization, Kallen argued, merely designates the aggregate product of a plurality of distinct ethnicities. Ross's America, a nation born from homogenous Anglo-Saxon stock, was a fantasy. His fear that natural selection would wreak dysgenic havoc on American Anglo-Saxon stock was little more than a chimera.

Having discredited the notion of racial homogeneity in the nation's history, Kallen turned his attention to the question of American racial homogeneity in the future. Focusing his attention on the notion of *Americanization*, Kallen observed that the term connotes "the fusion of the various bloods, and a transmutation by 'the miracle of assimilation' of Jews, Slavs, Poles, Frenchmen, Germans, Hindus, Scandinavians into beings similar in background, tradition, outlook, and spirit to the descendants of the British colonists." The goal, Kallen clarified, was to absorb that Americanism whose "spiritual expression" is found in the "New England school." Proponents of this ideal, he explained, believe the goal of assimilation would be attained through education, and, more importantly, through intermarriage, which would blend "all the European stocks" into a new "American race."[33]

Both racist nativists and optimistic Americanizers believed in the future evolution of a new American race, albeit with different understandings of its significance. For Ross and his ilk, it was something to fear. For liberal proponents of the melting pot, it pointed to "a newer and better being whose qualities and ideals shall be the qualities and ideals of the contemporary American of British ancestry."

Both the hopes and the fears attached to this future development, Kallen asserted, were groundless. There would be no new American race. Noting the prevalence of ethnic stratification in the country as a whole, Kallen remarked that "the likelihood of a new 'American' race is remote enough, and the fear of it unnecessary. But equally remote also is the possibility of a universalization of the inwardness of the old American life. Only the externals succeed in passing over." Moreover, Kallen argued, the intrinsic and ineradicable qualities that attach to ethnicity will, in the end, assert themselves no matter how one might try to deny them. Those who appear to be Americanized, like certain Jewish writers, he wrote, "protest too much." They tout it "like an achievement, a tour de force," but nevertheless reveal in their writing "a dualism and the strain to overcome it." Even Ross's anxiety regarding American Anglo-Saxon civilization, Kallen wrote, is a case in point of the inevitability of "ethnic nationality returned to consciousness."[34] The non-British elements in American society have provoked a reawakening of Kallen's ethnic self-consciousness.

The hopes and fears pinned to the coming of a new American race, Kallen argued, ignore a basic fact of nature. Ethnicity is heritable and an inalienable quality within every individual: "Behind him in time and tremendously in him in quality are his ancestors; around him in space are his relatives and kin, looking back with him to a remoter common ancestry. In all these he lives and moves and has his being. They constitute his, literally, *natio* [i.e., ethnicity]." The term *American*, by way of contrast, functions simply as "an adjective of similarity." Kallen wrote, "Similar environments, similar occupations, do, of course, generate similarities: 'American' is an adjective of similarity applied to Anglo-Saxons, Irish, Jews, Germans, Italians, and so on. But the similarity is one of place and institution, acquired, not inherited, and hence not transmitted. Each generation has, in fact, to become 'Americanized' afresh, and, withal, inherited nature has a way of redirecting nurture." American identity, in other words, takes on cultural shape only in the hyphenate form, prefixed by the ethnic group of origin (thus, for example, Irish-American, Jewish-American, German-American). "Inherited nature"—meaning the psychophysical inheritance of ethnicity—inevitably asserts itself.[35] Racial homogeneity, then, neither existed in the past nor will it exist in the future. Ross's claims for the past and fears for the future, Kallen asserted, were both without basis in fact.

On Population Pressure

Ross wrote with alarm about the "undue growth of cities," which was exponentially increasing the demographic pressures on "American stock." In his estimation, "American stock" in the cities had been steadily diminishing, while "foreign stock" had come to constitute three-fourths of the cities' populations. Ross provided statistics from the 1910 US Census on the relative distribution of "native white stock," "foreign stock," and "foreign-born." American urban life, as Ross saw it, was infested with foreign stock, and was now a tale of "congestion, misliving, segregation, corruption, and confusion." This, however, was only true of the urban crush created by immigrants in "motley groups like Pittsburgh." Ross opined that in cities like Indianapolis, a "native center" where American stock still prevailed, such social issues did not exist. The trend, Ross feared, was only getting worse. Native-born white stock was being crowded out of its natural environment and supplanted by a morally degenerate alternative. Ross believed that the general mixing of people together in concentrated urban areas had seeded the growth of cultural disintegration. The urban melting pot created a kind of internal rot that was beginning to become manifest in public life.[36]

Although Kallen granted that the massive influx of immigrants in recent decades had wrought a demographic transformation in America, he could not have disagreed more with Ross's pessimistic observations. In his address to the American and Western Philosophical Associations, Kallen had observed that the American urban environment was patently not a melting pot. In both rural and urban populations, he argued, ethnic groups were stratified "first of all geographically, the layers of the races of Europe following the streams of migration westward; then, industrially; different nationalities follow different employment, and, finally, socially, the upper classes being in the long run identical with the earlier comers."[37] Kallen reiterated this claim in "Democracy versus the Melting Pot," asserting that the different nationalities that immigrated to America tended to stick together in their own groups, not as ideological separatists or isolationists, but naturally, as their psychophysical inheritance asserted itself.[38]

The qualities of city life that so alarmed Ross reflected no deep internal, cultural rot. These had only external and superficial significance: "The *common* city life, which depends upon like-mindedness, is not inward, corporate, and inevitable," Kallen explained, "but external, inarticulate, and incidental, a reaction to the need of amusement and the need of protection, not the expression of a unity of heritage, mentality, and interest."[39] City life was not a proving ground of one native, settled race facing persistent demographic pressures on that environment. It yielded no single unity of mind that could support this charge. The city was an environment in which different ethnic groups negotiated their own needs and interests in relation to each other, in the political and educational spaces they shared. Concessions to "the Irish vote," "the Jewish vote," "the German vote" were a feature of political life, as was the existence of compromise school committees that represented different ethnic groups. The city, Kallen believed, could in fact be a model of cooperative democracy in action, not a hostile environment in which natural selection, operating through the forces of population pressure, would threaten the life of native-born white stock.

On Sexual Selection

Another alarming aspect about the melting pot for Ross was dysgenic sexual selection. He warned of the general diminishment of Americans' good looks through miscegenation: "It is reasonable to expect an early falling off in the frequency of good looks in the American people," Ross wrote. "It is unthinkable that so many persons with crooked faces, coarse mouths, bad noses, heavy jaws, and low foreheads can mingle their heredity with ours without making personal beauty yet more rare among us than it actually is." Ross noted with particular concern the natural physical weakness of Jews: "On the physical side the Hebrews are the polar opposite of our pioneer breed. Not only are they undersized and weak-muscled, but they shun bodily activity and are exceedingly sensitive to pain." Ross contrasted Jews with Americans: "Natural selection, frontier life, and the example of the red man produced in America a type of great physical self-control, gritty, uncomplaining, merciless to the body through fear of becoming 'soft.' To this roaming, hunting, exploring, adventurous breed what greater contrast is there than the denizens of the Ghetto?" American stature, physique, vitality, and morality were therefore going to suffer from the admixture of immigrant blood. Ross believed that "the competition of low-standard immigrants is the root cause of the mysterious 'sterility' of Americans." American fecundity suffered, he argued, chiefly where immigrants arrived. Every race, Ross opined, after it has become Americanized, is attacked by "fatal sterility." Ross concluded that the forces of sexual selection were contributing to race suicide: "A people that has no more respect for its ancestors and no more pride of race than this deserves the extinction that surely awaits it."[40]

Kallen's rebuttal to this consists of two parts. First, he argued that incidences of mixed marriage were statistically insignificant: "In the mass, neither he [the immigrant] nor his children nor his children's children lose their ethnic individuality. For marriage is determined by sexual selection and by propinquity, and the larger the town, the lesser the likelihood of mixed marriage."[41] Kallen believed that ethnic groups naturally preferred endogamy. Second, Kallen appealed to history to make the point that mixed breeding had never been a factor in the development of ethnic groups:

> The notion that the [Americanization] programme might be realized by radical and even enforced miscegenation, by the creation of the melting-pot by law, and thus by the development of the new "American race," is, as Mr. Ross points out, as mystically optimistic as it is ignorant. In historic times, so far as we know, no new ethnic types have originated, and what we know of breeding gives us no assurance of the disappearance of the old types in favor of the new,

> only the addition of a new type, if it succeeds in surviving, to the already existing older ones. Biologically, life does not unify; biologically, life diversifies; and it is sheer ignorance to apply social analogies to biological processes.[42]

In Kallen's view, no new ethnic groups had originated since historic times. They predated civilization. Theoretically, he allowed, a new ethnic type could arise through mixed breeding, but this was not likely to happen.

Kallen accepted a primordialist view of ethnicity—that is, the view that ethnic groups have existed since before the dawn of civilization, and are a permanent fact of human social life. He contended that the Americanization program would not lead to "a unison of ethnic types." Rather, it would at most lead to "a unison of social and historic interests," but even this would come at a great cost. It would be "established by the complete cutting-off of the ancestral memories of our populations."[43] It required, in Kallen's view, enforced homogenization, which would only result in what he had described as a dysfunctional "dualism and the strain to overcome it."

Having argued that natural selection processes did not play a role in the creation or development of ethnicity, Kallen presented his alternative vision. He believed that his solution to the problem of creating social cohesion affirmed the biological impulse toward diversity. Kallen felt that the time had passed that the New England Brahmins could claim to represent the American type: "At the present time," he wrote, "there is no dominant American mind." The reality with which America had not yet come to grips was that the *natio*, or ethnic group, was "the fundamental fact of American life." America was de facto composed of a plurality of such groups, and it must therefore adopt a prospective rather than a retrospective stance with respect to its cultural cohesion. Kallen took the Jews to be the paradigmatic example of ethnicity asserting itself despite the outward appearance of assimilation: "Once the wolf is driven from the door and the Jewish immigrant takes his place in our society a free man and an American, he tends to become all the more a Jew. The cultural unity of his race, history, and background is only continued by the new life under the new conditions . . . In sum, the most eagerly American of the immigrant groups are also the most autonomous and self-conscious in spirit and culture."[44] The social experiment of enforcing Americanization, which had been self-imposed by the Jews themselves, had resulted only in an even greater sense of autonomy and self-consciousness.

Thus, Kallen arrived at his fundamental thesis: "Starting with our existing ethnic and cultural groups," he wrote, America as a nation should free and strengthen "the strong forces actually in operation." It should "seek to provide conditions under which each [ethnicity] may attain the perfection that is proper to its kind." What troubled Ross and so many others, Kallen wrote, "is not really inequality; what troubles them is *difference*."[45] America, Kallen countered, must embrace diversity. Diversity, he insisted, was guaranteed by evolutionary fiat.

As we have seen, Kallen believed that the psychophysical inheritance of the ethnic group ensures that even were America to succeed in cutting off the immigrant from his or her past external associations, it would not eliminate the persistent influence of the group psyche on the individual. Like Freud, Kallen adopted an approach that "transcended the limitations of the debates about biological determinism and yet remained framed by them."[46] Inherited memory, for these Jewish thinkers, served as the foundation of personality for the individual as for the group, but it did not thereby circumscribe the life and personality of either the individual or the group within the confines of a racially delimited range of emotions or behaviors. Ross, on the other hand, ultimately placed humanity at the mercy of the mechanistic and impersonal forces of natural selection. For him, racial memory and personality did reflect a nonmalleable typology.

With this distinction in mind, we now turn to the concluding section of "Democracy versus the Melting Pot":

> What is inalienable in the life of mankind is its intrinsic positive quality—its psychophysical inheritance. Men may change their clothes, their politics, their wives, their religions, their philosophies, to a greater or lesser extent: they cannot change their grandfathers.

> Jews or Poles or Anglo-Saxons, in order to cease being Jews or Poles or Anglo-Saxons, would have to cease to be. The selfhood which is inalienable in them, and for the realization of which they require "inalienable" liberty, is ancestrally determined, and the happiness which they pursue has its form implied in ancestral endowment. This is what, actually, democracy in operation assumes. There are human capacities which it is the function of the state to liberate and to protect.[47]

Democracy, then, by taking into consideration the value of difference, the prevalence of diversity, and the intrinsically positive role that psychophysical inheritance played in the life of people, would promote a government characterized by cooperation rather than competition. Kallen believed that democracy, once properly aligned with biological processes, had the potential to usher in a new moral economy that would value diversity without itself descending into the competitive natural order of Ross's universe, of Tennyson's "Nature, red in tooth and claw," of the war of all against all.

The Scientific Basis for Cultural Pluralism

Evolutionary theory gave Horace Kallen a scientific basis to articulate the grounds for full and equal Jewish group participation in civic life. He turned his understanding of the evolutionary significance of social cooperation, coupled with his belief in ethnic psychophysical inheritance, into a scientific justification for how Jewish ethnicity serves a positive function for American democracy. It served as the scientific underpinning to his theory of cultural pluralism. Using the language of evolutionary theory, Kallen sought to carve out a space for Jews in the United States by highlighting the survival value of cooperation and the necessity of fostering it. He connected this evolutionary principle to the values of American democracy, thus aligning the ideals of the nation with the processes of nature. By nurturing natural ethnic diversity, America thereby enhances its own strength and vitality.

Kallen's Jewish readers, as refracted through the *American Israelite* and the *American Hebrew*, read him as a defender against anti-Semitism and as a critic of the assimilationist agenda of Americanization. Although Kallen's stand against racism and his affirmation of Jewish identity were of interest to Jewish readers, his use of evolutionary theory to support his views remained in certain respects his own idiosyncratic formulation. Nevertheless, Kallen's voice should be considered as one in a chorus that articulated an evolutionary paradigm for Jewish identity. Having been featured in the prominent periodical the *Nation* and then discussed in nationally circulating American Jewish periodicals, Kallen's unique construction of Jewish identity helped to drive the developing discourse that led to the perception of ethnicity as a defining feature of American Jewish identity.

· 4 ·

A Discontent of Hope

> If the turbulence of the times within you takes form in a discontent of hope, it makes of you an optimist, a revolutionary, a perfectionist.
>
> —Horace Kallen, *Culture and Democracy in the United States* (1924)

CONCERTGOERS packed into Aeolian Hall in New York City on Tuesday afternoon, February 12, 1924, to hear the bandleader Paul Whiteman's "modern American orchestra" perform a program titled "An Experiment in Modern Music." Among the featured pieces was the world premiere performance of George Gershwin's "Rhapsody in Blue." "I heard it as a sort of musical kaleidoscope of America," Gershwin later recalled, "of our vast melting pot, of our unduplicated national pep, of our blues, our metropolitan madness."[1] His fusion of jazz with concert idioms was an immediate sensation, and it was performed eighty-four times by Whiteman that year, marking its appearance as one of the most important musical events of the decade. The popular reception of Gershwin's piece, which had originally been entitled "American Rhapsody," established his centrality to American modernism.[2] In the same year in which Gershwin's "Rhapsody in Blue" made its appearance, the term *cultural pluralism*, coined by Kallen, made its print debut in what has become regarded as his seminal work, *Culture and Democracy in the United States* (1924).[3]

Culture and Democracy in the United States is a compilation work of six essays that Kallen had written over the course of the previous decade, dating back to his 1915 "Democracy versus the Melting Pot."

In the latter essay, Kallen had posed the question of how to create social cohesion in musical terms, a point that is particularly relevant to raise here. "Our spirit is inarticulate, not a voice, but a chorus of many voices each singing a rather different tune," Kallen wrote. "How to get order out of this cacophony is the question for all those who are concerned about those things which alone justify wealth and power, concerned about justice, the arts, literature, philosophy, science. What must, what *shall* this cacophony become—a unison or a harmony?" Unison, Kallen made clear, implies the imposition of will and the eradication of difference. Harmony, however, implies the preservation of difference. "What do we *will* to make of the United States—a unison, singing the old Anglo-Saxon theme 'America,' the America of the New England school, or a harmony, in which that theme shall be dominant, perhaps, among others, but one among many, not the only one?"[4]

In the concluding section to that article, Kallen offered his well-known orchestra metaphor to answer this question:

> As in an orchestra, every type of instrument has its specific timbre and tonality, founded in its substance and form; as every type has its appropriate theme and melody in the whole symphony, so in society each ethnic group is the natural instrument, its spirit and culture are its theme and melody, and the harmony and dissonances and discords of them all make the symphony of civilization, with this difference: a musical symphony is written before it is played; in the symphony of civilization the playing is the writing, so that there is nothing so fixed and inevitable about its progressions as in music, so that within the limits set by nature they may vary at will, and the range and variety of the harmonies may become wider and richer and more beautiful.

The ethnic groups of society are, as it were, instruments within the orchestra of America. The music is emphatically not a "unison," but features the interplay of individual instruments that create "harmony and dissonances and discords." Kallen referred to a conceptual divide between a musical symphony and the symphony of civilization, insofar as a musical symphony depends upon fixed writing; here, too, there is a parallel to "Rhapsody in Blue." Although the composition later became a fixed musical score, its world premiere included improvisational clarinet and piano playing, thus partially bridging the very gap that separated a musical symphony from the symphony of civilization. Kallen's metaphor for American civilization thus finds an accidental resonance in Gershwin's modernist masterpiece. The uniquely American blend of sound that is "Rhapsody in Blue," which showcases the individuality of instrumental sounds, is cultural pluralism's closest musical analog.

Culture and Democracy in the United States is typically evaluated in the context of immigration and ethnic studies. This is evident even from its publication history. Thus, for example, Arno Press, a now-defunct reprint house whose focus was on reference materials for libraries, republished *Culture and Democracy in the United States* in 1970 as part of a series called "The American Immigration Collection." The series name alone, in fact, appears on the hardback cover; the actual book title appears only on the side binding. When Transaction Publishers, an academic publishing house specializing in the social sciences, republished it in 1998, it was as part of a series called "Studies in Ethnicity."[5] These publication decisions indicate that scholarship has assigned Kallen's book to the specific canon of immigration and ethnic studies. Our aim here, however, is to show how *Culture and Democracy in the United States*, considered in its original publication context with Boni & Liveright, is embedded within, and is a contribution to, American modernism.

Considering Kallen as a modernist social critic sensitizes us to the network of relationships in print culture that Kallen cultivated during the years in which he developed his most important contribution to American social and political thought. As well, it helps us to contextualize his self-understanding as a contributor to the ongoing project of modernity. Finally, it adds another layer to our understanding of Kallen's self-construction as a Jewish-American, as someone who believed that each term in the hyphenated phrase is a relational term and can be understood only in relation to the other.

Approaching Kallen's work in this light is rendered all the more necessary considering that he quite literally wrote the definition of modernism. Written for the relatively new *Encyclopaedia of the Social Sciences* in 1933, Kallen's definition of modernism quickly became the operative definition for its time and created the backdrop for future developments concerning the concept. He wrote:

> Modernism may be described as that attitude of mind which tends to subordinate the traditional to the novel and to adjust the established and customary to the exigencies of the recent and innovating. . . . The modernistic attitude, in sum, arises where a fission develops in the social or intellectual order because a new invention or discovery has become powerful enough to impose adjustment to itself upon the resistant environment which it has entered as an interloper. The process of adjustment begins in some individual or small group whose life or work has been dislocated. Automatic at first, it soon gets rationalized into a program which wins adherence for a wider and wider range of personalities and locations.[6]

Modernism, for Kallen, describes the process in which innovation—whether artistic, scientific, or technological—forces a resistant social environment to undergo an adjustment to accommodate it. The modernist intellectual is someone who, like Kallen, prescribes an adjustment to the new conditions of life characterized by the rise of industry and science and the spread of democracy and humanism. Cultural pluralism is a modernist innovation, connected to American modernist art and literature, because it insists on an adjustment in the teeth of a highly resistant social and political environment.

Kallen's thesis thus functions as a modernist critique. He saw himself in a special relationship with his reading public, functioning much like the art critic he described in 1930:

> One cannot overstress the event that in the end it is the public whose decision determines whether a work of art or a school of criticism shall survive or perish; that schools of criticism absorbed in their warfare against one another, and movements in the arts absorbed

> in the development of their methods and realization of their purposes, behave as though their publics were not there at all or were passively waiting for their light and guidance. This is a delusion. On the record of history and of biography, the public is always present, and actively present. An artist might conceivably produce and exist without a public. A critic never could. He is a middleman, he intervenes between artist and public and creates a triangle of which he is the third member. He is the complication in the life of art.[7]

Kallen credited the public with agency, as a decision-making body that confirms or condemns works of art and schools of criticism. He saw himself as the critic, as the middleman who intervenes and creates an interpretation for the public. Kallen interpreted values in art as he interpreted values in society, and presented his ideas to the reading public, who, he wrote, were not merely present, but "actively present." Ultimately it was the public who would decide the fate of Kallen's views. The specific reading public that Kallen sought to engage was the politically left-wing, educated, and self-educating intelligentsia. These were the people who were likely to respond positively to Kallen's ideas and to take action in response. This, as we shall see, is why Kallen published his more significant social criticism in the *Nation*, became intimately involved in the management of the *Dial* in the wake of World War I, and published several books with Boni & Liveright.

For Kallen, modernism's importance lay not only in its innovative potential but also in the way that it creates and communicates social values. As a pragmatist, he evaluated the significance of modernist art through his perception of its relative contribution to society. "Art converts values into existences," Kallen argued in 1914. "It realizes values, injecting them into nature as far as may be." In Kallen's view, art converts values from theoretical abstraction into material reality. Its innovations make way for the birth of new values, bringing them into tangible existence. Art "realizes values *in* existence," he claimed. Without art, in other words, existence is meaningless. For Kallen, art injects value into existence. It thus served him as a replacement for the role that some might assign to religion. For him, existence and values are united in the world of art, creating meaning in life. Here Kallen articulated the philosophical link that connects art to the social criticism with which he was engaged. His notion of democracy in America took especial note of the conditions of existence and of realizing values in that existence.[8]

Kallen's involvement in the modernist movement was extensive. In addition to corresponding with literary modernist giants like Sinclair Lewis and T. S. Eliot, he was especially interested in artwork produced by Jewish artists like that of his friend, the painter and sculptor Maurice Sterne (1878–1957). Sterne had begun experimenting with modernism from the early 1900s, and during the 1920s he divided his time between Italy, where Kallen stayed as his guest in 1927, and New York, where he taught at the Art Students League.[9] Sterne's reputation as one of the foremost artists in America was established with an exhibit of his work in 1926 at the Scott and Fowles Gallery, and reinforced in 1933 when he was the first American painter to be honored with a retrospective exhibit at the Museum of Modern Art (MOMA) in New York City.

The retrospective featured pieces selected from sixty-seven different collections, including Kallen's own. Kallen authored the MOMA brochure's introduction to the Sterne exhibition. He wrote that an artist is usually known because he or she "exemplifies some aesthetic philosophy or some psychological theory of perception and technological theory of execution. The very names of the schools signalize their extra-pictorial preoccupations: 'Impressionism,' 'Post-Impressionism,' 'Cubism,' 'Futurism,' 'Orphism,' 'Vorticism,' 'Synchronism,' 'Dada,' 'Expressionism.'" Members of these schools are really "metaphysicians and psychologists," Kallen continued, who speak "to the *cognoscenti*; they make no communication to the masses of men."[10] Such an elitist approach was anathema to Kallen. His criticism of the art schools, that they "make no communication to the masses of men," was the same criticism that Kallen leveled against the various schools of philosophy, which, he charged, operate as "a ceremonial liturgy of professionals as artificial and detached from the realities of daily life as bridge or chess."[11] Kallen appreciated Sterne's work because, much like his own social philosophy, "it exemplifies no school; it calls for no special psychological or aesthetic theory," and, most importantly, "it speaks with the same clarity and appeal to the masses as to the experts." Kallen valued his work because, as he saw it, it applies "to the exigencies of the present hour the enduring meanings of the past."[12]

Kallen's summation of the value of Sterne's modernist art reveals at least as much about Kallen as it does about Sterne. Kallen sensed congruence in agenda between modernist art and his self-expression as a modernist thinker. Just as Sterne's work exemplifies the modernist "process of adjustment" that he signals in his encyclopedia definition, so, too, does cultural pluralism propose a cultural adjustment to bridge the current social fission, by recognizing the "enduring meaning" of ethnicity in the present context of American democracy. In this respect, cultural pluralism is a prose analog to modernist art. It was to be an experiment to create new value out of lived experience, articulating a necessary social adjustment upon a resistant environment to revitalize democracy.

Values and Radical Empiricism

Kallen's pragmatic approach to art and its perceived relationship to values is rooted in the "philosophical Darwinism" that he had first articulated in "Hebraism and Current Tendencies in Philosophy" (1909). William James and Henri Bergson, he wrote there, were both engaged with the task of developing a philosophy of evolution. Kallen claimed to have learned from James that the articulation of a new value arises as a result of "spontaneous variation," and that its subsequent longevity marks it as "fit" in the struggle for survival, and he claimed to have learned from Bergson that perceiving the contingency of reality occurs not through contemplation but through lived experience.[13]

Notwithstanding their several commonalities, Kallen identified Bergson's dualistic antithesis between spirit (the fundamental level of reality in Bergsonian metaphysics) and matter as the central feature that distinguishes his thought from James's radical empiricism.[14] Kallen did not presuppose, as did Bergson, a fundamental unity of being separate from its expression in the world of time and space. Rather, following James, Kallen accepted speciation and differentiation at face value.

Kallen's understanding of James's radical empiricism may be fruitfully compared to his conception of art. Just as he had written about Sterne's art, that it "exemplifies no school," so, too, Kallen wrote elsewhere, James sought "to build no system."[15] James's radical empiricism rejected the metaphysics of traditional philosophy in favor of a scientifically infused philosophical program. Radical empiricism, Kallen explained, was best described as an attitude rather than as a system. It aims "to describe reality as it comes to cognition, to apprehend experience in its purity," rather than as part of a metaphysical system. For the radical empiricist, there is no total whole to reality, but only "an aggregate of eaches, each with a vote that it casts primarily for itself, each involving novelties, chances, mutations, and discretenesses. . . . Thus, although recognizing human values, and indeed making them central, radical empiricism refuses to distort the world . . . that these values may be eternally conserved. . . . It acknowledges . . . the right and the will and the struggle to be."[16]

For James, "nothing could be more repugnant than a conception of individuality like [Bergson's]," Kallen explained. "James assumes the Darwinian hypothesis, naturally: what is human in man is a spontaneous variation, a mutation upon the subhuman surviving by force of its inward power. What matters to him, however, is this: that, whatever the origin of individuality, whether it be primary or derived, once it *occurs*, *it* is the thing that counts, not its source."[17] Individuality, then, is not merely a way station on the journey to a life of the spirit as Bergson would have it; it is, as James asserts, of ultimate significance by virtue of its existence. The Jamesian view of individuality fundamentally shaped Kallen's worldview.

The parallels to Kallen's characterization of art are readily apparent. Art, like radical empiricism, acknowledges "the reality of immediate experience," Kallen wrote. In "injecting" values into nature, art does not "claim for its results greater reality than nature's. It claims for its results greater immediate harmony with human interests than nature." Radical empiricism finds existence to be morally neutral. So, too, in art, "existence is without value and is converted into value."[18]

Value and existence, as in art, become fused in the aspect of intelligence as the seat of the "creative act, the inventiveness, of the human spirit." In a definite rejection of Bergson, Kallen wrote, "Not the immediate push of society or the remoter onrush of an élan, but the constant choices of the individual, urge humanity forward." James's "pluralistic insistence on individuality," rooted in an (ostensibly) Darwinian view of evolution, leads to the conclusion that "the moral universe, too, is not a monarchy but a federal republic."[19] Values are thus conceived not as a product of a monolithic and immutable exposition of divine law, but as part of a pluralistic universe in which new ideas are spontaneous variations introduced by the "constant choices" of the individual and must compete in the struggle for survival. Values are not part of a systemic and undifferentiated whole, but appear as "a federal republic," or an "aggregate of eaches." Conceived thusly in subjective and relativistic terms, the path is cleared for the artist (and not the theologian) to play his or her part in urging humanity forward.

Because Bergson's evolutionary metaphysics minimizes the import of individual distinctiveness and posits a higher order of an undifferentiated whole, it was not well suited to support a social theory that values pluralism for its own sake. For Kallen, as for James, individual distinctiveness carries ultimate significance. Diversity, difference, and distinctiveness must therefore be accepted as inevitable and constitutive aspects of reality, and the consequent plurality to be considered as an "aggregate of eaches." This Jamesian approach to the world finds its musical echo in "Rhapsody in Blue." As a composition, it, too, is a whole formed out of an aggregate of diverse, different, and distinct instruments and sounds, and (at least, in its first performances) it left room for spontaneous variations of musical ideas. Kallen's perception that reality is constituted by an "aggregate of eaches" was at the core of his attempt to reframe American democracy in such a way that it accorded with his understanding of the nature of reality in the post-Darwinian mold. He would consider his thesis of cultural pluralism as a "spontaneous variation" on society's palette of values, and would test its validity by its ability to survive and thrive in the uncertain environment of public opinion.

A Time of Transition

The appearance of "Democracy versus the Melting Pot" in 1915 marks an important moment in Kallen's biography, for it was with that article that he began to assert his presence in the public sphere as a social critic and politically engaged public intellectual. Kallen was not content to limit himself to the world of academia, a world that he saw as fettering free speech and hobbling American democratic principles. Although Kallen had been at the University of Wisconsin since 1911, he had been unhappy there almost from the beginning. In April 1918 Kallen finally resigned. The immediate impetus for his departure was the lack of academic freedom on American campuses that peaked during the World War I years. Kallen advocated for the rights of pacifists at a time when it had practically become treason to suggest that America need not enter the war. When faculty members at the University of Wisconsin issued a statement condemning Senator Robert La Follette for his antiwar stance, Kallen publicly resisted pressure from both the administration and the faculty to become a signatory, making life very difficult for him there.[20] Kallen's departure had been building for years, however. Reflecting on his impending departure, Kallen's friend and mentor, the Harvard psychologist Edwin B. Holt, wrote, "I regret very much on some accounts that 'the axe has fallen'! Though on others I am not so sure that it is not a fortunate thing to have the Gordian knot cut."[21] Kallen appears to have decided to bring things to a head with the publication of a politically volatile piece in the *Nation* in March 1918 concerning controversy over La Follette and freedom of speech. As Kallen wrote to his friend at the *Dial*, the editor George Donlin, "My most recent irregularity is my article in the *Nation* on the political situation in Wisconsin. They may kick me out before I get out in consequence. That is one reason for hurrying my resignation if that is possible."[22]

The year 1918 was a trying time for Kallen. His father had passed away in December 1917, and his future career was uncertain. Kallen's life was in turmoil. He began to work through the conditions under which he would become a politically engaged social scientist, philosopher, psychologist, and author. In April 1918 Kallen wrote to Holt about the uncertainties he faced: "I shall be out of this, I think, by the end of the month. Precisely what to do I do not know for the present—for the present there is some work in the way of propaganda and war stuff which may keep me going for a little while. Of course, I am more anxious than ever to get into the affray and to have a peck at the Hun: But mostly he needs mental killing and I suspect that I shall continue with that. Certainly I do not want to have any teaching responsibilities, that is a deadly thing under any circumstances."[23] Kallen was still relatively unsettled in 1919, as he indicated to Rachel Jastrow, wife of the psychologist Joseph Jastrow and sister to the Zionist leader Henrietta Szold: "There is nothing to report except a disorderly turmoil in my career since I left Madison."[24]

Kallen found work with President Wilson's Inquiry, informally called the House Commission, a group of academic advisors convened to advise the president on postwar national policy: "On the House Commission I had reports on the Jewish question and on the League of Nations. I was kept busy on that until peace was declared," he wrote to Jastrow. "Then I went into the enterprise of organizing liberal opinion in behalf of the League of Nations—through the League of Free Nations Association. I am still doing a good deal of that, making my living meantime by lecturing to forums etc., and writing. It is not much of a living, but it keeps me going."[25] Kallen dived into political activism as a writer. He wrote reports for the House Commission, and he published two political treatises supporting Wilson's efforts to create a League of Nations, entitled *The Structure of Lasting Peace* and *The League of Nations Today and Tomorrow*.[26]

It seemed for a short while that Kallen had found a niche as a political propagandist. As he wrote to Jacob Billikopf, executive director of the American Jewish Relief Committee, Kallen believed that he was eminently suited to working on behalf of the American government abroad: "There is hardly anybody, I suspect, who has a more living realization of the positive implications of Americanism and of our purposes in the war, than I," he wrote.[27] In January 1918 Kallen sent President Wilson a copy of *The League of Nations, Today and Tomorrow*, and requested that Wilson allow him to dedicate to him his forthcoming publication, *The Structure of Lasting Peace.* Wilson responded that although he appreciated Kallen's request, he had nevertheless to decline: "I hope that you will believe that, though I am obliged to decline, it is through no lack of genuine appreciation. I must decline merely because I cannot venture to associate my name with any particular plan, for fear the association would be misinterpreted. I feel obliged to confine myself in this matter to my own official utterances."[28]

Kallen's direct involvement in American government and politics, however, did not last long. He had simultaneously become involved with a group of intellectuals who were embarking on an exciting new venture in education, the New School for Social Research. With the possibility of combining his philosophical activism with teaching now before him, Kallen's professed dislike of teaching evaporated: "At present, I have had a windfall in the way of a collection of lectures for the New School of Social Research," he wrote to Jastrow. "This may become a very great instrument of democratic opinion. I do not know any more about it than I tell you."[29] Kallen's future would soon become tied to the New School, where he remained until his retirement in 1970.

The *New Republic* and the New School for Social Research

Kallen was not the only academic who was frustrated by the restrictions on academic freedom that prevailed on American university campuses. James Harvey Robinson and Charles Beard, historians at Columbia University, resigned their positions after colleagues were fired for publicly opposing the United States' entry into World War I. Although Robinson and Beard personally supported America's entry into the war, they, like Kallen, were outraged by the lack of freedom of speech. They quickly found an intellectual home with the intellectual circle associated with the *New Republic.*

The *New Republic*, like the *Nation*, was a weekly magazine of political and cultural commentary with left-of-center leanings. It was founded in 1914 by Herbert Croly, author of the influential *The Promise of American Life* (1909), which attacked laissez-faire policies and helped to shape the Progressive Era agenda of increasing government involvement in social reform. Croly actively sought out like-minded intellectuals to write for the *New Republic*, and now, in the wake of Beard's and Robinson's resignations from Columbia, he began to discuss with them the creation of an alternative to the existing university system—one that would offer academic freedom and would help to train future progressive leaders. Croly organized weekly planning meetings attended by leading intellectuals, jurists, and philanthropists. Kallen was among Croly's invitees.

Kallen also discussed with Croly the possibility of becoming a correspondent for the *New Republic* in Europe. "I should like very much to have an opportunity of talking over with you your proposed trip to Europe and the possibility of doing some work for the *New Republic* there," Croly wrote to Kallen in December 1918. "I should be very glad to do anything within my power to help you get over there, and I feel sure the work that you would send back would be very useful to the *New Republic*." The State Department frustrated Kallen's plans, however; its position was that the *New Republic* was already "oversupplied" with correspondents in Paris.[30]

Kallen then turned his attention more fully to the New School for Social Research. On January 20, 1919, Croly sent Kallen a telegram inviting him to teach at the school, and the following month the New School opened its doors.[31] The New School's progressive and scientifically minded founding faculty saw themselves as advocates of a "cosmopolitan and progressive humanism."[32] The New School was an anti-institutional institution that sought to provide a forum for new social critical perspectives on American life. Its aspiration to effect a fundamental social reconstruction was, however, short-lived. By 1923 the New School was forced to restructure itself for economic and other reasons. Alvin Johnson, associate editor of the *New Republic*, guided the New School toward developing a new curriculum centered around cultural subjects.

By the late 1920s psychology, art, and literature became the new focus, and courses in these areas were entirely modernist in orientation. The New School's faculty included preeminent modernists like the art critic Leo Stein (Gertrude Stein's brother), the composer Aaron Copland, the writer Waldo Frank, the literary critic Gorham Munson, the psychoanalyst Sandor Ferenczi, and the urban planner Patrick Geddes, among many others. They introduced students to a wide range of modernist developments, from art, music, and literature to urban planning and psychology. Kallen's lectures on Jamesian pragmatism and cultural pluralism, infused with the modernist perspective, were legendary by some accounts. Through Kallen and his colleagues Morris Cohen and Sidney Hook, the New School promoted philosophical pragmatism through the 1940s.[33] "The New School came to represent 'modernism,'" Peter Rutkoff and William Scott write, "broadly defined as artistic creativity, social research, and democratic reform."[34] Thus it was that, within the space of a decade, Kallen found himself in the heart of the premier institution in America for the study of modernist art and thought. Kallen's ties to modernism in America were fostered, albeit indirectly and accidentally, by his relationship with Croly and Johnson, editors of the *New Republic*.

The *Dial*

Kallen's engagement with modernism through print culture went beyond publishing articles and teaching. For a short time Kallen also became involved in the operations of the *Dial*, a magazine of literary modernism and Progressive politics. He played an important role in shaping the direction of the *Dial* during the second half of the 1910s. In 1916 Martyn Johnson, a Chicago decorator who had also been associated with the fledgling *New Republic*, purchased the *Dial*, which had been founded in 1880 but had recently begun to flounder. Johnson reoriented the *Dial*'s focus to literary modernism and Progressive politics. The *Dial* changed hands once again in 1919, when Scofield Thayer and James Sibley Watson Jr. bought it from Johnson. In the *Dial*'s final phase, from 1920 until it ceased publication in

1929, it became an important venue in which transatlantic modernist art and literature was introduced to an American audience.[35] Kallen's primary interest in, and involvement with, the *Dial* was in its penultimate phase, during the Johnson years. These were the years in which Kallen's blended interest in literary and political matters meshed with the magazine's interests.

Kallen had in fact already published in the *Dial* before Johnson took over.[36] His contribution signals the magazine's transformation at that time. Whereas the *Dial*'s reviews and literary criticism still revealed "the uneasy survival, passive and compromised, of the genteel tradition," as one scholar puts it, Kallen brought a fresh perspective that presaged the magazine's future liberation from that tradition.[37]

Johnson published his vision for the *Dial* on January 25, 1917. His editorial read:

> In announcing Mr. George Bernard Donlin as Editor the publisher takes occasion to make the following statement of the principles which will inspire the policy of the *Dial*. . . . The *Dial*, under its present management, will endeavor to carry on a fruitful tradition. It will try to meet the challenge of the new time by reflecting and interpreting its spirit—a spirit freely experimental, skeptical of inherited values, ready to examine old dogmas and to submit afresh its sanctions to the test of experience. If criticism is peculiarly needed, it is because criticism, with its sharply intellectual values, its free curiosity, and its necessary concreteness, can share almost equally with creative writing the privilege of revealing us to ourselves. And in a democracy such as ours no task is more worthwhile.[38]

Johnson laid out the conditions for the magazine's modernist orientation: it would reflect critically upon the times, be "skeptical of inherited values," and it would introduce a new "freely experimental" spirit. It was still "a fortnightly journal of literary criticism, discussion, and information," as the front page read, but Johnson made it clear that the *Dial* saw itself as having a social conscience as well. It had something to contribute toward American democracy. In accordance with its vision, it published literary criticism and political articles. For the next three years, until Thayer and Watson Jr. transformed it yet again, the *Dial* retained this blended orientation toward literature and politics.

Kallen was among those whom Johnson recruited from the outset to become regular contributors.[39] From that point on, he became an informal consultant, relied upon for his publishing and sales acumen. That he well understood the business of book publishing is evident from Kallen's correspondence with Johnson over the proposed publication of *The Structure of Lasting Peace*. Kallen, who compiled the book from a series of articles being published in the *Dial*, advised Johnson on the timing for its release: "If we are going to print the thing as a *Dial* book, I think that we had better follow the conventional procedure and get the book out a little while before the series is concluded. You know how it goes with the serial novels in the magazines: the books are out an issue or so before the serial is completed. The commercial advantage of that is obvious."[40] In the end, arrangements for its publication were made with Marshall Jones. Kallen prominently featured the book's connection to the *Dial* in the foreword, and wrote that he owed its inception and completion to its editor.[41]

Johnson consulted Kallen regarding his proposal to move the *Dial*'s offices from Chicago to New York: "I think you know that I am placing the *Dial* on the newsstands January 1st? I am also opening a New York office and I have a strong inclination to bring the *Dial* to New York next summer. I find that the salaries and manufacturing costs are cheaper here than in Chicago and the problem of my being here and Donlin there is very complicated. I shall be interested in hearing your reactions to these various ideas."[42] Kallen replied that although he agreed that they might have a New York office, he was against moving operations in toto. The *Dial*, Kallen felt, enjoyed a unique market in Chicago: "Things are lost in the shuffle in New York, while the *Dial* in particular has been an asset to the town of

Chicago." In December 1917 Kallen advised Johnson to "wait in this matter until we can talk it over."[43] Nevertheless, Johnson proceeded with moving the *Dial* to New York the following year.

Kallen's involvement in the *Dial*'s operations extended even to the hiring of associate editors. Thorstein Veblen, whom Johnson had wanted to recruit as an associate editor, was poised to accept a job with the War Labor Board. Kallen, however, persuaded Veblen to move to New York and join the *Dial*'s editorial board in June 1918 instead.[44] Kallen was also responsible for the hiring of an English professor at the University of Wisconsin, Clarence Britten, as an associate editor. "Thanks to your rather amazing interest in me, I am engaged here to assist Stearns," Britten wrote to Kallen. "I want to say 'thank you' in superlatives for suggesting me to Johnson."[45]

Kallen became particularly close with the young Chicago journalist George B. Donlin, whom Johnson had appointed editor in 1917. Donlin looked to Kallen as his mentor: "Now, my dear Kallen, I wish I could express with something like adequacy the gratitude I feel for the encouragement and help you have given me since I came to the *Dial*," he wrote to Kallen.[46] Tragically, Donlin fell ill with tuberculosis and was forced to resign just one year later. Johnson then decided to bring on Harold Stearns as editor. He informed Kallen of this in December 1917: "I don't know whether Donlin has written you about his going West for his health. His present plans, I believe, are to leave here about the 19th. I have been fortunate enough to secure Harold Stearns from the *New Republic*, who, during Donlin's absence, is to carry on the editorial responsibilities under the title of Associate Editor."[47]

Kallen cautioned that Johnson should reconsider hiring Stearns: "Confidentially, I am uncertain about Stearns," he wrote. "I knew him, I think, when he was in one of my classes at Harvard. As I remember him, he is too temperamental to be quite reliable, but it may be that time has stabilized him. However, hold off if possible and look around."[48] Kallen, meanwhile, wrote regularly to Donlin to keep him abreast of developments at the *Dial*'s offices: "The *Dial* will, I think, hold its own, but we are missing you sorely," he wrote in January 1918. "I spent a couple of days in the office with Johnson, Britten and Stearns. You will need to hold a pretty firm hand on Stearns. . . . Britten is, I think, a find. . . . I daresay Johnson wrote you of the plans to turn the *Dial* into a weekly, as soon as you are strong enough to take hold again. The whole enterprise turns on your getting well."[49] Donlin did not get well, however, and by the end of 1918, shortly after Johnson moved the *Dial* to New York, the magazine was struggling financially. Kallen wrote to Donlin that he had "formulated the plans for the reorganization of the *Dial* which it is now carrying out," but evidently those plans did not materialize because Johnson sold it to Thayer and Watson Jr. in 1919.[50] The Thayer-Watson *Dial* opened a very different chapter in the magazine's life. It would now ignore political issues and focus purely on aesthetics.[51] With that change, Kallen's centrality to the *Dial*'s management faded away. His view that modernist art and literary criticism should remain connected to social and political concerns did not reflect the magazine's new vision.

The years 1917–19 were a time of tremendous upheaval for Kallen, but during that time he made considerable contributions to American intellectual and literary modernism. These contributions were inseparably bound up with print culture. Kallen authored politically and philosophically provocative articles in national, liberal magazines like the *Nation*, the *New Republic*, and the *Dial*. He was deeply involved with the *Dial*'s editorial staff, which was devoted to literary modernism and Progressive politics. Kallen's relationship with Croly of the *New Republic*, a man who helped to shape Progressive Era politics in America, led to his career change, which, in turn, ultimately led him to an even deeper engagement with American modernism.

Kallen at the Intersection of Art, Science, and Publishing

Kallen's view that modernism's impact must be evaluated through the interaction of art, science, culture, and politics was shared with certain other modernist art critics, such as Amelia Defries of the Royal Institution in London. In a 1916 article in the *American Magazine of Art*, Defries, a proponent of civic art, wrote, "The place of art in relation to the life of the community and the city is being recognized by the politician, the biologist, and the sociologist as well as by the artist himself. Over and over again the Prime Mover in the Civic Movement has scorned the Utilitarians who pushed art out of the national life."[52] Defries, who would later write a biography of the renowned urban planner Patrick Geddes (published in the United States by Boni & Liveright), contacted Kallen in 1920, telling him that she had heard he wished "to correspond re[garding] progressive ideas." Defries wrote that she hoped "soon to see an effort made to organise a Federation or orchestration of all the progressive artists & Scientists, that these workers rather than unskilled labour, should lead."[53] For Defries, as for Kallen, the arts had social implications. She, like him, hoped to see artists and scientists in the vanguard of a socially progressive movement.

Kallen's response indicates his interest in the connection of art to science and industry and its practical bearing on life. The world of the arts, he wrote, reflects the great and growing social conflict in America. This had led him to reflect on "the bearing of art as an institution on the rest of life."[54] What particularly interested Kallen was the role of the artist as a cultural leader, articulating values and spurring social change. As a social philosopher, however, Kallen saw himself more in the role of the art critic than the artist. He drew a striking analogy between the political scientist and the theater critic in 1923: "May it not be rightly said, then, that political scientists are like critics at the play? Their reports of the performance will be fairly at one in naming the cast and recording the plot. But this naming and tracing is the least important thing about the reports. These become units of force in so far as they incorporate and utter also the reactions of the critics to their performance, their judgments of approval and condemnation. These are agencies in the fate of the play. They have power to make and to break, to sustain and to destroy."[55] Kallen perceived himself as an investigator in much the same way as he described critics at the play. He did not merely observe American social and political life. He asserted judgment as well. He saw himself as having agency in the fate of the political drama of America.

Kallen conceived of *Culture and Democracy in the United States* as a work of political science grounded in psychology. One year before its publication he made explicit his views on the connection between the sciences, and on the subjectivity and agency of the political scientist, in "Political Science as Psychology," published in the *American Political Science Review*. Political science, Kallen wrote, is best described as "the attentive response of various temperaments to a special pattern of associative action among men usually called citizenship. It is thus psychology twice over. It is psychology as the behavior of the political scientist; it is psychology as the behavior of the citizen." The political scientist, Kallen insisted, not only records observations but also, like a critic at the play, passes judgment on the results. The "distilled essence of a living political science," as he put it, would communicate not only the subject matter, but function at the same time as "an analysis, a judgment, a bid for change." Kallen saw political science as a force for change because its very presentation compels a reaction. It not only observes a living subject, in other words, but it partakes of the subject itself. It does not merely describe; it is self-consciously part of its own discourse. The facts are self-consciously re-presented, transvaluing the values they describe, providing, as Kallen cited James, "an option, momentous, living, and insecure."[56]

Kallen spent two years trying unsuccessfully to persuade various different publishers that *Culture and Democracy in the United States* was precisely the "bid for change" that America needed in the postwar era. He pitched his book, originally titled *The Meaning of Americanism*, to the biggest publishing firms in the United States—including E. P. Dutton; Harcourt, Brace and Company; Henry Holt; Macmillan; and George H. Doran—all of whom felt that Kallen had written a remarkable collection of essays, but they nonetheless could not envision a market for the book. Kallen then began to turn his attention to Jewish publishers, and approached B. W. Huebsch and Boni & Liveright. He urged them to consider his book's appeal "among the Americanization interests and among radicals and liberals generally," and, more specifically, Kallen believed it would find a niche as a university textbook. As he described it, *Culture and Democracy in the United States* would "present a radical pluralistic conception of the American state and American civilization." Kallen's book finally received a warm welcome from the one publisher who was willing to take a risk with it—Boni & Liveright. "I'm proud to be the publisher," Horace Liveright told Kallen. "It is a fine book."[57]

Boni & Liveright persuaded Kallen to change the title of his book, and he finally settled on *Culture and Democracy in the United States.*[58] Kallen removed the subtitles from the included essays; instead, only the book itself would have a subtitle—*Studies in the Group Psychology of the American Peoples.* That editorial decision marks a reconceptualization of Kallen's various essays. No longer would "Democracy versus the Melting Pot" be viewed as "A Study in American Nationality," as his original subtitle had it. It would now be repackaged, together with the other essays, as a psychological study.

The subtitle may have been intended to pique further sales interest, given the growing public interest in the findings of psychology at that time, but it also indicates Kallen's awareness of the political implications of that science. Racist anti-immigration activists, for example, used the findings of the Army Alpha and Army Beta intelligence tests to buttress their claim that America was becoming mentally feeble because of the influx of immigrants. Half of the draftees tested as "morons," and African Americans and immigrants from Southern and Eastern Europe appeared to have the mental age of preteens.[59] As early as 1922, the *New Republic* ran articles by John Dewey and Walter Lippmann that ridiculed the attempt to quantify American minds.[60] Kallen approvingly cited the latter's articles. He had a very different approach to American group psychology. As a functionalist psychologist, Kallen was not interested in the question of mental variability; his focus was on the question of group mental adaptation to the changed social conditions of modernity. Various forms of maladaptation to the conditions of modernity were already in evidence in American society, he argued, from fear-based xenophobic racism to the misguided optimism of assimilationism. He postulated an adaptation that would not attempt to impose homogeneity upon a naturally diverse environment, but would accept the naturalness of diversity, the salience of group difference, and would seek to foster intergroup cooperation.

By virtue of its publishing pedigree alone, *Culture and Democracy in the United States* must be considered part of the growing literary modernist movement in America. Kallen's publisher, Horace Liveright, was, as his biographer Tom Dardis puts it, a "firebrand" who became one of the foremost publishers of modernist literature in the 1920s.[61] Liveright was responsible in many ways for the creation of the modern American literary canon. He published Ezra Pound, T. S. Eliot, Sherwood Anderson, Eugene O'Neill, and several other Nobel Prize–winning authors. No stranger to scandal, Liveright was not only a risk-taking gambler, but his firm was also one of the speakeasies of the day, at which liquor flowed freely. Liveright was also a risk-taker in publishing. Over the objections of his staff, for example, he published Sigmund Freud's "racy" *General Introduction to Psychoanalysis* in 1920. This attracted the attention of the New York Society for the Suppression of Vice, causing a scandal that helped to increase sales of the book.[62] With respect to Kallen, Liveright recognized in him "a fellow progressive troublemaker," one scholar observes. Like his other authors, Kallen was a "radical," someone who "got at the root of things."[63]

Boni & Liveright had become a significant publishing house by the early 1920s, due in large part to Liveright's willingness to take risks. Firms like E. P. Dutton and Henry Holt, among others, were conservative bastions, run by old families and old money. They represented the entrenched Anglo-American literary heritage, and they generally ignored the trends in literary experimentation taking place in Europe. Given the prevalent anti-Semitism among the established publishing firms, Jews like Liveright had to strike out on their own if they wished to enter the publishing world. Jewish firms like Boni & Liveright did not necessarily pursue the publication of Jewish authors or Jewish interests, but their willingness to take risks and to challenge the establishment marks their different ethno-cultural vantage point. They were publishing on the margins, as it were, just as Jews were socially and culturally placed at the margins.

Jewish publishing firms were alienated from the conservative publishing establishment. They had nothing to lose by trying something new, since they had no contacts or contracts with established writers. Moreover, Jewish publishers were attracted to the rebellious literature of modernism that protested convention, and they were also aware that the intellectual needs of millions of non–Anglo-Saxon Americans were not being met. It is they who were primarily responsible for bringing literary modernism to America.[64] Liveright, a publisher with a talent for finding audiences for authors who challenged society, was a good fit for Kallen.

Boni & Liveright numbered among a small group of Jewish publishers who cultivated a similar set of authors and audiences, intent on "promoting pluralism to a liberal readership," for, as one scholar observes, "the ascendance of reactionary forces in 1924 worked against *and* gave rise to Jewish publishers' pluralist sympathies."[65] The fact that Kallen's book did not immediately cause a revolution in American self-perception is not so much a statement about Kallen as an individual as it is a statement about the difficulties faced by liberal pluralists generally, both authors and publishers. Not only was the Johnson-Reed Act legislated in 1924, but universities like Harvard and Columbia established admission quotas for Jewish students, and the Ku Klux Klan reached its peak with three million members. Kallen was enmeshed within a larger matrix of pluralist authors and Jewish publishers who worked against the American political mainstream, publishing works like *In the American Grain* by William Carlos Williams, *The New Negro* by Alain Locke, and *The Book of American Negro Spirituals*, edited by James Weldon Johnson.

Attentiveness to *Culture and Democracy in the United States*'s subtitle, *Studies in the Group Psychology of the American People*, reveals an orientation important to Kallen that has been lost in the subsequent republications of the book, which, in resituating it within their own realms of discourse, omitted the original subtitle. *Culture and Democracy in the United States* was, in Kallen's estimation, the product of "a living political science," and offered "a critical analysis of the behavior of men in their civic relationships." Kallen's particular focus was the civic relationships among different groups in America and how group mentalities influenced those relationships. Calling his book a "study" of these relationships did not imply that he understood the book to be a dispassionate and objective analysis. Rather, it was unapologetically written as an impassioned plea for reasoned pluralism and tolerance in a frenzied, irrational, and fearful time. It was an intervention, the intervention of a social critic. It was "an analysis, a judgment, a bid for change."[66] As a psychologist, political scientist, and Jew, Kallen was deeply invested in staking out his claim for America. His experiment of cultural pluralism was a social thought experiment, and, as a pragmatist, the validity of his hypothesis had to be tested for its functionality. The press provided Kallen with the opportunity to test his hypothesis, by communicating his message to a readership that could "react to it as a force." Kallen conceived of political science as a force for change because its very presentation could stimulate a reaction.

Reviews in a range of academic, political, and literary journals were, on the whole, tepid. Priced at $3, a modest 394 copies in the United States and 6 in Canada were sold in its first year. Sales dropped dramatically to 37 copies the following year. By 1930 just 812 copies had been sold. Liveright had lost over $750 on *Culture and Democracy in the United States*, prompting him to decide not to reprint it. Kallen's hopes to initiate widespread discussion about cultural pluralism did not materialize. Gradually, however, the notion of cultural pluralism did penetrate American consciousness, becoming a commonplace by midcentury.[67]

Pragmatic Modernism and Jewish Identity

For Kallen, the role of the modernist intellectual was to prescribe an adjustment to the new social conditions of life. Cultural pluralism is just such a modernist innovation. The "shock and defamiliarization" brought on by the modern condition, Kallen believed, had caused a dysfunctional psychological reaction in America, born of irrational fear and anxiety.[68] His solution to the dilemma was to affirm social differences, advocate for social cooperation, and reestablish the grounds for American democracy. Kallen hoped that art, literature, psychology, and political science would play a role in agitating for changes that would heal the torn social fabric.

Kallen, as a modernist and a pragmatist, responded to the turbulence of the times with "a discontent of hope."[69] His was a quintessentially meliorative approach, for he did not perceive his radical solution to the problems of society to register a complete break with the past. Rather, Kallen sought to contextualize his approach as consistent with the developmental process of democracy and true to the makeup of American society. By stressing historicity and continuity, Kallen may also be said to have recontextualized America and democracy into a mode compatible with post-Darwinian realities.[70]

Kallen's involvement with Boni & Liveright marks the culmination of a process that had begun almost ten years prior, when he first became deeply involved with the modernist movement through his relationships with editors. With *Culture and Democracy in the United States*, Kallen entered an interconnected web of relationships that brought pluralists and modernists together with Jewish publishing houses. The course of modernism in America was fundamentally shaped by the involvement of firms like Boni & Liveright.

Jonathan Sarna writes that Jewish publishers in America had two main goals. These were "to forge a new Jewish cultural center in America and to integrate American Jewry into a nationwide community [of Jews] bound together by a culture of print."[71] To these, we may now add a third goal. Although Jewish publishing houses like Boni & Liveright, Viking, Random House, and Alfred A. Knopf did not necessarily evince any particular concern for Jewish issues, their existence and their continued close relationships with one another grew out of the Jewish experience in America. They rebelled against their marginalization in American society and culture by the Gentile establishment, and, in the process, helped to promote modernist literature in America.[72] As American Jewish publishers, then, they perceived a need to carve out space for Jews within American society, in the process creating a nationwide multiethnic community bound together by a culture of print. Kallen's self-understanding as a Jew was wrapped up with this goal. His sense of Jewish identity was intimately tied to his vision for America, his commitment to cultural pluralism, and his hopes for modernism as a progressive social influence. The story of *Culture and Democracy in the United States* constitutes, to borrow from Kallen's metaphor, his unique instrument with "its specific timbre and tonality." It is his Jewish contribution to an "American Rhapsody."

· 5 ·

On Job, Secularization, and Psychology

Behold, He will slay me; I have no hope. Nevertheless, I will maintain my ways before Him.

—Job 13:15

"WE WILL SHOW YOU that you cannot conceive of a completed society without conceiving of its theatre," proclaimed Thomas H. Dickinson, founding director of the Wisconsin Dramatic Society and Kallen's colleague at the University of Wisconsin, in 1913. "The one is the temple of the other." Under Dickinson's enthusiastic direction, and inspired by Senator Robert La Follette's vision of supporting democracy through creative self-education, the Wisconsin Dramatic Society spearheaded a grassroots creative effort to stimulate the growth of regional drama, distinctively American in flavor, with artistic, social, and spiritual relevance. Dickinson's "temple" would also serve the spiritual needs of theatergoers. "We will be no less spiritual than yesterday if we worship in the voting booths, the laboratories, the parks, the theaters," he asserted. "Yesterday every man had a prayer book in his wallet. Today he has the manuscript of a play in his trunk."[1]

Kallen asked the Wisconsin Dramatic Society to stage a play that he wrote in that same year. Dickinson's political and religious sentiments resonated with Kallen's view regarding the value of the arts and their ability to realize values, supplanting the role that traditional religion had played in people's lives. Kallen's offering fit the mission of the Dramatic Society, which was to promote the work of local artists, and in particular to encourage the University to play an active role in supporting the local community. The production of his play, *The Book of Job*, was announced in the December 24, 1913, issue of the *New York Times* and in the January 2, 1914, issue of the *Jewish Exponent*: "This probably will be the first time 'Job' ever has been given on the modern stage. . . . Mr. Kallen said he has not dramatized the work, but simply restored it to the form in which it was originally written for the ancient Hebrews."[2]

In this chapter, we shall see that Kallen's effort to "restore" the biblical text of Job into its purportedly original dramatic form was inspired in part by his desire to challenge the assumption of cultural superiority granted to Greek literature, by assigning to Jewish literature a pedigree as culturally elevated as that of the esteemed Greek legacy. Kallen was also inspired by Job as a religious text, but not in the sense normally associated with the term. For him, Job became the fundamental Torah of his secular revelation. Kallen's identity as a Jew and an American is recorded in his changing interpretation of the book of Job over the course of fifty years. It is a journey that began with his original interpretation that Job is a drama modeled after a Euripidean tragedy, and his staging of it with the Wisconsin Dramatic Society, in which Kallen himself played the part of Job.[3]

On the face of it, it seems odd to treat Kallen, an arch-secularist, as a religious figure. His alignment with the secular Jewish intellectuals who gathered around the *Menorah Journal* has led historians like Michael Meyer to see Kallen as representative of an ideological camp within American Judaism that stood opposed to Jewish religious institutions.[4] On this reading of the historical record, Kallen stands beyond the periphery of ideas and influences that permeated and changed American denominational Judaism. He was someone whose views were simply rejected by them. His well-known anticlericalism and hostility to organized religion is not, however, the important aspect of his legacy for religious discourse. Kallen stood within the networks of ideas and relationships that shaped American culture and American Judaism, and he was an active participant in the larger push toward the secularization of American society that slowly unfolded over the first half of the twentieth century. Kallen made on impact on how American Jews engaged with secularism, not only within the obvious circles of Socialists, Communists, and other nonreligious groups but also within the liberal denominations of American Judaism.

In keeping with a general social trend, many Jews had become secular-minded and this-worldly, with faith in the tools of science to address the problems of life. What was needed, Kallen felt, was a profound readjustment, from Judaism to *Hebraism*, which term implied for him the totality of Jewish life, encompassing but not circumscribed by religion, and compatible with a post-Darwinian worldview. Hebraism's roots lay buried deep in the Jewish past, and Kallen believed that he could recover them from the literary remains of the book of Job.

Job's exceptional nature in the biblical canon, and its ambiguous message about the nature and quality of God's providence and the human condition in relation to it, has led, in modern times, to its being used as a text to either subvert the religious tradition or to support (and even transform) it.[5] Kallen, it will be remembered, was quite disenchanted with religion and skeptical of religious institutions. For Kallen, Job served as a kind of proof text for secularism. American civic and university life in that period, however, was steeped in Protestant religious and cultural sensibilities that deeply affected Kallen and may well have contributed to drawing his attention to the text. Charles William Eliot, president of Harvard, for example, once opined that the book of Job is "unsurpassable as literature."[6] Similarly, for Kallen, the significance of Job lay not in its status as a religious text, but in its character as literature. He desired to find within Jewish literary and philosophical tradition a level of cultural sophistication to match that of the Greek tradition. As a secularist, Kallen would have needed a nontheistic reason to find Job meaningful. This he found in his interpretation of the book of Job as the archetypal expression of the Hebraic worldview, and of Job himself as a proto-modernist.

Kallen Secularizes Job

In his seventies, Kallen reflected back on the books that he had written that best represented his worldview. To *The Book of Job as a Greek*

Tragedy (1918), he awarded pride of place. Kallen's interest in Job may be traced back to 1911, when he read Nathaniel Schmidt's *The Messages of the Poets: The Books of Job and Canticles and Some Minor Poems in the Old Testament, with Introductions, Metrical Translations, and Paraphrases.* Schmidt, professor of Semitic languages and literature at Cornell University, highlighted what he found to be the "modern" elements in Job. It shifts its interest "from heaven and hell to earth," Schmidt wrote, highlighting humanity's insignificance in the universe. He was struck by "the determination of Job . . . to abide by the interpretation imposed by the facts," and concluded that "Job spoke to the modern mind as he had never spoken before."[7]

The shift in focus "from heaven and hell to earth" is suggestive of the shift from the "transcendent frame" of experience to the "immanent frame" of experience claimed by the philosopher Charles Taylor to mark the fundamental conceptual change that characterizes modernity and our "secular age." With the advent of modernity, Taylor argues, the conditions for human flourishing began to be conceived in nontheistic terms for the first time. This focus on the human condition rather than on divine will resonated powerfully for Kallen. Schmidt's translation and his commentary clearly made an impression on him: "I am glad that my interpretation of 'Job' interested you," Schmidt wrote to Kallen. Schmidt had laid the groundwork for Kallen to read the book of Job as a text that speaks to the modern mind.[8]

Within two years, Kallen had developed his thinking concerning Job as an expression of Hebraism in the post-Darwinian mode, in which humanity was "forced to recognize that he is but a part of nature," as Schmidt had put it. In a 1913 letter to Henry Hurwitz, chancellor of the Intercollegiate Menorah Association and founding editor of the *Menorah Journal*, Kallen accepted his invitation to become a member of the Menorah College of Lecturers and he offered to prepare lectures under the general heading "The Meaning of Hebraism." Significantly, among Kallen's five suggested subtopics for Hebraism in the ancient world was "God and Nature in Job."[9]

At Hurwitz's urging, the Harvard Menorah Society staged a production of Kallen's play in 1916. Kallen, together with Hurwitz, was intent on promoting *The Book of Job* as an expression of the humanistic spirit of Jewish culture. For Kallen, it represented an assertion that Jewish culture existed on a par with Greek tradition. This struck a responsive chord with the *Jewish Exponent*, which responded to Kallen's reconstruction of Job with an almost palpable display of pride. Kallen "differs from the views of most of the big men in literature today," it announced. "They assert that in their whole literature the Jews have not a single drama." Kallen had refuted their views with his argument that, in its "original form," the book of Job "has all the characteristics of a drama written by a Hebrew writer in the Greek language." The *Jewish Exponent* thus regarded Kallen's thesis as a muscular assertion of Jewish participation in world literature and culture.[10]

Kallen wrote an introductory essay for *The Book of Job as a Greek Tragedy*, which, as he wrote to Hurwitz, "contains the total summary of my studies in the Hebraism of antiquity, and represents my conclusions concerning its natural development and significance."[11] In it, Kallen argues that the composition of Job follows the plan of a Greek Euripidean tragedy, but that it had been "modified by the literary tradition and spiritual quality of the Jewish race into something new and different." It exemplifies the ripened wisdom of the Jewish "theory of life," Kallen believed, revealing "a humanism terrible and unique," in which "the soul of man comes to itself and is freed. . . . It is without illusion concerning the quality, extent and possibilities of the life of man, without illusion concerning his relation to God. It accepts them, and makes of the human soul the citadel of man—even against Omnipotence itself—wherein he cherishes his integrity, and so cherishing, is victorious in the warfare of living even when life is lost."[12] This was quite unlike Greek humanism, Kallen argued, which declared "an ultimate happy destiny for man in a world immortally in harmony with his nature and needs." This Greek "anthropomorphosis," as he put it, constitutes a great illusion obscuring our ability to see the world truly as it is, and substituting for reality a future-oriented delusion of purposeful design.

Kallen was particularly drawn to the idea that Job is modeled after a Euripidean drama. In his introductory essay to the *Book of Job as a*

Greek Tragedy, he draws connections to structural parallels between Job and Euripidean tragedies, and surmises that the Jewish author of the book of Job was likely to have seen enacted a Euripidean play. Personal notes made while developing his thesis strongly suggest the influence of A. E. Haigh's *The Tragic Drama of the Greeks* (1896).[13] Haigh made much the same argument for Euripides that Kallen made for Job. For Haigh, Euripides was "a realist in art," who painted "men and women 'as they are.'" Euripides was, for Haigh, cosmopolitan in outlook, and, of all the Greek poets, "the most modern in his feelings and sympathies," giving "a faithful representation of the chequered character of human existence." Moreover, in Haigh's view, Euripidean dramas exemplify the culmination of the gradual secularization of Greek dramas. Though they treat of sacred subjects, they are "secular in tone." They concentrate "upon the facts of human nature, rather than upon the problems of religion," giving "a fresh development to tragedy, by transferring the conflict to the human soul. . . . He was the first to let us behold, in the recesses of the heart, the conflict between duty and passion, and between virtue and vice," revealing the "spectacle of a soul at war with itself," and, supplying "the basis of some of the greatest of modern tragedies, such as Hamlet, Macbeth, and Faust."[14]

Kallen made detailed notes of Haigh's argument, but did not suggest any of it in his book. Instead, he merely remarks, "That the thought of Job has Euripidean analogues need not be argued. The injustice of divinity, the unhappiness of mankind, the desirability of death, the rebellion and the ultimate or primal mystical perception which consoles,—these are the commonplaces of Euripides' thinking." Further on, Kallen observes, "The author of Job, like Euripides, knew the wisdom of conveying his heterodox doctrine by means of a seductive orthodox setting, and of so putting the seal of ultimate approval on the heterodoxy."[15] It remains a matter of speculation whether Kallen's silence regarding Haigh's thesis is because he rejected it, or, as seems more likely, he preferred to reserve those insights for a Jewish provenance. He needed a confrontation between Hellenism and Hebraism.

For Kallen, Job functions as a modern commentary on the human condition. It exemplified for him what he had argued in "Hebraism and Current Tendencies in Philosophy" (1909).[16] In the post-Darwinian world, humanity had to learn to adjust to living in an unjust world not specifically designed to satisfy human needs. Job, Kallen believed, had understood this presciently. Hebraism had remained a suppressed source of wisdom, he believed, because the appeal of illusion maintained by Hellenism had triumphed in the religious imagination. Greek thought, in other words, colonized Judaism by virtue of its (and religion's) seductive but illusory view of the universe. Kallen believed that only the advent of the scientific age had exposed the illusions of Hellenism, allowing Hebraism to resurface to conscious awareness. Both Job and science achieved a view of reality free from illusion, albeit by different means. Science creates disillusion by conquering nature through knowledge, but "the Hebraic mind had in Job attained disillusion without such compensating mastery of nature: its science was childishness. It had attained disillusion only with mastery of self, and such an excellence is too rare and difficult ever to become a common virtue of mankind."[17]

Kallen's careful alignment of Job with Hebraism captures the signal importance that *The Book of Job as a Greek Tragedy* had for him. As an example of Jewish literary and dramatic genius par excellence, it supported his identification with Judaism in a secular, cultural, and cosmopolitan modality. It served as a testimony to the value of the Jewish worldview, expressing the very foundation of what Kallen perceived to be the essential feature of Jewish psychophysical inheritance.

The Book of Job as a Greek Tragedy includes an additional introduction written by the renowned Harvard scholar George Foot Moore. The fact that Moore endorsed Kallen's book is significant. "Moore himself embodied the Menorah Association's ideal," Daniel Greene observes. "As a Christian who taught Jewish history and world religions at Harvard, Moore legitimated Jewish studies within an elite American setting." Moore found Kallen's thesis that Job was originally written in the Euripidean style to be an "ingenious hypothesis," and saw fit to discuss it in his course lectures. This legitimated Kallen's thesis in the very epicenter of American academe.[18]

Claude Montefiore, a founder of Liberal Judaism in Britain, however, wrote a scathing review of *The Book of Job as a Greek Tragedy* for the *Harvard Theological Review.* Assessing the viability of Kallen's hypothetical reconstruction of Job as a Euripidean tragedy, Montefiore concluded that it must be regarded as a failure. He recognized how deeply personal was Kallen's connection to Job: "Dr. Kallen, like the rest of us, is deeply impressed with the greatness of Job. And his just admiration, as it seems to me, has led him on to find in Job his own philosophy of life. What *he* thinks is the true moral of life, what *he* thinks is the right explanation of the riddle of the universe, that he discovers already expounded by the author of Job. As the Hero of the Gospels has often been made to preach the particular sort of religion and of Christianity which is most congenial to each commentator in turn, so is Job made to preach the philosophy of Dr. Kallen."[19] Montefiore was quite right. Kallen's view of Job was not echoed by any other contemporaneous Jewish thinker.[20] It is entirely Kallen's.

Kallen read Job as articulating a resolution to his perception of the confrontation between Hellenism and Hebraism. Job represented for him an archetypal model of the kind of healthy growth that results from intercultural exchange. As Kallen wrote in *Culture and Democracy in the United States*, "Cultural values arise upon the confrontation, impact, and consequent disintegration and readjustment of different orders, with the emergence therefrom of new harmonies."[21] He saw in Job the flowering of Jewish humanist cultural values arising from just such an impact and readjustment. The lived vitality of Judaism derived not from God's revelation at Mount Sinai, but from the ongoing discursive exchanges between cultural groups. This idea, undeveloped as of yet, would become, as we shall see, the kernel of his understanding of secular religion.

Montefiore's reaction to Kallen was extreme. He wrote that even were Kallen's teaching correct, there is one thing that it is not: "It is not Judaism." Montefiore may have granted him a place within secular nationalism, but Kallen's "subversal and denial of Judaism" precluded Montefiore from validating his work as a contribution to Jewish thought.[22] Interestingly, however, Kallen's hypothesis of the intermingling of the Hellenic and Hebraic traditions did not excite Montefiore's ire. Indeed, in *Liberal Judaism and Hellenism* (1918), Montefiore had written that in today's world, religion, to be viable, must "absorb and adopt the Hellenic spirit." He believed that there was a "kinship between Hellas and Judea," and "therefore we can fuse the spirit of Hellas with our own."[23] Montefiore had no objection to uniting Athens and Jerusalem. It was Kallen's rejection of the possibility of reading Job as theodicy, and his assertion that the Joban God has no bias "in favor of one of living as against another, or in favor of one of his creatures as against another" that Montefiore could not abide.[24] For Montefiore, as for the Reform movement, Judaism was in the first instance a matter of faith in a covenantal relationship with God, which was precisely the point that Kallen disputed. Kallen's Job (like Schmidt's) shifted attention from heaven to earth, from the "transcendent frame" to the "immanent frame." Kallen had secularized Job.

For the *Menorah Journal*, on the other hand, such theological questions were entirely beside the point. It was interested in the advancement of Jewish literature and culture, and the appearance of *The Book of Job as a Greek Tragedy* became the impetus for the *Menorah Journal* to devote almost an entire issue to the subject. It flagged its intentions in its February 1919 edition, telling its readers that they could expect a "four-act" feature in the next number:

> From the Bible to Euripides, and from the classic alcoves of Cambridge University to the present-day theatre on Broadway, will be the range and scope of this group of articles. Professor Gilbert Murray, the world's greatest authority on Euripides, will give a sympathetic opinion on the theory of Dr. H. M. Kallen that the Book of Job was deliberately written on the model of a Euripidean tragedy. Dr. Max Radin, who has made a special study of Jewish life in the Greek and Roman periods, will treat Dr. Kallen's theory with less tender mercy. Stuart Walker, who, as this note is written, is presenting the

> "Book of Job" as a drama in a Broadway theatre, will give his theory of the dramatic value of the Old Testament classic for present-day theatre goers. In conclusion will be given a Menorah critic's impressions of Stuart Walker's production.[25]

The *Menorah Journal* delivered on three of its four promised pieces.[26] The promised critical review of Walker's production of Job never appeared.

Kallen's thesis was favorably received by Murray and vehemently rejected by Radin. Radin particularly objected to Kallen's reconstruction of the text as a drama. But it was precisely Kallen's presentation of Job as a play that most interested the *Menorah Journal*, as is made clear by an editor's note appended to Radin's article listing various productions of Kallen's play and encouraging readers to contrast Kallen's historical reconstruction with Stuart Walker's own artistic interpretation.[27] The *Menorah Journal* represented Kallen's work as both a scholarly piece and a dramatic performance, highlighting Job as a literary and cultural artifact. In this way, it helped to underscore Kallen's larger project, which was to inject a historical consciousness of Jewish humanism into American Jewry. The *Menorah Journal*'s so-called four-act feature suggests that it saw in Kallen's and Walker's plays not only a way to recover a Jewish literary cultural heritage but also a way to contribute to the continued growth and vitality of Jewish culture.

The *Menorah Journal*, which insisted the study of Jewish literature is just as valuable as the study of the traditional Greco-Roman canon, saw Kallen's "restoration" of Job to its purported original Euripidean form as a valuable contribution to their efforts to foster such study. Kallen's Job preserved Hebraism even as it participated in Hellenic culture. It was, in other words, a model for how he envisioned Jewish ethnic participation in American society. Jews absorbed American culture, but preserved their identity despite the pressures of Americanization. Kallen's Hebraic-Hellenic Job mirrored the creation of a hyphenated Jewish-American identity. It expressed, dramatically, Jewish ethnicity. This is what Job signified for Kallen during the 1910s and 1920s.

Despite Montefiore's strong claim that Kallen's thesis had nothing to say to a Jewish audience, the *Menorah Journal* certainly disagreed. Additionally, Kallen's play received some additional attention from his friend, the prominent rabbi and Zionist leader Stephen S. Wise. His Free Synagogue hosted a fundraising effort for the United Palestine Appeal in 1926, a cause close to Kallen's heart, at which the synagogue mounted a production of *The Book of Job*, starring a Broadway cast.[28] Kallen's view of ethnicity was quite literally on display.

Psychology Renarrates Religion

Kallen's Job was a prophet of psychological man. Job recognizes that human existence is contingent not on proper faith or on moral living, but on the impersonal flux of life. This, for Kallen, constitutes the Joban revelation. On this reading, Job recognizes the impossibility of establishing a covenantal relationship with God, and understands that he must face the absurdity of existence by stint of his personal courage and integrity. He therefore exclaims, "Behold, He will slay me; I have no hope. Nevertheless, I will maintain my ways before Him" (Job 13:15). The "destiny of man," Kallen concluded, is to "maintain his ways with courage rather than with faith, with self-respect rather than with humility or better perhaps, with a faith that is courage, a humility that is self-respect." It is precisely the moral indifference of the universe that encourages human moral and spiritual growth. "Hence, when Yahweh reveals himself to Job as the creative providence sustaining even the most impotent of living things and destroying even the strongest," Kallen clarified, "Job realizes that not prosperity but excellence is the justification of human life, and the very indifference of Yahweh comforts him."[29]

The internal life of man is thus discovered to be the true locus of salvation. "His [Job's] attitude declares that the validity of each man's struggle to live has to be an inward validity never to be sanctioned from any outer source," he wrote in 1927. "It consists in a kind of self-acceptance, . . . in being true on the basis of what one finds within one's self, not on the basis of what one finds outside one's self." This self-awareness, in turn, becomes the ground for human fulfillment and happiness. The disillusion of the modern scientific age has made it impossible to maintain that, despite all evidence to the contrary, the world was made for our ends. Rather, happiness and fulfillment follow from the work of self-integration.[30] Kallen thus applied a functionalist psychological interpretation of religion to Job. The ultimate significance of Job's secular revelation lies in its functionality. The Joban response represented, for Kallen, the ground for a psychologically healthy response to the realities of existence.

De-Christianizing America

During the 1920s and 1930s, Kallen developed this functionalist psychological interpretation of religion into a commentary on the nature and place of religion in America more generally, and he made a significant contribution to the discourse on this subject. He chastised religious institutions for their anemic response to modern conditions. He read the historical record as one of religious institutions' warfare against science and retarding the human struggle for freedom, and he argued that a proper understanding of religion's psychological function would enable people to free religion from institutional control.

Kallen believed that religious institutions were fundamentally out of step with modernity. In addition to criticizing Jewish religious institutions, he also targeted Christian institutions. Kallen launched his strongest offensive against religious institutions in *The Warfare of Religion against Science* (1931), one of Haldeman-Julius's Little Blue Books pocket book series. Little Blue Books, the creation of one of America's most successful publicists, Emanuel Haldeman-Julius (1889–1951), was an especially popular series in the 1920s. It was pitched to the poor and working class as a "University in Print," intended to serve as a self-education and self-help series priced at an affordable five cents per book. The series grew to include more than two thousand titles and sales totaled in the hundreds of millions.[31]

The notion that religion and science are locked in perpetual conflict, a thesis popularized in the latter half the nineteenth century by John William Draper and Andrew Dickson White, was not the only way, or even the most popular way, in which religion and science were perceived to interact. Many Protestant pastors and churches viewed science as compatible with religion, and some went so far as to integrate science and scientists into their religious worldview. Kallen acknowledged this in *The Warfare of Religion against Science*, citing the example of the Riverside Church in New York City, led by Pastor Harry Emerson Fosdick. In an overt attempt to proclaim the compatibility of religion and science, the Riverside Church had recently erected an edifice that featured carvings of scientists (including Einstein) amid carvings of angels and other more traditional religious icons. Kallen also addressed himself to the writings of the University of Chicago theologian Henry Nelson Wieman, and sharply attacked the "new type of theologian who is all eloquence about the glories of scientific method in religion, the uses of experimentation and the like, until one might think that religion had come to terms with science and become a laborer in its vineyard following its ways." This type of thinking, Kallen claimed, was misguided and misleading: "The 'props' which are used to shore religion up, even when borrowed from science, are used willy-nilly with the purpose at the same time to break science down." Kallen believed that science thus co-opted would ultimately end up by serving religion's needs.[32]

Kallen's dismissal of the possibility of integration between religion and science led him to claim all the more strongly that White and Draper did not go far enough in exposing religious institutions as alone the aggressor: "The history of science and scientists," he insisted, "is a history of complete pacifism and nonresistance toward religion. Nay, more, it records much friendliness and cooperation; when scientists do actively consider religion, they do so to bring it aid and comfort, to sustain and to strengthen it."[33] Kallen argued, as a secularist and atheist, that religious institutions were intrinsically opposed to free will and free thought and that they indoctrinated rather than served people.

Kallen then extolled the virtues of science's purported objectivity. This, interestingly, contradicted his own assertion from a decade prior that, notwithstanding science's ideal of objectivity, the reality is that science is a subjective process.[34] *The Warfare of Religion against*

Science, however, was prepared as both an educational as well as a polemical piece for a working-class reading audience. As an author writing a popular tract, Kallen likely felt no need here to expand on the subtle differences between ideal and reality. Structuring a clear and absolute binary opposition between religion and science was an effective rhetorical strategy for addressing a mass audience.

Kallen concluded *The Warfare of Religion against Science* with an observation rooted in the Joban perspective:

> If man were not, in Job's words, born unto trouble, what would he be born to? If there were no warfare to man upon earth, whatever else could there be to him? Religion and science are opposite poles of the same energies, like cold and heat or dark and light. Where one is, the other cannot be, so long as the energies are actual, since both present merely locations and degrees of the movement of our vital forces, since both serve but as stances of the total propulsion of our living selves. From the quietness and securities of fixed and frozen faith to the quicknesses and inquiries of mobile, warm doubt and back again, up and down and round and round, our spirits move, all the days of our life."[35]

Kallen wished to persuade readers that conflict between science and religion was persistent and inevitable. The reason behind his refusal to entertain any other options becomes clear with his concluding lines: "The thin red line of life thrusts on, manifold, changeful, varied, a warfare and a trouble, division in its works and ways, death at its heart. Of this creative thrust religion and science are as the magnetic poles, not to be joined together while it can carry on."[36] Kallen needed religion and science to be in conflict because, to him, the conflict illumined the process of propulsion in the life of the human spirit.[37]

This process, first proposed, as Kallen would have it, in the book of Job, sees conflict as an essential aspect of growth. The absence of conflict implies death. Healthily managed, it promotes free inquiry, diversity, the growth of knowledge, and the development of personal integrity and excellence. The purported integration of science with religion, Kallen felt, was simply an instance of the church adopting a new strategy to reassert its old metaphysics, moral suasion, and social power. Kallen's invocation of the conflict thesis was designed to counter the integrationist strategy, and to expose the fallacy to his readers. He hoped thereby to challenge peoples' acquiescence to church institutions. Kallen's close friend, the philosopher George Santayana, to whom he had sent a copy of *The Warfare of Religion against Science* in Rome, drew this conclusion from his reading of it: "I have absorbed your counterblast to religion. As a popular tract it is capital, beating the eloquent parsons at their own game."[38]

Haldeman-Julius's assessment of popular culture, one scholar observes, ran counter to the commonly held narrative about the Roaring Twenties. That narrative dwells on the stereotypes of the Jazz Age and Lost Generation; that is to say, on the moral dissoluteness and general disillusionment of the period. Haldeman-Julius, however, believed that the American people were fundamentally optimistic, moral, and socially progressive. They espoused "practical (as distinguished from religiously dogmatic) values."[39] The phenomenal success of the sales of the series shows that Haldeman-Julius properly understood American intellectual taste. The American people were seeking to self-improve, and his "University in Print" series was the key to that self-improvement.

Kallen similarly believed that he was addressing a socially progressive readership interested in self-improvement. His presentation was informed by the Joban philosophy of life he had articulated over a decade prior—a philosophy of freedom. That Kallen understood his essay primarily as a meditation on freedom is further confirmed by his inclusion of it seventeen years later in *The Liberal Spirit* (1948), a collection of essays concerning the problem of freedom in the modern world. The conflict between science and religion thus provided the raw material for Kallen to show "how the continuing crisis of freedom may be overcome by faith acting without illusion."[40] Kallen intended to illumine what he believed to be the necessary conditions for human freedom. His participation in the discourse concerning the place of religion in America thus engaged a broad readership, which was encouraged to think through the relationship between science and religion, and to consider the consequences of that relationship.

Beyond commenting generally on the engagement of science and religion, *The Warfare of Religion against Science* also marks a Jewish intervention in American religious discourse, registering a protest against Protestant religio-cultural hegemony. In this respect, the book fit with Haldeman-Julius's publishing vision. Haldeman-Julius, a second-generation American Jew, had early on appreciated the popular appeal that the Little Blue Books series would have for an American audience that "had tired of Christian piety," Andrew Heinze writes. "Seeing himself as a successor to Voltaire and Paine, Haldeman-Julius launched a thirty-year freethinking crusade against religious dogma in general and Christianity in particular." Haldeman-Julius's attacks utilized the science of psychology as support for his secularizing vision, and the Little Blue Books series "subjected Jesus himself to psychiatric examination." The result was to distill "an American Jewish propensity to identify the 'true' values of America with those leaders who had ceased to be true Christians. . . . From Joseph Jastrow to Emanuel Haldeman-Julius, Jews showed themselves eager to enter the marketplace of readers and, in that arena, to use psychology as a weapon against Christian domination of American culture." *The Warfare of Religion against Science* thus marks Kallen's participation in what has been described as the de-Christianization of America that took place during the mid-twentieth century.[41]

Functionalist Psychology Secularizes Religion

Kallen did not write for just the working-class market. Four years before *The Warfare of Religion against Science*, he published *Why Religion* with Boni & Liveright in 1927 for a middlebrow readership. Whereas Kallen's popular tract intended to describe the relationship between science and religion, in *Why Religion* he sought to educate readers concerning the psychological foundations of religion. Kallen's interest in applying the science of psychology to understand religion was consistent with broad popular interest in the mind and personality in American culture during the 1920s and 1930s. Books on psychology, such as James Harvey Robinson's *The Mind in the Making* (1922), were bestsellers. By the 1920s many Americans had come to believe that psychology held the key to understanding the self, society, and religious experience.[42]

In addition to this popular phenomenon in American culture, a special affinity between American Protestantism and psychology had been established. It was a trend begun at the turn of the twentieth century, sparked in large measure by William James's *The Varieties of Religious Experience* (1902). James and his followers, as one scholar puts it, "renarrated religion through psychology."[43] By 1927 psychology came to occupy such an important place in American Protestantism that it provoked H. Reinhold Niebuhr to protest in the *Christian Century*, the most influential American Protestant journal of the first half of twentieth century, against the "sterile union" of psychology and religion that had resulted from the "revolution introduced by William James and his followers."[44]

The selling potential of books on psychology was not lost on Boni & Liveright. It marketed *Why Religion* as "a notable contribution to the psychology of religion," and it highlighted in particular the connection between Kallen and James on the dust jacket: "This book, by a gifted disciple and interpreter of William James, takes up, after two decades of scientific advance, the unanswered questioning that was stirred by the famous *Varieties of Religious Experience*." James's *Varieties* was subsequently republished by Modern Library, founded by Boni and Liveright, in 1929.[45] Kallen's book was thus part of a larger discourse being circulated in the late 1920s by Boni & Liveright (among others) concerning the relationship between psychology and religion.

James, Dewey, Kallen, and Wieman, of the Chicago Divinity School, all understood that relationship in pragmatic, or functionalist, terms. *Functionalism* was born with the appearance of Dewey's *The Reflex Arc Concept in Psychology* (1896). It constituted an effort to model scientific psychology upon the Darwinian evolutionary paradigm, and became the dominant school of psychology in America for the first three decades of the twentieth century.[46] Although its practitioners agreed on the guiding principle of analyzing function and usefulness, functionalist psychology nevertheless supported a variety of opinions with respect to the study of religion. It allowed a secular humanist like Kallen and a religious humanist like Henry Nelson Wieman to interpret religion in very different ways.

Kallen's perspective relied heavily on James's idea that the truth-value of belief lies not in the content of that belief, but in the function that it serves. Belief is a form of mental adaptation. It reflects the choice of one option from among a variety of options, and, in its more significant form, is driven by a pressing need to make a choice. It is the psychological ground for salvation, not because that salvation is directed toward an ultimate good, but because it is discovered by the psychological benefits derived, as he learned from William James, from the act of believing:

> Now, in this sense, in this very atheistic and non-institutional sense, religion is one of the conditions of both progress and happiness. Without this projection of the will to believe by means of symbols into the unknown in space and time and matter, there can be churches, there can be static and rigid organizations of society, there can be habit-bound communities and individuals, but there cannot be a free, flexible, changing life, there cannot be progress, there cannot be happiness. Progress and Happiness are grounded on a religious foundation, but religious in complete contrast to the traditional meanings of that word. This is the living religion of the firing line, of the danger-points of life, and at the firing line there can be no finalities and no infallibles. There can be nothing but faith in a projection, in an imagined content of value; faith that carries on only by its own momentum and by no other. Religion in this sense is at the core of personality, is the spirit of society as these move dangerously from one phase of existence to the next.[47]

Religion so construed serves a real psychological need. Its validation comes not from supernatural authority, but from the religious experience itself. Indeed, for Kallen, the supernatural is not an objective fact, but an emotional one. Religion, in the noninstitutional sense, becomes the core of personality by virtue of the function it serves in giving purpose, meaning, and hope.

Here, too, Job serves for Kallen as a paradigm. Job, to him, was the first person to undergo that internal process of integrating this religious perspective into a healthy psychological outlook and a robust sense of self. Kallen maintained that Job teaches that it is necessary to find within oneself the strength to self-validate and to make peace with living in an unjust world. The book of Job, he wrote, depicts what to him was this primary psychological sense of religious meaning:

> With this self-acceptance, it becomes possible to accept without self-reproach the universe also. Thus, a view of the nature and destiny of man in a world not made for him becomes charged with religious meaning, and religious meaning in the primary sense of the term. The Supernatural is invoked to resolve an insuperable crisis of which it is itself the occasion and the cause. All the forces are in issue. Into the unseen we project our conception of what we are and of what life and the world are and what they do to us. And then we judge them; in the light of our integrity which we hold fast and will not let go, we judge them. However, judging, we are free to take trouble no more, we accept life, we accept ourselves. Then such harmonies as are possible between us and the residual worlds get established, actual ones are perfected. Life gets integrated. No longer are we at war with our nature because we are at war with its conditions. The conflict between the ground of our existence and its intent has lapsed. Heart and head, so to speak, have been reconciled. If happiness names anything, it names this state of self-acquiescence, of reconciliation and self-integration.[48]

Kallen's Job now no longer speaks only to a Jewish audience with the unique insights of Hebraism. Job teaches something far more universal about the substance of religious meaning. Job is a prophet of humanism. Human fulfillment is discovered through self-integration. Job is psychological man.

With *Why Religion*, Kallen's understanding of religion's psychological underpinnings entered the growing popular discourse concerning religion's relationship with psychology in America. In fact, it provoked an extended response from Henry Nelson Wieman. Wieman, a former Presbyterian minister, shared much in common with Kallen philosophically. He, too, had been influenced by William James, Josiah Royce, Henri Bergson, Ralph Barton Perry, and John Dewey. Wieman believed in treating the subjective religious experience as the critical factor in religion, and he wished to interpret the significance of religion from an empirical analysis of that experience. The conclusions that Wieman drew, however, were quite different from those of Kallen. Wieman conceived of God as a creative process, and he maintained that belief as such is worthless if it is not directed toward the supreme good. He argued that it is possible to construct a viable theocentric orientation from the empirical data provided by human religious experience.[49]

Wieman, a founder of process theology in liberal American Protestantism, first began to develop his ideas in *The Wrestle of Religion with Truth* (1927). In it, Wieman devoted an entire chapter to responding to *Why Religion*. Kallen became, for Wieman, a useful foil against whom he could contrast his own thinking: "We believe Kallen has correctly stated the facts," Wieman wrote, "but we do not agree with the inferences he draws from them. Religious belief is certainly full of illusion and these illusions console and inspire. But we do not believe they have the value Kallen attributes to them." While Wieman accepted the Jamesian premise that belief involves selective action in response to certain stimuli, he insisted that it must be "rightly directed." Wieman rejected Kallen's use of the term *salvation*, which, he noted, "is not necessarily directed toward the supreme good." Without metaphysical content, Wieman found it to be meaningless. "The supreme good will be found only as we learn how to select stimuli and develop systems of response to stimuli in such a way as to give rise to the most delightful of all possible worlds. . . . In this sense God, the ultimate cause or condition, enters into the supreme good, since he is that which gives rise to the best possible world when man makes right adjustment to him." Wieman thus applied a functionalist approach to his religious worldview, but he understood progress and happiness to be achieved only when the mind was directed toward the "supreme good."[50]

In a review written for the *Journal of Philosophy*, Kallen criticized Wieman's "arbitrarily assumed metaphysical assumptions." Kallen considered Wieman a representative "of a growing mode of ratiocination which protesting loudly that religion is in need of clear and distinct modern ideas, adds to the current obfuscation and obscurantism by befogging such clear and distinct ideas as it has." Kallen particularly noted Wieman's Christian bias: "Religion may be non-specific, but Jesus is still the Most High; the religious experience may imply solitary worship, but the church is still necessary; science may be the only source of verifiable truth, but the Bible is the precious concentration 'of these many centuries of worship and experimental living.' One religion is no truer than another, but missionaries—of course, Christian ones—have a peculiar justification, as has 'religious education' in the public schools. Life consists in adapting yourself to your environment, but adapting yourself to your environment is the same as 'getting right with God.'"[51] Wieman was self-contradictory, Kallen claimed. Moreover, Wieman's argument expressed a Christocentric point of view. For Kallen, the functionalist approach to religion must be devoid of any hint of metaphysics. As a participant in the discourse that led to the de-Christianization of American academic and public thought, Kallen's engagement with Wieman registers a Jewish voice of protest against American Protestant religio-cultural hegemony.

Engaging with Jewish Religious Humanism: Kallen and Cronbach

Why Religion did not stimulate a response among rabbis. Although popular psychology was fulfilling a religious function for many Americans, many American rabbis disdained religious humanism for what they perceived to be its anemic commitment to religion. In Reform Judaism, "religious humanism remained confined to a vocal minority," Meyer writes. "In both the [Hebrew Union] College and the

[Central] Conference [of American Rabbis] theism remained the dominant form of belief."[52] Given that Reform Judaism was considered the most prestigious form of Judaism in America, Kallen was simply outside of mainstream Jewish religious discourse.

The internal dynamics of the Jewish community, however, proved decisive in forcing change. Beginning in the late 1920s, a new generation of Reform Jews was growing increasingly interested in the ideas of psychologists.[53] The educated laity in Reform congregations, together with the vocal minority of religious humanist rabbis in the Central Conference of American Rabbis, brought pressure to bear upon the movement. In 1928 the Central Conference of American Rabbis took the unprecedented step of inviting a psychiatrist to speak at their annual convention. In 1937 Hebrew Union College began to offer a course in pastoral psychology.[54] In 1946 the Reform rabbi Joshua Loth Liebman, with the publication of his national bestseller, *Peace of Mind*, which offered a synthesis of religion and psychology, became not only the most celebrated rabbi in America but also "a rabbi to the American public." Liebman's "theological concoction," Heinze notes, "was a potent blend of Kaplan's philosophy [i.e., his functionalist view of religion], Freud's psychology, American democracy, and Liebman's favorite theme from rabbinic Judaism, the idea of men and women being in partnership with God."[55] The dynamics that led to this shift from placing functionalist psychology outside the bounds of Jewish religious discourse to placing it firmly within, and, moreover, representing Judaism with it to the wider American public, is a complex tale. The relationship between Kallen and the Reform rabbi Abraham Cronbach (1882–1965) is a part of this tale.

Abraham Cronbach was appointed to the newly created chair of Jewish social studies at Hebrew Union College in 1922, where he remained for the rest of his life. Best-known for his activism as a pacifist, Cronbach also introduced a religious humanist perspective to Hebrew Union College. Prior to his academic appointment, Cronbach had developed an interest in psychology from his work as a chaplain. In the same year that he joined the Hebrew Union College faculty, Cronbach published "Psychoanalysis and Religion" in the *Journal of*

Religion, in which he opened an inquiry into the psychoanalytic values undergirding religion. Reform Judaism had, from its inception, embraced the historical scientific school of study. Cronbach now called for the psychological study of religion, based on pragmatic principles. Like his liberal Protestant contemporaries, Cronbach hoped to find through such an exploration a basis for the unity of religion and psychology, founded upon common understanding and mutual respect.[56]

Kallen's first correspondence with Cronbach concerning Judaism in America began with a disagreement over Kallen's *Menorah Journal* article "Can Judaism Survive in the United States?" (1925). In that article, Kallen painted a bleak picture of the widening fissure between Jewish tradition and modernity: "As the ways of thinking and ways of behaving based on science and conditioned by industry enter into the texture of the daily life of Jews, Judaism and its institutions fall more and more into an innocuous desuetude," he claimed. "The survival of Judaism is postulated upon the inertia of a respect for the past and the energy of a fear of the future." Kallen upbraided rabbis for failing to adjust to the modern world of science and industry. In particular, he faulted the three liberal seminaries that were best positioned to address modern conditions—the Jewish Theological Seminary, Hebrew Union College, and the Jewish Institute of Religion—for providing rabbinical training wholly lacking in "American or generally Jewish as against Judaistic content."[57]

Kallen's article was one of a series of inflammatory articles launched by the *Menorah Journal*'s editor Elliot Cohen. Cohen, Hurwitz, and Kallen all published articles highly critical of the Jewish religious establishment. These articles changed the perception of the *Menorah Journal* by Reform rabbis, who came to see the journal as representative of an ideological camp opposed to Reform Judaism. Whereas it had once been possible to imagine an alliance between the allegedly nonpartisan *Menorah Journal* and Reform rabbis, matters had now deteriorated beyond repair. Reform rabbis spoke out against the *Menorah Journal*. Julian Morgenstern, president of Hebrew Union College, issued a strong condemnation of the *Menorah Journal*, and Abba Hillel Silver, another prominent Reform rabbi, wrote "Why Do the Heathen Rage?" as a rebuttal to the views of Cohen, Hurwitz, and Kallen. Although Hurwitz had promised Silver that the *Menorah Journal* would print his article, Cohen reneged on that promise. As a result, Silver resigned from the board of the Intercollegiate Menorah Association.[58] The rift between the secular intellectuals of the *Menorah Journal* and the Reform movement seemed complete. Morgenstern and Silver had made it clear that they felt that they had nothing positive to offer Reform Judaism. Whereas Wieman, as we saw earlier, included Kallen within the discursive boundaries of his construction of religion, Morgenstern and Silver excluded him (and Cohen and Hurwitz) from religious discourse.

The rift was not as complete as it first appears, however. Cronbach was one of the few who did not react to Kallen's article with outrage, and instead engaged his friend in a sustained dialogue concerning Judaism. Kallen wrote to him:

> Please believe that I am not anti-rabbinic; I have no feeling in the matter beyond a deep and growing anxiety about the future of the whole Jewish cultural complex in the United States, Judaism included, and an interest in a scientific approach to the study of conditions and remedies. I welcome discussion and am only too happy to recognize facts wherever and whenever they are pointed out. My judgment of the function of rabbis in [the] survival of Judaism is not one which I formed with pleasure; it is one which was forced on me by the situation. Any data that would justify revising it would be most welcome. . . . The situation in Judaism calls for scientific analysis and cooperative study of all who genuinely care about its future, not for personal recrimination and defensory [*sic*] tactics. . . . If you ever come this way I shall be glad to talk with you about these matters.[59]

Cronbach endeavored to persuade Kallen to amend his negative assessment of the rabbinate, but Kallen was unmoved. In his opinion, individual examples to the contrary were not sufficient to invalidate his conclusions about the group as a whole: "The statistical average is identical with no particular person," Kallen wrote. "Yet it does define the group."[60]

In Kallen's estimation, it was impossible to remain a rabbi and still subscribe to current scientific scholarship. "In my judgment, scientific scholarship leads to agnosticism and atheism," he wrote Cronbach. "Would your college follow it there?" In Kallen's mind, there was an inherent incompatibility between science and religion, which was precisely the point that Cronbach disputed. Nevertheless, Kallen wrote, this did not present an insurmountable obstacle to their relationship:

> At bottom, you and I are not so far apart as you pretend. The idea that we are is due to the notion that my papers are an attack and not a description, and that the rabbinate needs defense. It doesn't. It is what the economic & social situation has made it and seems satisfied. Meantime the Jewish tradition loses in vitality and significance. That is what bothers me, and why I study the rabbinate as well as the Jewries of the world. If I am irked at all it is by the Jewish policy of repression, of the traditional fear of *Hillul Hashem* [blasphemy]. Free, if necessary, violent discussion, open and thorough airing of views, oxygenation, seem to me essential to salvation. I hope they do to you.[61]

Kallen had found in Cronbach someone with whom he could engage in productive debate.

Cronbach was a popular teacher at Hebrew Union College, especially in the 1930s. The school culture under Morgenstern's presidency (1922–47) was markedly different from that which had characterized the rigid ideology of Kohler's presidency. It now supported a plurality of views and freedom of expression. Although Cronbach was the sole representative of religious humanism on the faculty, this did not mean that he lacked a sympathetic audience among his students. In fact, Meyer notes, Cronbach "exercised considerable influence on students" among those who were "intellectually uncomfortable with theism."[62]

On the occasion of Cronbach's tenth anniversary with Hebrew Union College, a student body committee organized to honor the popular teacher. The result was the publication of a compilation volume of Cronbach's writings, *Religion and Its Social Setting* (1933).[63] Kallen was the inspiration behind its publication, as was made clear by the chair of the Cronbach anniversary committee and student editor of the *Hebrew Union College Monthly*, Martin M. Weitz. Weitz wrote to Kallen, "Thanks again *very* much for your suggestion to make the Cronbach book and to help make as large a section of the liberal world as possible Cronbach-conscious—and too for your kindly and personal interest in me."[64] *Religion and Its Social Setting* foregrounds Cronbach's functionalist psychological approach to religion. Religion was an assertion of a person's perceived highest purpose, and whatever served that end may be called God. Religion must be evaluated by its effectiveness in preserving and ennobling values, not in its fidelity to supernatural revelation. Despite the fact that a majority at Hebrew Union College and in the Central Conference of American Rabbis subscribed to the theism propounded by Samuel S. Cohon, the college's professor of Jewish theology, Kallen believed that this student-led initiative signaled a developing change at Hebrew Union College.[65] He attributed this shift to the efforts of both Weitz and Cronbach. *The Hebrew Union College Monthly*'s "tone, attitude and interest are [a] far cry from what seemed to prevail at Hebrew Union College when I had an entertaining visit there back in 1915," Kallen wrote Weitz. "They seem to me to mark a very positive advance."[66]

Kallen and Cronbach regularly exchanged manuscripts and publications. Cronbach, for example, wrote to Kallen expressing his gratitude for his help in preparing "The Psychoanalytic Study of Judaism."[67] Kallen sent Cronbach a copy of *The Warfare of Religion against Science*. Cronbach thanked him for it, expressing "admiration" for his "brilliant powers." Although Cronbach could not bring himself to agree with Kallen's thesis, he nevertheless felt compelled to consider his point of view: "I ask myself the question: What really is so grievously wrong about religion that a man like Prof. Kallen should go to such pains as to show it up in such a desperately unfavorable light? A thing may be ever so excellent and yet something must be radically wrong if people are somehow inclined to ignore its excellences and to concentrate on its blemishes." Cronbach did not believe that the "dunce cap," as he put it, fit him as "a devotee of religion" and of science, but, he wrote, "I do say that religion greatly needs setting its house in order so long as there is something about it which makes a man like you willing and eager to institute such a comparison."[68] Cronbach announced his intention to share Kallen's work with his students, and hoped that he would be able to convince the administration to invite him to lecture: "I am going to lend your paper to my students. I wish I could get you to meet my students and wrestle it out with them. I have steadily been making efforts to get you invited to Cincinnati. But, alas, certain bygones refuse to be bygones. Nevertheless, I continue my efforts. I think that religion, MY religion, has everything to gain from a man like you. You are a purifyer [*sic*]. You are an assailant that can prompt needed improvements."[69] Kallen was still persona non grata at Hebrew Union College, but, through Cronbach, its students would now have the opportunity to be exposed to his ideas.

Cronbach sufficiently impressed Kallen such that, as noted earlier, he urged Weitz to publish *Religion and Its Social Setting* as part of their plans to honor Cronbach. At Weitz's behest, Kallen wrote the introduction to the book, and permitted him to publish an advance copy of it in the *Hebrew Union College Monthly* in order to promote its sales. Kallen's introduction glowingly described Cronbach's integration of science with religion, suggesting a new openness on Kallen's part to moving beyond the "warfare" model, as well as marking the introduction of Cronbach's psychological approach to Judaism. Kallen praised Cronbach's presentation of the "philosophical and psychological fundamentals" of Judaism. He also identified Cronbach as a modernist. Religionist critics of modernism, Kallen wrote, protest that God had become "nothing more than our highest social purpose," but, be this as it may, "the identification saved the substance of religion as a projection of feeling and integrated it with science as a way of thought." Cronbach's modernism, Kallen added, "stresses the emotional and the poetic," able "to assume for authority such Christian Modernists as Ames, Wieman and Coe, but to employ the anti-religious Freud as a support for the power and value of religious meanings." Cronbach's Judaism, Kallen concluded, may be called "Evangelical Judaism" with respect to human relations. The "good"

Jew is so not in proportion to his subscription to dogma, but in proportion "to the possibilities of stimulating friendships and reciprocal inspirations in all Jewish sections."[70]

Cronbach wrote appreciatively to Kallen, "So often have I been misinterpreted that I find it an honor and a joy when someone sets forth correctly what I am trying to say. You have expressed my thoughts better than I can express them myself. . . . It pleased me particularly that you used the phrase 'Evangelical Judaism.' I think your mind gave birth to that expression while you and I were seated on the porch of your domicile in Columbus Ohio when I had the privilege of being your guest and conversing with you in June 1930. That phrase is a most suitable peg on which to hang some useful ideas."[71] Kallen's support for Cronbach was rooted in their shared belief that religion articulates values and aesthetics. They were united by their shared commitment to humanism and the insights of psychology, although Kallen's humanism was secular and Cronbach's was religious.

Kallen viewed his new relationship with Weitz as an opportunity to further circulate his views among Reform rabbis. Kallen sent Weitz his new book, *Judaism at Bay* (1932), for which Weitz thanked Kallen and announced his intention to lead group discussions on it: "I plan to read parts of it to a small but interested group I have organized here for a discussion of 'Modern World Problems.'"[72] Through Cronbach and Weitz, Kallen's ideas circulated among religious humanists in the Reform movement. He entered into the larger discourse that eventually led to the inclusion of functionalist psychological thought in mainstream Jewish American religious thought.

Creation, Revelation, and Redemption

Kallen began his journey into the book of Job in the 1910s as a way to give shape to Jewish identity. As we shall see in the following chapter, Kallen retained the Joban text as his central Torah through the rest of his life. It would guide Kallen's Jewish identity, and he hoped it would shape Jewish identity in America and in Israel. Job, however, was not only a text that spoke to Kallen as an expression of Hebraism. It was also a text that illuminated the proper function of religion and articulated a redemptive humanism to rival traditional religion. Through *The Warfare of Religion against Science* and *Why Religion*, Kallen entered into discourse with Jews and non-Jews concerning the place of religion in America. In both of these works, Kallen rooted his argument in what he believed to be the Joban perspective. In *The Warfare of Religion against Science*, Kallen aligned the Joban view that life is defined by perpetual struggle with his belief in the "warfare" between religion and science. In Kallen's rhetoric, religion and science take on an almost cosmic significance, locked in a perpetual struggle that provides life's creative propulsion. In *Why Religion*, Job becomes the model of a healthily integrated personality. As we shall see in the following chapter, these various articulations of Job become further refined and integrated by Kallen over the next decades as he gradually fused together secularism, religion, democracy, and the American Idea. Job comes to articulate a vision of redemption for America, and for Israel. In a very real sense, then, we may suggest that Kallen's relationship to Job reflects the three stages of the traditional religious triptych of creation, revelation, and redemption. In this chapter, we have seen Kallen move from seeing Job as the creator of Hebraism to being the source of a psychological religious revelation. We turn now to the final stage—redemption, born of secularism, freedom, and democracy, and refracted through Job.

· 6 ·

On Secular Religion and Democracy

The only thing we have to fear is fear itself.
—Franklin D. Roosevelt, First Inaugural Address, March 4, 1933

DURING THE 1940S AND 1950S, Kallen's efforts to define the terms of religion's engagement with science and democracy intensified. By the 1950s he had synthesized secularism, religion, and democracy. This synthesis, however removed from established institutional Judaism, was still part and parcel of his self-understanding as an American Jew. Kallen came to see himself as a modern-day Job, concerned with individual integrity and engaged, as George Reisch puts it, in "an ongoing vigilant patrol of the epistemic shoreline," guarding against all forms of what he perceived to be fascist thought.[1] This evolution in Kallen's thinking was spurred in large part by the profound changes America underwent from the period of the Great Depression through World War II and on into the Eisenhower administration in the 1950s, and by the social and political consciousness of his academic home at the New School for Social Research.

During the Roosevelt administration, American citizens were deeply concerned that the country might not survive the threats posed by totalitarianism to American capitalism, liberty, and democracy. Strong totalitarian regimes in Italy, Germany, Japan, and Russia seemed more capable and energetic than liberal democracies. It was an age of fear, with the outcome for American capitalism and democracy uncertain.[2]

America's gaze was, for the most part, focused inward as it struggled with economic devastation and skyrocketing unemployment. But, in some quarters, there were those who looked upon Hitler's rise to power as a grave threat and were determined to take action. In 1933 the New School for Social Research, under the leadership of President Alvin Johnson, launched its University in Exile program to bring to the United States (primarily Jewish) academics dismissed from their posts due to laws enacted by Hitler's Nazi administration. Renamed the Graduate Faculty of Political and Social Science in 1934, Kallen served on its faculty—and, later, as its dean. He played a leading role in bringing émigré intellectuals to the New School and helped to organize their regular "General Seminar" sessions in which they discussed the prospects for democracy.[3]

It is in this social and intellectual context that Kallen developed a new and politicized reading of Job. In a 1934 radio broadcast, Kallen offered a novel interpretation of the same passage from Job that he had in years past found meaningful for other reasons, now finding that Job 13:15 offers a message of hope and strength against totalitarianism in the vein of Roosevelt's inaugural message that "the only thing we have to fear is fear itself." One listener's impressions of Kallen's message are recorded in the Chicago Unitarian magazine *Unity*:

> We tuned in on the radio the other day, and chanced to hear Dr. Horace Kallen drop the word of insight which we must pass on to our readers. Speaking on Facism [*sic*], Dr. Kallen made reference to the famous passage in the 13th chapter of "Job," which runs, "Though He slay me, yet will I trust in Him." The speaker then pointed out that this was a mistranslation; that, in the original Hebrew, the verse stated, "He will slay me; I have no hope; yet will I defend my integrity to His face." The first and familiar version, said Dr. Kallen, conveys perfectly the attitude of the loyal citizen in the Fascist state. Subject to a tyranny which he knows will absorb and crush him, destroy all his individuality in the interest of

> a totalitarian society, he yet puts his trust in the dictatorship and obeys it. The second version of the great biblical passage, the correct one, is a beautiful illustration, said Dr. Kallen, of the attitude of the man who would be free. It is the perfect slogan of liberty, as over against the repressive rule of either church or state. . . . Strike me if you will, . . . Yet am I the master of my own life. . . . We have never heard the case for liberty put more vividly than this.[4]

Kallen here used a biblical reference (in Jewish religious terms, he delivered a *dvar Torah*) to drive home a point about freedom and liberty. He aligned Job with democracy. It signaled a transition in Kallen's thinking. Over the course of the next twenty years, as we shall see, Kallen came to interpret Job as postulating the premise for democracy and cultural pluralism, an idea rooted in his original understanding of the book of Job as a product of the discursive exchange between the Greek and Hebraic worldviews discussed earlier.

Kallen sought to promote this view by once again staging a production of his dramatic rendition of Job. President Roosevelt's Works Progress Administration (WPA) inaugurated a bold program to support the arts in 1935. One of its programs, the Federal Theater Project (1935–39), was created to employ starving artists and actors, and drew in an audience of one million people each month.[5] In 1937 Ben Russak, assistant supervisor to the playreading department, wrote to Kallen that he, the department supervisor, and the director of the Play Bureau, were very excited to produce *The Book of Job as a Greek Tragedy.* Benjamin Zemach, who choreographed Kurt Weill's *The Eternal Road*, was enthusiastic about staging his play, and the avant-garde composer Ernst Toch was anxious to compose a musical score for it. The Broadway star Sam Jaffe, who had played the part of Job in the Free Synagogue's 1926 production, wished to do so again, but was prevented from doing so by a previous contractual obligation. Although two units of the Federal Theater (one in Boston) wished to produce *The Book of Job*, the funding, in the end, appears not to have materialized.[6] This eagerness to present Kallen's play no doubt had something to do with his considerable reputation within the arts community.

Indeed, Kallen had been solicited (and reluctantly agreed) to serve on the advisory committee of the Experimental Theater of the Federal Theater Project just the year before.[7] He was eager to see mounted a play that he felt had something important to say to America about freedom and individuality.

Kallen also remained invested in defending against what he perceived as the threat religion posed to science's independence. To him, the hallmark of modernity was the triumph of science and democracy over ecclesiastical control. Kallen, who had earlier identified Job as a proto-modernist in this respect, saw himself as adopting a Joban stance of resistance against the attempts of religious institutions to exert control in politics or in science. For this reason, he, together with John Dewey, vigorously opposed the Conference on Science, Philosophy and Religion. Founded in 1940, and sponsored by the Conservative movement's Jewish Theological Seminary under the leadership of Chancellor Louis Finkelstein, the Conference on Science, Philosophy and Religion sought to chart a progressive traditionalist religious path to unify science, philosophy, and religion, promote democracy, and articulate an American moral order.[8] Finkelstein also used it to cement Jewish with American religious values. The Conference on Science, Philosophy and Religion helped to popularize the notion that American values were based upon a common Judeo-Christian heritage, creating "a new ecumenism of American religions." Kallen and Dewey, however, opposed the Conference on Science, Philosophy and Religion because, to them, it represented a covert attempt to impose traditionalist religion on American intellectual life. For Kallen, the real enemy was the Catholic Church. He believed that the Conference's validation of neo-Thomist and Catholic doctrine represented a threat to American democracy.[9]

Kallen wrote a sharp rebuke to Finkelstein after the first conference. It seemed to him that, as a Jew, Finkelstein should take a leading role in promoting "active toleration," but, he wrote, he believed that the Conference on Science, Philosophy and Religion "made the painful impression of active intolerance, commented on as such in Protestant publications."[10] As one scholar puts it, Kallen feared that

Finkelstein "had made a devil's pact with the Catholic Church."[11] He explained his opposition to the Finkelstein conference in a letter to his friend, the philosopher Van Meter Ames:

> As I understand it, Einstein had been practically hounded into sending them a paper. In this paper, he gave his conception of God and Nature as they developed out of his feeling of the trend of science. Mr. Finkelstein denounced him then and there. That whole meeting was a clerical's holiday for Jesuits and neo-Thomists. It caused such a disturbance even among the timid Protestants that the latter meetings seem to have been shaped to overcome the bad feeling caused by the first. But all of them are designed so to harmonize science and religion that science is converted into the hand-maiden of the special orthodoxies whose interests the protagonists of the conference are trying to further. Dewey and I have consistently declined to participate in the meetings.[12]

Because Finkelstein had publicly denounced Einstein's "cosmic religion," Kallen perceived the Conference on Science, Philosophy and Religion to be intent on silencing dissenting voices. It showed up the duplicity of science-friendly religionists, in his eyes. Kallen felt that the Conference on Science, Philosophy and Religion wished merely to use science to further religious aims. It thus appeared to him to have totalitarian pretensions.

Alarmed by what they perceived to be the "alliance of Finkelstein with Catholic, neo-Thomist intellectuals and religious scientists," Kallen and Dewey, working with Unitarian minister Edwin H. Wilson, editor of the *Humanist*, convened the rival Conference on the Scientific Spirit and Democratic Faith in 1943. As Kallen conceived it, their conference would take up the cause of "democratic religions" against authoritarianism. Although their conference met only four times, concluding in 1946, those years helped to cement for Kallen his conception of secularism as religion.[13]

Those years also cemented for Kallen a connection between Jews and democracy. The Nazi regime's war against the Jews and against democracy spurred Kallen's thought in this regard. "The peculiar identification of Jews with democratic ideals and democratic ideals with Jews has been variously made at different times with different intent by friends and foes, both Jews and non-Jews. Sound or unsound, it is made," Kallen wrote in 1942. "Certainly, the Nazi cult aggressively couples the Jews with the democratic ideal. 'Degenerate Jewish democracy' is a phrase ever in the mouths of Hitler and his apostles at home and abroad, and their war upon the democracies is always a war against the Jews."[14] That same year, the Bloch Publishing Company informed Kallen that, since they had no present plan to reprint *The Book of Job as a Greek Tragedy*, they needed to secure his permission to turn in for scrap the book plate metal that they had been holding onto, in accordance with a new law passed to support the war effort. Kallen replied, "I hope it will be turned into bullets that will tear Hitler and his apostles apart."[15]

Although the enormity of the genocide underway was not yet appreciated, Kallen did understand that Hitler had declared war on the Jews. Because of Hitler, he wrote, the Jewish people had become viewed as the symbol of the "struggle of the democratic faith to make secure the equal right of different people to life, liberty, and the pursuit of happiness."[16] Hitler's identification of the Jews with democracy and democracy with the Jews, Kallen wrote with irony, is "the greatest honor which the Jews have received from friend or foe since Christianity was established as the prevailing religion of the Western World."[17] As Kallen read the historical record, since it was the democratic faith that had opened the doors of the ghetto and allowed Jews to participate in society, this meant that Jews do indeed have "a moral and spiritual stake in democracy."[18] Thus, free participation in democracy becomes an affirmation of Jewish identity, a point that Kallen saw as affirmed in Job.

Even in the United States, however, the Jewish "moral and spiritual stake in democracy" had not yet been adequately recognized. In an America in which political culture had assumed a generic Christian piety, Kallen saw a need to correct that bias in his ongoing fight for cultural pluralism. Thus, he wrote to President Roosevelt in 1945:

> Dear Mr. President:
>
> In your address today you employed an expression which troubles me and a great many of your other friends. You said, "There is no room in the world for German militarism *and* Christian decency." Among your auditors, I believe, were multitudes of men and women who are decent but not Christians. Some are Communists, some are Mohammedans, some are Confucians, some are Buddhists, some are Taoists, some are Agnostics, some are Judaists, some are Atheists. I am sure you did not mean to exclude them from the company of the decent and to confine decency only to those who are Christians. Your expression, which, I presume, is a convention of usage rather than the utterance of a point of view, unnecessarily shuts out from the democratic goals of the war too many people who are also offering blood and sweat and tears on the battlefields, in the factories, and in the homes. It seems to me that it would be more democratic to speak of human decency, and not to suggest that decency is a special characteristic of one section of the religious cults of the world.[19]

Just before World War II concluded, as the world began to absorb the chilling reality of the Holocaust and as the Jewish struggle for independence in Palestine was imperiled by the restrictions imposed by the infamous British White Paper of 1939 (also known as the MacDonald White Paper), Kallen cemented a connection between Jews and democracy in unequivocal terms:

> What do the Jews ask? Only that an honest effort shall *now* be made to save as many as possible of their brethren from the abominations of living death and the obscenities of cruel destruction which the Nazis perpetrate upon them. Only that Palestine, the one place of refuge guaranteed them by solemn treaty and the law of nations, shall not be shut to them. . . . They ask that, as democrats who not only fight and die for democracy but live their lives out building it up, the democratic community of their building shall not be sold into bondage to the fascist Arab [i.e., the small propertied class of feudal landlords], nor reduced to a mere tool of the imperialist Briton.[20]

The struggle for Jewish survival was inextricably connected to the struggle for democracy. Kallen envisioned this as a struggle for a democratic nation-state of Israel that would safeguard not only the Jewish people but also guarantee the freedom and prosperity of Palestinian Arabs. For that reason, he believed that "the cause of the Jewish Homeland and the cause of the Arab fellah are one cause."[21]

By the 1950s, Kallen saw himself as a defender of "democratic religions" like Judaism and Protestantism (and unlike Catholicism). From here, it was only a small step to declaring that the most democratic of all religions is democracy itself, for democracy provided the surety that no one religion would presume to dominate any other, and was itself a faith commitment in the workings of society. Kallen first articulated this idea in "Democracy's True Religion" (1951), which appeared first as an article in the *Saturday Review of Literature*, and later as a pamphlet published by Beacon Press.[22] In it, Kallen described the religion of the *American Idea*, a phrase he adopted from the Unitarian abolitionist Theodore Parker. "For the communicants of the democratic faith, this is the religion of religions, the common faith in the way of life which keeps impartial peace among them all and assures to each its liberty on equal terms with the others," Kallen wrote. "It is the one way in which each, although maintaining its unique and singular individuality, although cherishing its incommensurable difference, can yet live together with the others in such wise that it can grow in liberty and safety more certainly than if it sought to exist solo."[23] In this formulation, Kallen reiterated in large measure his original cultural pluralism thesis, but without reference to racial ideas. The thesis of cultural pluralism now rested on a common faith in democracy.

"Secularism is religion," Kallen declared provocatively. "It favors the betting of one's life on equal liberty for all men to believe, to inquire, to hear, and to teach, against the exclusive authoritarian claims of a special occupational class."[24] Kallen argued that secular religion, democracy, and science all express the same commitment to human freedom. Relying upon the definition of faith that he had set forth in *Why Religion*, Kallen saw in secularism precisely the same sort of demand for active commitment that described religious faith.

It requires of the believer to "bet" one's life on that proposition over the rival claims of sacerdotal authority, he argued. As such, it serves the same function as traditional religious belief and therefore qualifies to be considered a religion. Moreover, because secularism guarantees the freedom of all beliefs and all religions, it is a metareligion. The American Idea, secular, scientific, and democratic, was, for Kallen, the religion of religions.[25]

Kallen elaborated on these ideas in correspondence with his friend, the poet T. S. Eliot. The fact that he corresponded with someone of Eliot's stature is significant. Considering Eliot's cultural cachet and religious standing, Kallen's correspondence with him is a dramatic expression of his commitment to proselytizing American religion. Kallen's attempt to convince Eliot of the validity of his conception of religion signifies a discursive intervention at the very heart of modern culture. Eliot's anti-Semitism may make their friendship seem unlikely, but they were in fact close friends for several decades. Their surviving correspondence dates from 1927, and continues through 1960, but they had been close friends at Harvard from 1906 to 1911, so it seems likely that earlier letters have been lost.[26] Over the course of some thirty-three years, Eliot and Kallen corresponded about a wide range of topics, including philosophy, poetry, religion, cultural pluralism, and the nature of secularism. This correspondence is significant for Eliot scholars, constituting a record of Eliot's "sustained intellectual engagement with the role of Jews and Judaism in Western culture," as one scholar puts it succinctly, adding that Kallen's notion of cultural pluralism wrought a signal effect upon Eliot, leading to his "late enthusiasm for [cultural] diversity."[27] The correspondence is thus a striking testimony to Kallen's unflagging optimism that support for his beliefs, or, at least, respect for them, could be won out of reasoned conflict, even from a thinker as diametrically opposed on philosophic and religious issues as was Eliot. This had always been a hallmark of Kallen's thinking, from his onetime heated debate with his teacher Barrett Wendell to his early confrontations with Reform rabbis, and including his debates with Solomon Schechter, the architect of American Conservative Judaism, who, Kallen wrote, had exercised such profound influence "on the definition and pattern of my interest and activity in the Jewish scene" by virtue of the fact that "we were friendly enemies."[28]

Kallen likely hoped that he might be able to persuade Eliot to validate his notion of the American Idea as religion, or to convince him to take the idea as a serious alternative to his own worldview. "Please believe, dear Tom, that religion is as serious a word to me as it is to you," Kallen wrote. "Religions are many, and can be separated into two components, *faith*, and *the content of faith*." Kallen attempted to find common ground with Eliot by prioritizing the function of faith over its content: "What is common to the global miscellany of religions, then[,] is not *what* is believed, but *how* it is believed." Each religion's adherents bet their lives on its proposition for salvation. The American Idea, Kallen wrote, is no different. It signifies "the statement of faith concerning God and man and human relations expressed by the Declaration of Independence." Kallen argued that this faith has been a guiding creed for the American people, who have struggled "in the schools, the churches, the workshops, the halls of government and the courts to incarnate faith in fact. The Idea is American, and not British, not Swiss, not Scandinavian, the same way as an individual is American and not British or other."[29]

Kallen reiterated his conception of the American Idea as metareligion: "The American Idea can be, and is, not so much *a* religion, as religion, indeed the one reliable catholicity of religions, and the American religion insofar as Americans *are* Americans. For they are Americans, and not merely citizens of a particular sovereign state, in the measure of their commitment to the American Idea." Because it is a religion "wherein . . . diverse individual religions are united," he concluded, "it is religion at the opposite pole of . . . religious intolerance." The American Idea is by its very nature tolerant and pluralist, and, Kallen added, "it is for this reason too, that the Idea works as the creative propulsion of a national culture."[30]

Kallen, as we have seen, had located Hebraism prior to Judaism, and believed that religion is a product of culture. Eliot, on the other hand, was adamant that the reverse was true, and that culture was a product of religion.[31] This general point of disagreement carried specific implications for how to situate Judaism in America. As Eliot and Kallen discussed the relationship between democracy, the American Idea, and religion, the subject of Jews and Judaism remained an important subtext to this discussion. Eliot, fearing that Kallen's postulated religion for America invited totalitarianism and oppression, appealed to Kallen to consider the importance and value of the Jewish religion. Kallen responded by underscoring his belief that only the democratic religious idea ensured tolerance and freedom for all, preventing traditional revelatory religions from seeking totalitarian dominance themselves. The American Idea, Kallen wrote, "displaces Judaism's and Christianism's traditional arrogation of divine election with the belief that divinity, however conceived, plays no favorites and favors no one human conception of itself above any other."[32] At the end of their unresolved debate over the issue of Judaism as a religion and its relationship to the American Idea, Eliot observed somewhat ironically on April 2, 1955, "You know, it seems to me that you have been defending a religion called the American Idea—and that it is I who have been defending a religion called Judaism."[33]

Eliot and Kallen's extended correspondence bears witness to how central to their disagreement over American "religion" was the friction between a religious definition of Judaism and an ethno-cultural understanding of it. Their correspondence also offers a particularly crystalline view of how dramatically Kallen's connection to Judaism and his notion of cultural pluralism had evolved far beyond their original racialized context. When Eliot inquired whether Kallen's views on Jewish education would justify the creation of separate Jewish schools on a religious or racial basis, Kallen replied with a strong repudiation of the very notion of race:

> You use the word "race." I don't remember employing that word in anything I wrote you. To me the word stands for a fiction which men use mostly as an instrument of discrimination against other men. Biologically those are of the same race who can breed together; their diversities are primarily cultural, not biological. Racism, whether in

> the United States, in Germany, in Britain, in Africa, in India, or in Israel, postulates a non-existent biological ground for a caste-system or other fixed hierarchy of values which, I believe, violates the integrity of those whom it favors as of those whom it abuses. To me, "Jew," "Irishman," "Negro", "Indian," and so on, signify nothing racial. Each word denotes a singular configuration of beliefs, thoughts, rites, rotes, works, and ways which have been compounded into an ethos, that any individual can enter by birth, by conversion, or by immigration and naturalization. No one is born with an ethos. It is not an innate idea, but an acquired one. It is to a group what personality is to an individual—not an endowment but a pattern of existence attained by learning and self-commitment. . . . Experience has led me to conclude that they [Jewish schools] can do a better job, and thus enable the Jewish citizens of the United States to perform better their function in the teamplay [*sic*] of cultural heritages and communions which I believe underlies whatever is different and new in the culture of the American people. My experience is that hardly any one of the nation's component groups fails to cultivate some formation of its heritage, or to desire that its neighbors should see and appreciate it as a contribution to the spirit of America—*e pluribus unum*.[34]

Kallen had abandoned his early racial views some decades prior, so in that regard there is nothing particularly significant about the date on which he wrote this, but the clarity of this exposition and the intended recipient of the message make it a significant intervention in defining Jewish identity for a Christian audience.

The fact that Kallen and Eliot agreed to disagree is not in itself important. Kallen understood that what was of central importance was the mutual respect they had for each other's ideas, and their continued openness to dialogue. Thus, Eliot wrote of his admiration for Kallen, and Kallen, for his part, interpreted their disagreements to be of a constructive and friendly nature, for, as he wrote to Eliot, "you recognize that artists and thinkers sustain the integrity of their singular vision and action only as 'a sporting fellowship even among opposite minds.'"[35] In other words, the very act of disagreeing led each to develop and clarify, to "sustain the integrity," of their own thoughts.

In the 1950s American national piety consisted of a bland civil religion. President Dwight Eisenhower gave voice to this in 1954: "Our form of government has no sense unless it is founded in a deeply felt religious faith, and I don't care what it is. With us, of course, it is the Judeo-Christian concept, but it must be a religion that all men are created equal."[36] Whereas many Americans, like President Eisenhower, viewed America as the home to many different religions united in civility, Kallen insisted that secularism should communicate a more urgent and meaningful religious message. Americans, Kallen wrote, had "bet their lives on the American Idea," a yearning for human freedom, and America's diverse individual religions were united in their faith in human fulfillment through democracy.[37] Protesting the anemic expression of national civil religion, Kallen wrote, "Secularism cannot be freedom from religion; it must be freedom from coercion and exploitation by a particular religion. Secularism is freedom *of* religion to be different. Thus, again, Secularism Is the Will of God."[38] Stressing the lesson of Job, Kallen wrote that it was postulated "on the individual's concern for his own integrity, and on his consequent free movement between and among the diversity of group formations."[39]

The Joban postulate of secularism is precisely how Kallen also defined the American Idea. The "American Idea," he wrote in *Cultural Pluralism and the American Idea*, "lays the responsibility for his own freedom on the individual's will and courage, designating all association as voluntary, and postulating it on the individual's concern for his own integrity and on his consequent free movement between and among the diversity of group formations." Kallen's conception of the American Idea as American civil religion is perhaps the single most robust formulation from that time. He went so far as to propose the creation of a secular bible, which he called the Bible of America: "As a creed covenanted by all religions for the freedom of each, the Gospel of America receives, each generation, a fresh philosophical restatement, addressed to the exigencies of the times. As a plan of human relations in the human enterprise, it receives like repristination from the utterances of poets, statesmen, dramatists, men of letters. A sequence of such renewals makes up the Bible of the people of Israel, and of their Christian epigons. In the same way, a selected sequence may make up a Bible of America."[40]

This bible would contain the secular equivalent to the Pentateuch—the first five books of the Jewish and Christian Scriptures—and the poetic and wisdom writings: "Its book of Genesis would of course be the Declaration of Independence, which is also the simplest, clearest, most comprehensive, yet briefest telling of the American Idea," Kallen wrote. "It sets the theme and whatever follows is a variation upon it." He then suggested over thirty other possible texts from the American context to follow, including speeches, literature, and laws that variously addressed historic and current social justice issues such as slavery, racial discrimination, women's rights, and labor relations, as well as more general principles of human rights, democracy, and the separation of church and state. Kallen even suggested that one of his own essays might be included. "And the Bible might conclude in unfinished political Torah with the Universal Declaration of Human Rights adopted by the Assembly of the United Nations."[41] This Torah, as Kallen called it, would thus express the values and ideals of freedom and democracy. Although Kallen may not have won many adherents, he did gain attention. Those who disagreed with Kallen's conception of democracy as religion, like the sociologist Will Herberg, could not ignore his views. The disagreement, in fact, helped to advance the debates by forcing a further clarification of the alternatives.

In lectures delivered at Drew University in 1961, Herberg, author of the widely acclaimed *Protestant, Catholic, Jew* (1955), analyzed the paradox that America was "at once the most religious and the most secularistic of nations."[42] In the context of the 1950s, Herberg observed, the American Way had become the "operative religion" of Americans, and "conventional religion" (meaning normative Christianity and Judaism) plays a social function in helping people find a sense of belonging in a subcommunity. Whereas the ethnic subcommunity had provided Americans with the requisite sense of belonging in the past, Herberg argued, now that role had devolved to the Catholic, Protestant, and Jewish religious communities. The American Way represented the "what" of American religion, and belonging to one of the three established religions described the "how" of belonging.

Herberg used Kallen's *Democracy's True Religion* as a sounding board for his own ideas, just as Wieman had earlier clarified his views in response to Kallen's *Why Religion*. Herberg identified *Democracy's True Religion* as "the classic formulation of the benevolent syncretism [of religion and culture] that constitutes America's secularized religion."[43] Kallen's religion of the American Idea was in some ways the paradigmatic expression of the shared national piety of the era. In 1954, the same year that Kallen published *Secularism Is the Will of God*, Congress added "under God" to the Pledge of Allegiance. This piety, George Marsden observes, was born of "World War II patriotism, Cold War anxieties, inherited American ideals, similar religious and moral heritages, and a burgeoning economy that provided most people with at least the hope of sharing in the American dream. In such a setting, pragmatism could draw on shared moral capital."[44] But, Herberg wrote, theologians who were critics of American religion had "grave misgivings" about Kallen's claim that democracy was a viable "superreligion." They took belief seriously, and could not "easily be persuaded to dissolve it in the generalized religiosity of the American Way." For "theologically concerned" critics, argued Herberg, secularization in America had come to mean the emptying of meaningful content from religion.[45]

Although Kallen did not directly engage in dialogue with Herberg over this, he might have countered that, although he hoped to empty religion of its supernaturalist illusions, he nevertheless valued religious feeling and found in secularism a deep faith commitment. "As a Secularist," Kallen wrote, "I recognize the equal right of all the world's different faiths to be what they are as they are, so long as they do not cancel this right for themselves by refusing it to others."[46] Kallen's identification as a secularist did not negate his strong sense of connection to his Jewish identity, as is evidenced in part by his suggestion of a Torah for America. He distinguished between those whom he called "Judaists" and "Jews." The former are religious; the latter are, like Kallen, secular. The latter group, Kallen wrote, believes in "an ongoing transvaluation of the 'religious' tradition by the sciences of man and nature and by the industrial and other arts." Kallen perceived his secular religion to be an expression of such an ongoing transvaluation. This transvaluation was the key, he believed, to "the ongoing existence and growth of the distinctively Jewish group."[47] Kallen's belief in secularism was his contribution to the ongoing growth of the "distinctively Jewish group."

On Job and Liberty

By the 1950s the book of Job had come to represent for Kallen the essential expression of his faith in freedom and democracy. This he expressed in a popular radio broadcast series entitled "This I Believe," created in 1951 to address the fears and anxieties of the age. Broadcast from 196 stations in the United States and abroad two to three times per day, and repeated at intervals over several weeks, each five-minute episode featured the personal philosophy of different speakers.[48] Kallen's episode aired in 1953. He told his listeners that his beliefs had developed out of his reading of Job. "Now in my seventieth year, I am asked what have I bet my life on," Kallen said.

> Pondering the answer, I find that above all else, I believe in equal liberty for every person to believe, to change his beliefs, to tell his beliefs; and in reason, the one method by which this equality of all believers is most reliably confirmed and advanced. I believe that democracy is the free orchestration of mankind's equal liberty; that progress is their teamwork, that peace is their reciprocal guarantees. . . . Now to bet one's life on equal liberty for everybody as the goal, and on reason as the going to this goal, is to . . . live by a fighting faith in the freedom which Job bet his life on when he challenged the justice of the almighty and the almighty justified him.[49]

Whereas in the past Kallen had stressed reading Job as an expression of Hebraism's philosophical compatibility with modernity, he now highlighted Job's faith commitment. Kallen identified Job's faith with his. They both lived with a fighting faith in freedom.

Having cemented in his mind the connection between Job, faith, and democracy, Kallen sought to republish *The Book of Job as a Greek Tragedy* for the new era. The reissue would become part of Kallen's proselytizing efforts on behalf of the American Idea. In 1959 Kallen found a publisher in Hill & Wang, a firm that specialized in publishing dramas. Hill & Wang's interest may have been piqued because of the recent runaway success of Archibald MacLeish's *J. B.* (1958), a modern retelling of the book of Job, and so believed that there was a potential audience for *The Book of Job as a Greek Tragedy*.[50]

In the new preface, Kallen justified his republication by noting its uniqueness (and importance) as a dramatic rendering of the biblical text, which no one else had done. Referring to MacLeish's *J. B.*, Kallen characterized that play as part of the "matrix of orthodoxy" of which all recent commentators (including Josiah Royce and Carl Jung) seemed to be a part. They focus on the prologue of the biblical tragedy, Kallen explained, which fit the natural human tendency to want a happy ending. This natural "hunger of the heart," he wrote, "impelled the canonical masking of the Tragedy of Job by the form the Bible preserves it in," and "has motivated the bulk of its traditional reinterpretations." Kallen, on the other hand, wished to preserve "the tragic intention of the Tragedy of Job." The Joban conclusion, Kallen added, is "neither reconciliation nor submission, but recognition."[51]

The most striking part of Kallen's new introduction is when he refers to Robert Frost's *A Masque of Reason*, a 1945 comedy purporting to be the forty-third chapter of the book of Job, with its theme, as Kallen put it, of "the tragedy's vital heresy." He wrote that the humanism in *A Masque of Reason* is true "to the spirit of the Hebrew Tragedy of Job," and that it established why, "of all books in the biblical canon, the poetic drama of Hebrew Job concurs best with whatever is modern and not merely contemporary in the faith of modern man."[52] Through his references to *J. B.* and to *A Masque of*

Reason, Kallen linked *The Book of Job as a Greek Tragedy* to American dramatic literature. He did not include any religious commentators or theologians in his treatment of modern interpretations. Kallen situated his republication of Job as American drama and literature, in the tradition of Robert Frost and Archibald MacLeish. Only, with Kallen, it was also a secular religious offering. He made sure to send T. S. Eliot a copy of it, who expressed his delight at receiving it.[53]

Kallen particularly hoped that *The Book of Job as a Greek Tragedy* would influence attitudes and policies in Israel. He had felt long before the establishment of Israel that his favorite passage from the book of Job aptly captured in psychological, emotional, and ethical terms the Jewish struggle for a homeland, which had seemed an unrealizable dream. Thus, Kallen wrote in 1932:

> Societies and nationalities are no more immortal than individual men and women. But neither the one nor the other dies by giving up the struggle voluntarily. The author of the Book of Job had a deep insight into both the psychology and the ethics here involved. "Behold, He will slay me," he makes his hero declare. "I have no hope. Nevertheless, I maintain my ways before Him . . . Mine integrity hold I fast and will not let it go. My heart shall not reproach me so long as I live." I know not how many times I have cited these verses. They are the sum of wisdom to me, with respect to all things, and also with respect to the position of the Jews in relation to the Jewish homeland. The vision of the homeland is the center of Jewry's integrity. It must be held fast if Jewry is to survive as a sane people in what seems to be becoming an insane civilization. . . . Zion becomes more precious as Zionism becomes more futile.[54]

Now that the Zionist dream had been realized, however, *The Book of Job as a Greek Tragedy* took on a new importance for Kallen. It would now serve to support the fledgling (and embattled) Israeli identity. As an ideal of democracy and freedom, the American Idea knows no national boundaries, and its applicability to Israel was almost self-evident to Kallen. He awaited the publication of *The Book of Job as a Greek Tragedy* in paperback, as Kallen wrote to Arthur Wang in June

1959, so that he could take copies with him to Stockholm, where he was to speak on "Cultural Pluralism in the Modern World" before the World Jewish Congress. That venue would allow Kallen to distribute his ideas to an international assembly of Jewish representatives, which he hoped would translate into further sales opportunities abroad. "I am particularly concerned that there should be a market in Israel," Kallen wrote. "Regarding Israel, perhaps you could arrange sales on the basis of certain reserve funds which the United States Government makes available for the purpose of distributing American books and American ideas."[55] Kallen believed that since *The Book of Job as a Greek Tragedy* was self-evidently about the American Idea, the American government might help to finance the distribution of his book as part of their propaganda efforts.

In "Whither Israel" (1951), Kallen described "the [Israeli] governmental dilemma between, on the one hand, a solidarity to be created by appeasing protagonists of religious intolerance and coercion and, on the other hand, remaining loyal to the principle of equal liberty for the different." He worried that Israel might acquiesce in militarization and in the political empowerment of the religious bloc, thereby undermining its fundamental commitment to democracy and embracing totalitarianism. Kallen appreciated that Israel was caught on the horns of a terrible moral dilemma: "The alternatives are to accept the murder of freedom at the hands of its foe or to kill freedom in order to save it from the foe." The book of Job, Kallen wrote, described the attitude of courage and faith that Israel should adopt. Although the future was uncertain, Israel must maintain its faith in freedom. If it were to transpire that Israel were destroyed, then at least it "will have held fast to its integrity and not paid for some form of physical survival with moral suicide."[56] Kallen thus offered his Joban philosophy as a moral guide to sustain Israel's commitment to freedom and democracy in 1951.

In 1959, on the heels of a visit to Israel sponsored by the Theodor Herzl Foundation and the American Association for Jewish Education to inquire into the type of society that the new nation was in the process of creating, it seemed particularly apropos. As Kallen reflected in his sympathetic report from that trip, published as *Utopians at Bay* in 1958, Israel seemed to Kallen to embody the faith, struggle, and integrity of Job. "The total impression I left Israel with, was of a somewhat strayed Utopian fellowship of believers, intrepid, embattled, and unyielding, working and fighting with every means within their reach, to transubstantiate the image of the things they hope for into the actualities they live with, to transvalue the faith which is the evidence of their things unseen into the visible events and tangible facts of everyday existence," he wrote. "Be the outcome of their struggle what it may, it presently discloses an ethos of valor and devotion which seems to me a moving testimony to what is most hopefully human in mankind's struggle for its own humanity."[57] Job thus captures the integrity of the selfhood of the Jewish people, its struggle to achieve its own vision, and to keep its individuality and its character even as it secures the freedom and security of all other peoples and faiths in its homeland. This marks the fighting faith of Israel.

Thus, over the course of fifty years, the book of Job remained at the heart of Kallen's self-fashioning as a Jew. From announcing Job's presence as a drama in Jewish literature, to finding in Job an expression of philosophical Darwinism, and on to reading Job as a prototypical version of the American Idea, Kallen's personal changes are recorded in his changing interpretations of Job. These changes in Kallen's self-understanding, in his sense of personal identity as a Jew, as an American, and as a human being, describe his own struggle for survival: "When we say we struggle for our own survival, it isn't primarily the survival of the body that we struggle for," Kallen once said. "It's for a certain identity, a certain pattern, of the action of the body, of the living and thinking and feeling that are expressed in words and in habits of life and in ideals."[58] For Kallen, that struggle entailed discursive engagement with a wide spectrum of American life.

As a consequence of Kallen's engagement with print culture, and with a wide spectrum of American intellectual life, including religious and cultural leaders like Cronbach, Wieman, Eliot, and Finkelstein, whose receptivity to his ideas varied, Kallen's story is enmeshed in the larger story of American and Jewish religious discourse. By examining the social circulation of Kallen's ideas, we gain appreciation for the protean quality of secularism and the engagement of science and religion. The discourses cause a renegotiation of the meaning of the terms, and help to constitute culture. Kallen's interventions in the discourses concerning the engagement of science and religion, the meaning of freedom and democracy, and the function of secularism, were not only personal reflections—they were also contributions to the development of Jewish life in America.

◆ ◆ ◆

Epilogue

Science, Religion, and Integrity

> Rabban Gamliel would proclaim and say: Any student whose inside is not like his outside will not enter the study hall.
>
> —Talmud, Berakhot 28a

"DID YOU WORK THIS OUT YOURSELF; I mean this relation of your Jewishness to your Americanism?" Ira Eisenstein asked Kallen in a 1970 interview. Kallen replied, "I lived it out. The thought came as a realization of what I had lived." Asking why one should be Jewish was as irrelevant to Kallen as asking why one should be alive. Rationalizations of living (Jewishly or not) are needed only when that life is challenged, he opined. Otherwise, it is simply an ongoing activity. Eisenstein pressed Kallen on this point, arguing that Jewish identity is indeed challenged, for many Jews no longer see any point in belonging to Jewish group life. Kallen replied, "And what is their way of life? Isn't it highly concentrated in the activity of rejecting whatever Jewishness is a constituent of their personality? . . . They wage a constant internal warfare." Rejecting Jewish identity, in other words, becomes an unhealthy variation of Jewish identity. "If one is healthy, living is an ongoing internal orchestration of future with past. It is to maintain the well balanced healthy personality, that is labelled 'integrated.'"[1]

Kallen's views concerning Jewish identity may be faulted for their inadequacy to address the multiplicity of Jewish identity narratives that have exploded in recent decades. Although Kallen had dropped the vocabulary of race from his lexicon many decades before, he still retained a view of Jewishness bounded by what Andrew Winston calls "self-essentialization."[2] "How do you stop being a Jew?" Eisenstein asked. "You don't," Kallen replied.[3] Winston pointed out that self-essentialization is a common phenomenon among members of marginalized groups. A number of theoreticians of Jewish identity describe this growing phenomenon among Jews, which sees particular expression in the unexpected re-racialization of Jewish identity, especially among American Jews.[4]

Notwithstanding this element of self-essentialization, Kallen left Jewish identity otherwise unbounded. Kallen offers up a nuanced way of looking at Jewish identity that suggests that Jewishness does not lie in any particular propositional content. It is not defined by religion, biology, or by anything in particular. In keeping with Professor William James's maxim of "live and let live" (a maxim Kallen amended to "live and help live") so, too, Kallen believed that living Jewishly needs no particular justification. "The living makes its own meaning, *is* the meaning, is all the meaning there can be. For each person it consists of this and no other singularity of faith and works struggling on, maintaining its integrity."[5]

For Kallen, the American Idea brought him back to a positive integration of Jewish identity with American identity. They both contributed to the ongoing orchestration and coordination of his life, and to his commitment to democracy and the principle of live and help live. Kallen joined Jewish and American identity together under the rubric of secularism, and called himself a secularist rather than a Judaist by faith.[6] Science and print culture served as effective communicative tools for Kallen to promote his ideas, and these also became expressions of his Jewish identity as lived experience.

In 1933, reflecting on the relationship of the individual to the different social fields in which he lives, Kallen focused his attention on what he called "the living man," the one who exists in subjective relationships:

> Broadly speaking, the relation may be compared to the relation of a moving searchlight to the objects which it illuminates. The point of

illumination is the lamp, but the field which is illuminated is outside the lamp. As the lamp swings, the beam moves. Now one thing is illuminated, now another. The lamp, the light and the fields lit up are as the living man, his responsiveness and the social institutions he responds to. The lamp by illuminating them cuts them out of their context and establishes them in a special relationship to itself. They, being illuminated, limit and define the lamp's special field. Lamp and field determine each other reciprocally but not necessarily.[7]

The living man corresponds to the lamp, his responsiveness corresponds to the light, and the social institutions he responds to correspond to the fields. Taken together, they represent a totality of experience that is determined by the quality of the dynamic and reciprocal relationships between the living man and the fields of his engagement.

For Kallen, this implied the necessity of struggle—a struggle for the survival of integrity and individuality. The field of struggle was no longer nature but rather human relations, "enchanneled in the establishments of civilization itself."[8] Kallen's fashioning of Jewish identity entailed a Joban struggle to maintain his integrity and to support the integrity and diversity of the Jewish community. It also entailed modulating consistency with change. Kallen's early racialized view of Jewish identity was replaced by a faith in humanism in his later years, and these different ideas were connected through his changing conception of cultural pluralism. Kallen reflected upon the role of change in the struggle for identity:

When we say we struggle for our own survival, it isn't primarily the survival of the body that we struggle for. It's for a certain identity, a certain pattern, of the action of the body, of the living and thinking and feeling that are expressed in words and in habits of life and in ideals. So that, if you agree that human beings are different from each other, that each is struggling to live long, to make a personal history, and that that struggle which we call struggle for self-preservation is basically a process of self-alteration, because as soon as you stop altering, as soon as you really stay unchanged,

> you're dead. The living change, they alter. The dead are immortal. They can't die again, they never alter.[9]

Kallen's struggle to establish his place as an American Jew largely unfolded in the public square of the press. As a result, it became part of the American Jewish community's discourses concerning its sense of identity. As American Jews began to think through the implications of science and secularity, American Jewish modernity was born.

What I Believe and Why (1971), published when Kallen was eighty-nine years old, records a question posed to Kallen concerning the relationship of science to faith: "In the light of *the worldview that modern science is unfolding*, what grounds have you for religious convictions about cosmic reality?" Kallen responded, "I do not consider that modern science is unfolding one and only one worldview, or that it is committed to any. Science, insofar as it *is* science, is an ongoing method of inquiry, changing and improving as it goes on."[10] In a similar vein, Kallen had argued that democracy, insofar as it is a religion, requires a faith commitment to a process rather than to an object. Kallen had grown to believe that, properly construed, science and religion are not so much delimited fields of knowledge as they are orientations to living. So, too, was Kallen's sense of self as a Jew predicated not on a specific defining characteristic, but on his commitment to struggling to live as a Jew. Jewish identity describes an ongoing method of inquiry in its own right, with its vitality registered in the ongoing diversification of expressions of Jewish living.

Physics, Art, and Becoming

As Kallen saw it in 1933, philosophical Darwinism, which affirmed freedom, chance, individuality, and the flux of life, found further confirmation in the new developments of the physical sciences. They were "undergoing a revolution which restored chance, individuality and freedom to paramountcy," he wrote. "This revolution was initiated by the labors of Einstein and Planck and is still in process." Kallen felt that the physicists themselves, however, were not ready to face the implications of relativity and indeterminacy for the human condition:

"It has not yet influenced the hearts of men courageously to accept the individual, the relative, the contingent and to make the most of their opportunity." Instead, Kallen wrote, physicists such as Arthur Eddington, James Hopwood Jeans, and Robert Andrews Millikan "sublated" the insights of physics, chemistry, and astronomy "into the aspect of a divinity that shapes our ends happily."[11] As Kallen saw it, they allowed religion to subvert and co-opt science into serving an illusory teleology. He, by way of contrast, insisted on seeing indeterminacy as fundamental. The new scientific context merely confirmed for Kallen the Jamesian perspective on individuality and freedom that he had embraced all along.

In an undated interview held sometime after Einstein's death in 1955, Kallen contrasted his interpretation of relativity with that of Einstein:

> Einstein was first and last a determinist. I'm not. Einstein insisted that the articulation of cause and effect was made more precise rather than less precise by means of the concept of relativity, and he looked for the achievement of what he called the Unified Field in which the determinism would be more explicit and complete than ever. . . . The cosmic determinism is analogous to the determinism that's in Spinoza's philosophic system. And the identification of the two is a very important thing in the interpretation of Einstein's basic philosophic intention. Now, I myself am disposed to hold . . . that relativity makes a break, if one can see it, with the deterministic postulate, and that it had relations to the implications of the quantum theory.
>
> I think that he was so committed to the determinist postulate and so certain that the causal sequence could be discerned that he thought that the suggestion of chance could not be a deception on the part of the universe. Now, I agree that it could not be a deception, but for me, the consequence is that chance is real.[12]

Kallen suggested that Einstein could not admit the possibility that his theory of relativity showed that chance is real. He again articulated his commitment to a worldview of flux and chance—a premise basic to his views on freedom and individuality. These were views that, in the first two decades of the twentieth century, Kallen had held were the philosophical consequence of Darwinism, but now he found their philosophic home in the consequences of relativity and quantum theory. As ever, Kallen's continuing interest in science was in its utility in interpreting the human condition.

From about 1967 on, during the last decade of his life, Kallen found in the kinetic art of the Israeli artist Ya'acov Agam someone who had succeeded in translating quantum theory into an important affirmation and instantiation of individualism in the flux of life. Kallen called Agam the "Painter of Becoming." He regarded his work as an exemplar of the ethos of modernity, representing the artistic expression of Hebraism. Kallen preserved an article reporting on one of Agam's installations, in which a man is pictured wearing a shirt with the same color vertical stripes as the painting behind him. As the subject sways back and forth, a camera captures the movement as one blur of motion. The subject's position is indeterminate, and he is different from moment to moment. The elapse of time, the piece seems to be saying, allows us to perceive the continual process of "becoming."[13]

Einstein famously spoke of space-time; Kallen preferred to reverse the terms and speak of time-space. "I regard time as being more fundamental," he said, and "closer to basic reality."[14] Time was more fundamental for Kallen because he was interested in the human story of "becoming." Agam's approach to time, Kallen felt, affirmed his views on Hebraism and becoming. Agam himself confirmed the identification of his art and his concept of time with Hebraism. In another newspaper clipping that Kallen preserved, Agam is quoted as saying, "Today, in all forms of art, we fight against the past and against time. That's why whenever you look at a work of art, it recalls something that happened before. There is a different approach, the Hebrew concept. Its basic approach to life holds that man came from dust and returns to dust. Hebrew civilization teaches us that we cannot fight for eternity, we cannot fight time." Agam then connected this idea to Heisenberg's uncertainty principle: "According to Heisenberg's principle," says Agam, "it is impossible to measure the mass of a particle at the same time you measure its speed. If you can measure its speed, you can't measure its weight. We are forever without a total view of reality. We can only know it in part and in stages." . . . "A scientist," in Agam's view, "approaches life and reality today as a possibility. Life is a possibility, and it is important to try to create a visual expression to fit this new approach to modern science."[15] Agam had, in essence, captured in his art Kallen's Hebraism and his understanding of the modern ethos. Connecting science and philosophy through art allowed him to instantiate the contingency of identity in moments of time.

What it meant for Kallen to be a Jew, to be a human being, to be alive, and to live in the modern world is captured in this idea of "becoming." Kallen's continual "becoming" was the music of his "self-orchestration." We have seen how Kallen's views on race shifted, from craniometry to the psychophysical, and then to distancing himself from racial ideas and biology altogether. His views on religion shifted. His position in both Jewish and non-Jewish society shifted. Also, Kallen's relative influence in these various fields changed. However, through all of these changes, Kallen preserved his Joban "integrity," or, to refer once again to Kallen's orchestra metaphor, the "specific timbre and tonality" of his individuality.

Kallen as a Religious Thinker

This faith commitment to the uncertainties of becoming while staying grounded in one's integrity and individuality carries with it implications for Jewish living more generally. As Kallen worked through the conditions of his identity as a Jew, he also charted a path to Jewish living that corresponds with what Hilary Putnam theorizes as a pragmatist orientation to religion and ethics. Putnam points to Peirce, James, and Dewey as having provided the blueprint for such an approach. Ethical and religious inquiry may proceed along the lines of the scientific principles laid out by these thinkers—the principles of experiment, fallibilism, and communication. The principle of experiment is that ideas must be tested in practice. Cultural pluralism was, accordingly, a social hypothesis to be validated through experience, not through speculation. Cultural pluralism was never intended to be merely an abstract concept—it developed and was validated through lived experience.[16] The principle of fallibilism locates religious experience not in the absolute certainty attendant upon revelation, but in the uncertain and tentative manner in which one lives one's life. Religious inspiration, in this light, "uses the whole personality of a time-bound and culture-bound human being, who expresses what she or he takes to be truth in a language full of both cultural assumptions and personal idiosyncrasies."[17] Kallen's religious inspiration was that secularism and democracy are the best expressions of the principle of "live and help live."

The principle of communication states that truth "aspires to be public. Whatever your existential commitments may be, if you claim truth for them, you must be willing to discuss them." Kallen's oeuvre is one long record of his lifelong adherence to this principle. An idea "must happen and take a place in somebody's biography before it can figure as a concept in the architecture of a system intended for everybody," Kallen wrote in *Art and Freedom*. "The man's ideas, his philosophic faith with its logical system, serve him in fact as instruments of relation with the multitudes in their diversity and inner collectivity." Putnam joins this principle to James's "live and let live" because it entails a moral commitment to, in James's words, "be tolerant, *at least outwardly*, of everything that is not itself intolerant."[18] This commitment undergirded Kallen's entire philosophy.

Putnam argues that Wittgenstein, Kierkegaard, and Maimonides all teach that "your religion is not just a matter of what you say and what you publicly do, but a matter of the whole spirit in which you live your life." Kallen frames religion in similar terms, as a decision to bet one's life on certain values.[19] He bet his life on his conception of the modern ethos as Hebraism, embracing openness in science, creativity in arts, democracy, and moral autonomy and integrity. Kallen should be taken seriously as a religious thinker.

This is an important way of reframing the reception of Kallen, because scholarship has usually focused attention on the programmatic limitations of his thinking. Kallen's principle of "live and help live" is perhaps unsatisfying as a programmatic answer. But Kallen's views concerning the future prospects for, and desirability of, Jewish group cohesion should be understood not as a practical program but as a faith assertion. His self-professed faith of secularism was an expression of living Jewishly.

We began with Noah Efron's question of why science has proved so appealing to Jews. We have seen that for Kallen this is because science served as an instrument of relation to others. It could be plumbed for values and it was the shared intellectual currency through which the meaning of individuality and social solidarity could be shaped. It served as a liberating tool. In its ideal form, it offered openness where traditional religious life had seemed to him to stifle and constrain. More importantly, it could be deployed to make the case for Jewish incorporation into the civil sphere, a construction of social solidarity that, Jeffrey Alexander writes, is predicated on a secular faith. Through science, Kallen participated in what Jakob Egholm Feldt describes as a contribution discourse, which required that Jews demonstrate their civility.[20] The field of engagement with that discourse was science and print culture.

What Lionel Trilling describes as the modern moral frame of "authenticity," Kallen calls "integrity."[21] Kallen's life is emblematic of how Jewish identity is in constant flux. It emerges from what Charles Taylor describes as a discourse of recognition.[22] Kallen's philosophic faith in science, art, democracy, and secularism as approaches to preserve one's freedom and individuality are captured most simply in his idea of Job: "Perhaps the image of all art and of all science, of the entirety of civilization, the shining symbol of the first luster and the last of the human spirit, is . . . the man of Uz named Job, confronting the infinite and infinitely heedless Power which to him is God, to others Nature, declaring: 'Behold, he will slay me; I have no hope. Nevertheless will I maintain my ways before him.'"[23]

Notes

◆

Bibliography

◆

Index

◆ ◆ ◆

Notes

Introduction

1. Trilling, *Sincerity and Authenticity*; Taylor, "Politics of Recognition," 37.

2. Sander Gilman observes that the twentieth century gave rise to two models of multiculturalism that acquired a global resonance—the "hybrid" and "cultural diversity" models. He identifies Kallen as an originator of the latter. Daniel Greene shows how cultural pluralism grew out of American Jewish thought and was particularly linked to second-generation American Jews in the university who sought to spark a Jewish cultural renaissance. David Weinfeld describes cultural pluralism as "lived experience," rather than simply an abstract philosophical program, and, in tracing its development through Kallen's friendship with Alain Locke, provides an important corrective to Eric Goldstein concerning Kallen's place in American racial discourse. Kallen has been central to discourse concerning ethnicity in America and has been subjected to powerful critiques by scholars such as Werner Sollors and David Hollinger because of his apparent ethnocentrism and fixed notion of identity. Sarah Schmidt's valuable biography of Kallen chronicles his creation of a distinctively American form of Zionism, but Noam Pianko points out that Kallen's nationalism also developed out of a transatlantic discourse with British internationalists, thus linking him to the mix of cosmopolitan idealism with a paternalistic sense of noblesse oblige that that legacy implies. Jakob Egholm Feldt makes Kallen his protagonist in his treatment of transnationalism as a cultural intervention rooted in a migration perspective that views reality from a perspective simultaneously universalistic and particularistic. See Gilman, *Multiculturalism and the Jews*, 45; Greene, *Jewish Origins of Cultural Pluralism*; Weinfeld, "What Difference Does the Difference Make?"; Goldstein, *Price of Whiteness*, 179; Sollors, *Beyond Ethnicity*; Hollinger, *Postethnic America*; Schmidt, *Horace M. Kallen*; Pianko, *Zionism and the Roads Not Taken*; Egholm Feldt, *Transnationalism and the Jews.*

3. Howsam, *Old Books and New Histories*, 4.

4. Kallen, "Retrospect and Prospect," 251–52.

5. Hilary Putnam defends this pragmatist approach to religion. He argues that it is possible to articulate a faith commitment that arises out of Peirces's scientific

principles of experiment, fallibilism, and communication. It is a faith commitment without dogma, metaphysics, or certainty. See Putnam, "God and the Philosophers."

6. Kallen, *Individualism*, 6–7.
7. Higham, *Send These to Me*, 206.
8. Quoted in Higham, 206–7.
9. Kallen, *Individualism*, 10.
10. Kallen, "How I Bet My Life," 197; Kallen, "Promise of the Menorah Idea," 10.
11. Konvitz, "In Praise of Hyphenation and Orchestration," 17.
12. Kallen, "How I Bet My Life," 195, 197; emphasis in original.
13. Higham, *Send These to Me*, 209–10.
14. Toll, "Horace M. Kallen," 66.
15. Dewey, *Reflex Arc Concept in Psychology*.
16. The boxing image seems particularly apt because as a teenager Kallen sometimes engaged in street fighting, boxing in Boston's Scollay Square (an area now known as Government Center). See Weinfeld, "What Difference Does the Difference Make?" 35.
17. Veblen, "Intellectual Preeminence of Jews in Modern Europe"; Hollinger, "Why Are Jews Preeminent in Science and Scholarship?"; Bell, *Winding Passage*, 75.
18. Efron, *A Chosen Calling*, 7.
19. Kallen to Cronbach, January 4, 1928.
20. Hollinger, "Amalgamation and Hypodescent," 1366.
21. Alexander, *Civil Sphere*, 4.
22. Alexander, 54–55.
23. Kallen, *Secularism Is the Will of God*.
24. Alexander, *Civil Sphere*, 550.
25. Kallen, *Creativity, Imagination, Logic*, 198.
26. Quoted in Goren, *Dissenter in Zion*, 106.
27. Kallen, "Democracy versus the Melting Pot," 220.
28. Russell, *New Hopes for a Changing World*, 181.
29. Konvitz, "In Praise of Hyphenation and Orchestration," 19.
30. Kallen, *Creativity, Imagination, Logic*, vii.

1. Race, Hebraism, and Civility

1. "Is There a Jewish Race?"; "There Is No Jewish Race!"
2. "Question of Race."
3. Frank, "Jews, Multiculturalism, and Boasian Anthropology"; Morris-Reich, *Quest for Jewish Assimilation*; Matthews, *Quest for an American Sociology*.
4. Brown, "All, All Alone," 169.
5. Soltes, "Yiddish Press," 193; Diner, *In the Almost Promised Land*, 30–31.

6. Diner, *In the Almost Promised Land*, 89, 91.

7. Gerstle, "Protean Character of American Liberalism."

8. Gerstle, *American Crucible.*

9. Toll, "Horace M. Kallen," 73.

10. Weinfeld, "What Difference Does the Difference Make?"; Greene, *Jewish Origins of Cultural Pluralism.*

11. Higham, *Send These to Me*, 210. This claim is contested by Weinfeld.

12. Goldstein, *Price of Whiteness*, 35–36, 179; Weinfeld, "What Difference Does the Difference Make?" 168.

13. Cohen, "'Maccabaean's' Message," 164–65.

14. Young, *Colonial Desire*, 60.

15. Leonard, *Socrates and the Jews*, 10, 120, 127.

16. Fried, "Creating Hebraism, Confronting Hellenism."

17. Kallen, "Ethics of Zionism," 65, 67.

18. Ripley, *Races of Europe*, 390; see Efron, "Jewish Genetic Origins," 13–14.

19. He named Lucien Wolf and Konstantin Ikow. Kallen, "Ethics of Zionism," 67–68.

20. Efron argues that the Khazar theory has been at the forefront of scientific discourse about Jewish origins from that time into the present. See Efron, "Jewish Genetic Origins," 20–26.

21. Goldstein, *Price of Whiteness*, 179.

22. Gilman, *Case of Sigmund Freud*, 221.

23. Kallen, "How I Bet My Life," 197.

24. Kallen, "Ethics of Zionism," 64.

25. Kallen, 63–64, 68.

26. Wundt, *Elemente Der Völkerpsychologie*; see Klautke, *Mind of the Nation.*

27. Kallen, "Ethics of Zionism," 64, 71.

28. Efron, *Medicine and the German Jews*, 159, 164–65.

29. Pinsker, *Auto-Emancipation*, 3–4.

30. Lightman, "Spencer's American Disciples"; Francis, "Reforming Spencerians."

31. Macpherson, *Herbert Spencer*, 176.

32. Kallen, "Ethics of Zionism," 62; Interestingly, the idea that social organization proves at times to be an effective unit of selection has begun to resurface in sociological discourse. See Turner, "Herbert Spencer's Sociological Legacy."

33. I am indebted to Christopher Green, professor of psychology at York University, Toronto, for pointing me to the connection with Baldwin, and I am grateful to Andrew Winston, emeritus professor of psychology at the University of Guelph, Ontario, for his insight and assistance.

34. This is not to suggest that Kallen was gesturing toward the "Baldwin effect." He made no move to suggest that an organism's individual learning would,

through reproductive selection, affect the evolution of a species. See Simpson, "Baldwin Effect."

35. Baldwin, *Darwin and the Humanities*, 41.

36. Baldwin, 43; emphasis in original.

37. Kallen, "Zionism and the Struggle Towards Democracy," 379.

38. Quoted in Efron, *Defenders of the Race*, 90.

39. Kallen, "Judaism, Hebraism and Zionism," 182.

40. Kallen, 183.

41. Sarna, "American Jewish Press," 542; Madison, *Jewish Publishing in America*, 19; Vizetelly, "American Hebrew."

42. Kallen, "Value of Universal Judaism," 276–77.

43. Raisin, "On 'Universal Judaism'"; emphasis in original.

44. Schulman, "Last Word on the Rabbinical Conference," 3, 6–7; emphasis in original.

45. Kallen, "Judaism, Hebraism and Zionism," 181, 183.

46. "Persons Talked about."

47. See, for example, Kallen, "Judaism by Proxy."

48. Kallen, *Judaism at Bay*.

49. Kallen, "Hebraism and Current Tendencies in Philosophy," 497–98.

50. Kallen, 498.

51. James, "Great Men, Great Thoughts"; Francis, "Reforming Spencerians."

52. Hook and Konvitz, *Freedom and Experience*, viii; also quoted in Konvitz, "In Praise of Hyphenation and Orchestration," 19.

53. Jewett, *Science, Democracy, and the American University*, 12.

54. "Jews: A Study of Race and Environment."

55. "Jewish Race"; "No Jewish Race."

56. Myers, "Is There a Jewish Race?"

57. "Race and Environment."

58. See, for example, Jacobs, "Mendelism and the Jews"; "Jewish Race Problem"; Lipsky, "Are the Jews a Pure Race?"

59. Kallen, "Promise of the Menorah Idea," 11.

60. Kallen, "Jewish Publication Society."

61. Kallen.

62. "Hobby Horse of Race," 70.

63. Covitt, "Anthropology of the Jew," 391; "Anthropological Explanation."

64. Paul, *Controlling Human Heredity*.

65. Hart, *Healthy Jew*, 106.

66. Pearson to Kallen, January 6, 1908.

67. Kallen, "Judaism, Hebraism and Zionism," 183; emphasis in original.

68. Kallen, 183; emphasis in original.

69. Jacobs, "Mendelism and the Jews."
70. Reichler, *Jewish Eugenics*, 11, 17–18.
71. Rosen, *Preaching Eugenics*, 109.
72. "Jews a 'Recessive' Race Type."
73. Galton, "Photographic Composites"; Jacobs, "Jewish Type."
74. Jacobs, "Mendelism and the Jews."
75. Boas to Kallen, November 20, 1933; Kallen to Boas, November 21, 1933.
76. Efron, *Defenders of the Race*, 160.

2. Transnational Social Psychology and Nationality/Ethnicity

1. Kallen, "Third Annual Convention Luncheon," 130.

2. Egholm Feldt, "New Futures, New Pasts," 859.

3. See, for example, Smith, *Ethnic Origins of Nations*; Hutchinson, "Ethnicity and Modern Nations."

4. Korelitz, "Menorah Idea."

5. Sollors, *Invention of Ethnicity*, xiii; Kallen, "Nationality and the Hyphenated American"; Greene, *Jewish Origins of Cultural Pluralism*; see Hapgood, "Jews and American Democracy"; Bourne, "Jew and Trans-National America"; Dewey, "Principle of Nationality"; Zimmern, "Nationality in the Modern World"; Simon, "Religion and Nationality"; Berkson, "Community Theory of American Life."

6. Toll, "Ethnicity and Freedom," 161; Greene, *Jewish Origins of Cultural Pluralism*, 35, 39; "What Is the Menorah Movement?" 294; Hurwitz, "Menorah Movement," 50.

7. Greene, *Jewish Origins of Cultural Pluralism*, 16.

8. Greene, 31; see also Fried, "Creating Hebraism, Confronting Hellenism."

9. Kallen, "Third Annual Convention Luncheon"; emphasis in original.

10. Kallen to Hurwitz, July 26, 1916.

11. Kallen, "Promise of the Menorah Idea," 13.

12. Alexander, *Civil Sphere*, 8.

13. Dalton, *Theodore Roosevelt*, 462.

14. Intercollegiate Menorah Association, *Menorah Movement*, 84. Jacob Schiff, a prominent philanthropist and Jewish communal leader, was present at the dinner.

15. Intercollegiate Menorah Association, 83.

16. Toll, "Ethnicity and Freedom," 160; Toll, "Horace M. Kallen," 63; Greene, *Jewish Origins of Cultural Pluralism*, 67–74.

17. Kallen, "Promise of the Menorah Idea," 13. This perspective would later be adapted by Rabbi Mordecai Kaplan to serve his Reconstructionist program.

18. Intercollegiate Menorah Association, *Menorah Movement*, 84; emphasis in original.

19. Greene, *Jewish Origins of Cultural Pluralism*, 68.

20. "Editorial Statement," 1–2.

21. Krupnick, "Menorah Journal Group"; Korelitz, "Menorah Idea"; Alter, "Epitaph for a Jewish Magazine."

22. Alter, 55.

23. Greene, *Jewish Origins of Cultural Pluralism*, 13.

24. Hall, "Yankee and Jew," 87, 89.

25. Hall, 90.

26. Eliot, "Potency of the Jewish Race," 141–42.

27. Eliot, 144.

28. Kohler, "Third Annual Convention Luncheon," 129.

29. Board of the Hebrew Union College Literary Society to Kallen, January 6, 1915. Fifty years later, Kallen was awarded an honorary degree at Hebrew Union College's New York school, which points to the tremendous institutional changes that took place during the intervening decades. See Office of Public Relations to Kallen, March 15, 1965.

30. Kroeber, "Are the Jews a Race?" 290–91, 293.

31. Kroeber, 294.

32. Intercollegiate Menorah Association, *Menorah Movement*, 84.

33. "Editorial," 218.

34. "Editorial," 218; see Askowith, "Letter from the Menorah Journal," for the *Menorah Journal*'s response. It did not address the question of race, but strongly asserted that the *Menorah Journal* did not take sides on debatable issues.

35. Fishberg, *Jews*; Fishberg, "Assimilation," 25.

36. Fishberg, "Assimilation," 25, 27.

37. Fishberg, 29, 37.

38. Kallen to Mack, January 19, 1915.

39. Kallen to Mack, January 19, 1915; emphasis in original.

40. Kallen, "Zionism and the Struggle Towards Democracy," 379; Kallen, "Zionism and Democracy," 656.

41. Greene, *Jewish Origins of Cultural Pluralism*, 13.

42. Reprinted in Hart, *Jews and Race*, 256–57.

43. Efron, *Defenders of the Race*, 156.

44. Kallen, "Eugenic Aspects of the Jewish Problem," April 12, 1918, 655.

45. Weindling, "Evolution of Jewish Identity," 121, 123; Efron, *Defenders of the Race*, 160.

46. Reprinted in Hart, *Jews and Race*, 264.

47. Hirschler, "Basis for Jewish Consciousness."

48. Slavet, "Freud's Theory of Jewishness," 96; see also Sulloway, *Freud, Biologist of the Mind.*

49. Pianko, *Zionism and the Roads Not Taken*, 41–42.

50. Sluga, *Nation, Psychology, and International Politics*, 50.

51. Kallen, *Structure of Lasting Peace*, 29–30.

52. Kallen, 31.

53. Pianko, *Zionism and the Roads Not Taken*, 42.

54. Sluga, *Nation, Psychology, and International Politics*, 48.

55. Sluga, 45.

56. Quoted in Sluga, 45.

57. Konvitz, "In Praise of Hyphenation and Orchestration," 18.

58. Himmelfarb, *Jewish Odyssey of George Eliot*, 124.

59. Omer-Sherman, "Thy People Are My People"; Kotzin, *Judah L. Magnes*, 31, 345n40.

60. Schmidt, *Horace M. Kallen.*

61. Eliot, *Daniel Deronda*, 1236–37.

62. Kallen, "Eugenic Aspects of the Jewish Problem," March 29, 1918, 558.

63. Kallen, *Structure of Lasting Peace*, 30–31.

64. Kallen, "Democracy versus the Melting Pot," February 18, 1915, 194.

65. Eliot, *Daniel Deronda*, 1444.

66. Eliot, 1525–26.

67. Eliot, 1520–21.

68. Kalonymous, a common medieval Jewish name, was also Kallen's original family name. See Konvitz, "Horace M. Kallen," 145.

69. Eliot, *Daniel Deronda*, 1654, 1664.

70. Eliot, 1724–25.

71. Eliot, 1725, 1664; Kallen, "Democracy versus the Melting Pot," February 25, 1915, 220.

72. Kallen, *William James and Henri Bergson*; Kallen, "Nationality and the Hyphenated American," 79.

73. Kallen, "Nationality and the Hyphenated American," 80.

74. Kallen, 82.

75. Kallen, 80–81.

76. Kallen, 80.

77. Sollors, *Invention of Ethnicity*; Anderson, *Imagined Communities.*

78. Kallen, "Nationality and the Hyphenated American," 82–83.

79. Smith, *Ethnic Origins of Nations*, 15, 97.

80. Smith, 154.

81. Kallen, "Nationality and the Hyphenated American," 86.

82. Brandeis, *Jewish Problem.*

83. Schmidt, "Zionist Conversion of Louis D. Brandeis"; Schmidt, "Horace M. Kallen and the 'Americanization' of Zionism"; Schmidt, "Horace M. Kallen: The Zionist Chapter"; Schmidt, *Horace M. Kallen.*

84. Quoted in Mason, *Brandeis*, 442, 446.
85. Brandeis, *Jewish Problem*, 5–6.
86. Brandeis, 4–6, 8.
87. Brandeis, "Palestine and the Jewish Democracy."
88. Schulman, "Why American Jews Consider Zionism Undesirable," 40.
89. "Outlook's Opinion," 42.
90. Matthews, *Quest for an American Sociology*, 128.
91. Matthews, 36–37.
92. Shore, *Science of Social Redemption*, 83, 117.
93. See Green, "Darwinian Theory."
94. Goldberg, *Modernity and the Jews in Western Social Thought*, 99.
95. Berkson, *Theories of Americanization.*
96. Berkson, "Community Theory of American Life."
97. Berkson, 311.
98. Berkson, 311–12.
99. Berkson, 316.
100. Berkson, *Theories of Americanization*, 101–2.
101. Dewey, "Principle of Nationality," 203–4.
102. Berkson, *Theories of Americanization*, 117–18.
103. Kallen, "'Americanization' and the Cultural Prospect"; *pace* Greene, *Jewish Origins of Cultural Pluralism*, 89, who suggests that Kallen was persuaded by the mid-1920s to adopt the point of view of his critics—Berkson, Dewey, and Drachsler.
104. Kallen, "'Americanization' and the Cultural Prospect," 162–63.
105. Grant, *Passing of the Great Race.*
106. Hutchinson, "Ethnicity and Modern Nations," 653.

3. Darwinism and Democracy

1. Kallen, "Democracy versus the Melting Pot," February 18, 1915; Kallen, "Democracy versus the Melting Pot," February 25, 1915; see, for example, Sollors, *Theories of Ethnicity.*
2. Gleason, *Speaking of Diversity*; Greene, "A Chosen People in a Pluralist Nation"; Hattam, *In the Shadow of Race*; Higham, *Send These to Me*; Hollinger, *Postethnic America*; Konvitz, "In Praise of Hyphenation and Orchestration"; Pianko, "True Liberalism of Zionism"; Schmidt, *Horace M. Kallen*; Sollors, "Critique of Pure Pluralism"; Toll, "Horace M. Kallen."
3. This chapter appears, in modified form, in Kaufman, "Horace M. Kallen's Use of Evolutionary Theory."
4. Kallen, "Democracy versus the Melting Pot," February 18, 1915; Kallen, "Democracy versus the Melting Pot," February 25, 1915; Ross, *Old World in the New.*

5. For a fuller treatment of Ross's legacy, see Weinberg, *Edward Alsworth Ross and the Sociology of Progressivism*; Keith, "Foundations of an American Discipline."

6. Kallen, "Democracy versus the Melting Pot," February 18, 1915, 191.

7. US State Department, "Milestones."

8. Paul, "Darwin, Social Darwinism and Eugenics," 214–39.

9. Dewey to Kallen, March 31, 1915; emphasis in original.

10. Bourne, "Trans-National America"; Bourne, "Jew and Trans-National America"; Holt to Kallen, April 20, 1915; Kallen to Hurwitz, 1915.

11. Kallen to Hurwitz, 1915.

12. "'Nation's' Jubilee."

13. "Editorial," *American Israelite*, February 25, 1915.

14. "Editorial."

15. "Democracy versus the Melting Pot," March 5, 1915.

16. "Editorial: 'The Orchestration of Humanity.'"

17. Hart, *Healthy Jew.*

18. Kallen, *Culture and Democracy in the United States.*

19. Abstract in Bush, "Joint Meeting of the American and Western Philosophical Associations."

20. Bush, 94–95.

21. Bush, 95; emphasis in original.

22. Ross, *Old World in the New*, 30.

23. Ross, 17, 19.

24. Ross, 167.

25. Ross, 148, 160, 164–66; Kallen, "Democracy versus the Melting Pot," February 18, 1915, 193.

26. Darwin, *Descent of Man.*

27. Perry, *Moral Economy.*

28. Kallen, "Moral Economy."

29. Kallen, "Ethics of Zionism."

30. Kallen, "Judaism, Science and the 'New' Thought."

31. Kallen, "Judaism, Hebraism and Zionism," 182.

32. Kallen, "Democracy versus the Melting Pot," February 18, 1915, 191.

33. Kallen, 192–93.

34. Kallen, 193–94.

35. Kallen, 193–94.

36. Ross, *Old World in the New*, 239–40.

37. Quoted in Bush, "Joint Meeting of the American and Western Philosophical Associations," 95.

38. Kallen, "Democracy versus the Melting Pot," February 25, 1915, 220.

39. Kallen, "Democracy versus the Melting Pot," February 18, 1915, 192; emphasis in original.

40. Ross, *Old World in the New*, 287, 289–90, 300, 304.

41. Kallen, "Democracy versus the Melting Pot," February 18, 1915, 194.

42. Kallen, "Democracy versus the Melting Pot," February 25, 1915, 219.

43. Kallen, 219.

44. Kallen, 217–18.

45. Kallen, 219; emphasis in original.

46. Gilman, *Case of Sigmund Freud*, 226.

47. Kallen, "Democracy versus the Melting Pot," February 25, 1915, 220.

4. A Discontent of Hope

1. Pollack, *George Gershwin*, 297.

2. Oja, "Gershwin and American Modernists," 648–50.

3. Kallen, *Culture and Democracy in the United States.*

4. Kallen, "Democracy versus the Melting Pot," 96, 110; emphasis in original.

5. Kallen, *Culture and Democracy in the United States*, 1970; Kallen, *Culture and Democracy in the United States*, 1998.

6. Kallen, "Modernism," 564, 568.

7. Kallen, *Indecency and the Seven Arts*, xiv–xv.

8. Kallen, "Value and Existence in Art and in Religion," 273–76.

9. "Three American Philosophers Exploring Rome in Motor Car."

10. Kallen, "Maurice Sterne and His Times," 7.

11. Hook and Konvitz, *Freedom and Experience*, viii.

12. Kallen, "Maurice Sterne and His Times," 8, 11.

13. Kallen, "Hebraism and Current Tendencies in Philosophy," 498.

14. Kallen, *William James and Henri Bergson.*

15. Kallen, "James, Bergson, and Traditional Metaphysics," 239.

16. Kallen, *William James and Henri Bergson*, 27–28.

17. Kallen, 222–24; emphasis in original. Kallen misattributed spontaneous mutation to Darwin.

18. Kallen, "Value and Existence in Art and in Religion," 273, 276.

19. Kallen, *William James and Henri Bergson*, 229–30, 233.

20. "Dr. Horace Kallen, Philosopher, Dies"; Konvitz, "In Praise of Hyphenation and Orchestration," 18.

21. Holt to Kallen, February 28, 1918.

22. Kallen, "Politics, Profits, and Patriotism in Wisconsin"; Kallen to Donlin, March 18, 1918.

23. Kallen to Holt, April 9, 1918.

24. Kallen to Jastrow, February 28, 1919.

25. Kallen to Jastrow.

26. Kallen, *League of Nations*; Kallen, *Structure of Lasting Peace*.

27. Kallen to Billikopf, March 5, 1918.

28. Wilson to Kallen, September 30, 1918.

29. Kallen to Jastrow, February 28, 1919.

30. Croly to Kallen, December 21, 1918; Croly to Kallen, June 12, 1919.

31. Croly to Kallen, January 20, 1919.

32. Rutkoff and Scott, *New School*, 17–18.

33. Rutkoff and Scott, 27, 38, 79.

34. Rutkoff and Scott, 38.

35. Bell, *Winding Passage*, 75; Joost, "Dial in Transition," 287–88; Westbrook, *John Dewey and American Democracy*, 233; Wolin, *Rhetorical Imagination of Kenneth Burke*, 16–17.

36. Kallen, "Cosmic Systems and Philosophical Imagination."

37. Joost, "Dial in Transition," 283.

38. "An Announcement."

39. Clayton, *Forgotten Prophet*, 232.

40. Kallen to Johnson, January 24, 1918.

41. Kallen, *Structure of Lasting Peace*, vii.

42. Johnson to Kallen, December 3, 1917.

43. Kallen to Johnson, December 13, 1917.

44. Bell, *Winding Passage*, 75.

45. Britten to Kallen, December 28, 1917.

46. Donlin to Kallen, December 13, 1917.

47. Johnson to Kallen, December 11, 1917.

48. Kallen to Johnson, December 13, 1917.

49. Kallen to Donlin, January 11, 1918.

50. Kallen to Donlin, December 2, 1918.

51. Joost, *Scofield Thayer and the Dial*, 21.

52. Defries, "Stephen Haweis as a Civic Artist," 13.

53. Defries, *Interpreter Geddes*; Defries to Kallen, April 26, 1920.

54. Kallen to Defries, June 8, 1920.

55. Kallen, "Political Science as Psychology," 191.

56. Kallen, 190–91, 194.

57. Macrae to Kallen, August 4, 1922; Harcourt, Brace and Company to Kallen, August 21, 1922; Santon to Kallen, September 30, 1922; Kallen to MacVeagh, October 15, 1923; Latham to Croly, October 23, 1922; Kallen to Huebsch, October 28, 1922; Komroff to Kallen, November 10, 1923; Liveright to Kallen, April 5, 1924.

58. Kallen to Komroff, December 11, 1923.

59. Green, "Darwinian Theory, Functionalism, and the First American Psychological Revolution," 80.

60. Dewey, "Individuality, Equality, Superiority"; Lippmann, "Mental Age of Americans."

61. Dardis, *Firebrand.*

62. See Dardis; Gilmer, *Horace Liveright.*

63. Green, *Social Life of Poetry*, 686.

64. Gilmer, *Horace Liveright*, 8–9; Dardis, *Firebrand*, 51; see also Egleston, *House of Boni & Liveright.*

65. Green, *Social Life of Poetry*, 43; emphasis in original.

66. Kallen, "Political Science as Psychology," 190, 194.

67. Matthews, "Making America a Racial Crazy-Quilt"; Munro and Hanford, "Book Reviews"; O'Brien, "Book Review"; Roosevelt, "Professor Kallen Proposes to Balkanize America"; Russell, "Americanization"; Smertenko, "Course Charted"; "Book Reviews"; Boni & Liveright, "Royalty Statement," June 30, 1924; Boni & Liveright, "Royalty Statement," June 30, 1925; Liveright to Kallen, June 18, 1930.

68. Schoenbach, *Pragmatic Modernism*, 13.

69. Kallen, *Culture and Democracy in the United States*, 1970, 16.

70. See Rorty, *Objectivity, Relativism, and Truth*, 1:93ff.; Schoenbach, *Pragmatic Modernism.*

71. Sarna, "Two Ambitious Goals," 377.

72. See Gilmer, *Horace Liveright*, 8–9; Green, *Social Life of Poetry*, 44.

5. On Job, Secularization, and Psychology

1. Wisconsin Dramatic Society, "Rise of the Curtain," 5–6; Ewell, "Arts Wisconsin."

2. "To Stage 'Book of Job'"; "Domestic Notes."

3. Feuer, "Horace M. Kallen on War and Peace."

4. Meyer, *Response to Modernity*, 305.

5. Larrimore, *Book of Job*, 154ff.

6. Eliot, "Jewish Contribution to Modern Social Ethics."

7. Kallen, "Horace M. Kallen"; Kallen, *Book of Job as a Greek Tragedy*; Schmidt, *Messages of the Poets*, 105–6.

8. Taylor, *Secular Age*; Schmidt to Kallen, October 25, 1911.

9. Schmidt, *Messages of the Poets*, 7:102; Kallen to Hurwitz, October 27, 1913.

10. Hurwitz to Kallen, November 22, 1915; "Domestic Notes."

11. Kallen to Hurwitz, March 2, 1917.

12. Kallen, *Book of Job as a Greek Tragedy*, 7, 77–78.

13. Kallen, "Untitled," n.d.

14. Haigh, *Tragic Drama of the Greeks*, 217–26.

15. Kallen, *Book of Job as a Greek Tragedy*, 37, 68.

16. Kallen, "Hebraism and Current Tendencies in Philosophy."

17. Kallen, *Book of Job as a Greek Tragedy*, 78.

18. Greene, *Jewish Origins of Cultural Pluralism*, 96; Kallen, *Book of Job as a Greek Tragedy*, x; Wolfson to Kallen, March 17, 1918.

19. Montefiore, "Book Reviews," 221–22; emphasis in original.

20. Interestingly, a recent take on Job by a Reform rabbi echoes some of Kallen's ideas. See Fried, "Job and Leviathan," 30–48.

21. Kallen, *Culture and Democracy in the United States*, 202.

22. Montefiore, "Book Reviews," 223–24.

23. Montefiore, *Liberal Judaism and Hellenism*, 190, 230.

24. Kallen, *Book of Job as a Greek Tragedy*, 45.

25. "Editor's Note," 51.

26. Murray, "Job as a Greek Tragedy," 93–96; Radin, "A Mistaken Hypothesis," 97–103; Walker, "Book of Job on the Stage," 104–8.

27. "Editor's Note," 103.

28. Free Synagogue, "Free Synagogue Presents the Book of Job."

29. Kallen, *Book of Job as a Greek Tragedy*, 77.

30. Kallen, *Why Religion*, 282–83.

31. Kallen, *Warfare of Religion Against Science*; Palmer, *Emanuel Haldeman-Julius*; Heinze, *Jews and the American Soul*, 129.

32. Draper, *History of the Conflict between Science and Religion*; White, *History of the Warfare of Science*; Kallen, "Warfare of Religion against Science," 115.

33. Kallen, "Warfare of Religion against Science," 1948, 93.

34. Kallen, "Political Science as Psychology," 181–203.

35. Kallen, "Warfare of Religion against Science," 1948, 126–27.

36. Kallen, 127.

37. The tendency to essentialize "science" and "religion" persisted in scholarship until the 1970s, when studies like Moore, *Post-Darwinian Controversies* began to explore a nonessentialized approach. For an excellent overview of how religion and science came to be constructed as categories, see Harrison, *Territories of Science and Religion*.

38. Santayana and Holzberger, *Letters of George Santayana*, 296.

39. Herder, "Education for the Masses."

40. Kallen, *Liberal Spirit*, vi.

41. Heinze, *Jews and the American Soul*, 128–30; Hollinger, *Science, Jews, and Secular Culture*.

42. Hedstrom, *Rise of Liberal Religion*, 72–73.

43. James, *Varieties of Religious Experience*; Meador, "My Own Salvation," 282.

44. Quoted in Meador, 270; see also Hedstrom, *Rise of Liberal Religion*, 72. Both Meador and Hedstrom cite Niebuhr as evidence of the secularization wrought by psychology upon Protestant Christianity in America.

45. James, *Varieties of Religious Experience.*

46. Dewey, *Reflex Arc Concept in Psychology*; Green, "Darwinian Theory, Functionalism," 75–83.

47. Kallen, *Why Religion*, 286.

48. Kallen, 283.

49. Luker, "Wieman, Henry Nelson."

50. Wieman, *Wrestle of Religion with Truth*, 151–52, 158–59.

51. Kallen, "Wrestle of Religion with Truth," 277–78.

52. Meyer, *Response to Modernity*, 317.

53. Heinze, *Jews and the American Soul*, 208.

54. Meyer, *Response to Modernity*, 315.

55. Liebman, *Peace of Mind*; Heinze, *Jews and the American Soul*, 215, 230.

56. "Abraham Cronbach Papers"; Meyer, *Response to Modernity*, 317; Cronbach, "Psychoanalysis and Religion," 588–99.

57. Kallen, "Can Judaism Survive in the United States?" 545, 555.

58. Silver, "Why Do the Heathen Rage?" 364–87; Greene, *Jewish Origins of Cultural Pluralism*, 146–47.

59. Kallen to Cronbach, December 22, 1927.

60. Kallen to Cronbach, January 4, 1928.

61. Kallen to Cronbach, January 4, 1928.

62. Meyer, *Response to Modernity*, 302, 317.

63. Cronbach, Weitz, and Hebrew Union College, *Religion and Its Social Setting.*

64. Weitz to Kallen, April 3, 1933; emphasis in original.

65. Meyer, *Response to Modernity*, 317.

66. Kallen to Weitz, June 3, 1932.

67. Cronbach, "Psychoanalytic Study of Judaism," 605–740; Cronbach to Kallen, November 25, 1932.

68. Cronbach to Kallen, November 17, 1931.

69. Cronbach to Kallen, November 17, 1931.

70. Kallen, "Introduction to Forthcoming Volume," 5.

71. Cronbach to Kallen, April 2, 1933.

72. Kallen, *Judaism at Bay*; Weitz to Kallen, June 14, 1932.

6. On Secular Religion and Democracy

1. Reisch, *How The Cold War Transformed Philosophy of Science*, 170.

2. Katznelson, *Fear Itself*, 10.

3. Quoted in Katznelson, 49.

4. "Unity—April 2, 1934," April 2, 1934.

5. Musher, *Democratic Art*, 3.

6. Russak to Kallen, July 2, 1937; Toch to Russak, July 17, 1937; Russak to Kallen, September 4, 1937.

7. Kallen to Loving, January 15, 1936.

8. Beuttler, "Organizing an American Conscience."

9. Gilbert, *Redeeming Culture*, 86–87, 92.

10. Quoted in Gilbert, 85.

11. Gilbert, 85.

12. Kallen to Ames, April 27, 1943.

13. Gilbert, *Redeeming Culture*, 84, 87–89.

14. Kallen, "National Solidarity and the Jewish Minority," 21.

15. Fisch to Kallen, September 1, 1942.

16. Kallen, "National Solidarity and the Jewish Minority," 21.

17. Kallen, "National Being and the Jewish Community," 77.

18. Kallen, "National Solidarity and the Jewish Minority," 21.

19. Kallen to Roosevelt, March 1, 1945; emphasis in original.

20. Kallen, "Jewish Right, Christian Power," 98.

21. Kallen, 98.

22. Kallen, "Democracy's True Religion," July 28, 1951, 6–7; Kallen, *Democracy's True Religion.*

23. Kallen, *Democracy's True Religion*, 1951, 9–10.

24. Kallen, 15.

25. Kallen, *Why Religion*, 90; Kallen, *Secularism Is the Will of God.*

26. See Omer, "Defending a Religion Called Judaism," 322. See also Omer-Sherman, "Rethinking Eliot, Jewish Identity, and Cultural Pluralism"; Schuchard, "Burbank with a Baedeker, Eliot with a Cigar"; Perloff, "A Response to Ronald Schuchard." Omer's "It Is I Who Have Been Defending a Religion Called Judaism" inspired a debate among literary scholars in a special section of *Modernism/Modernity* in 2003 (10, no. 1), in which Ronald Schuchar and six other scholars debate the issue. Anecdotes related by Schuchard make it clear that Eliot's respect for Kallen was deep and genuine. Omer-Sherman and Schuchard take Eliot's correspondence as evidence that he did not see Kallen as his "pet Jew," which is a common trope with anti-Semites like Ezra Pound. Marjorie Perloff, however, rejects their interpretation. Our purpose here, however, is not to evaluate Eliot's views but to explore Kallen's ideas and intentions more thoroughly.

27. Omer, "Defending a Religion Called Judaism," 322, 328.

28. Kallen, "Retrospect and Prospect," 248.

29. Kallen to Eliot, December 23, 1954.

30. Kallen to Eliot, December 23, 1954.

31. Eliot to Kallen, November 26, 1954.

32. Kallen to Eliot, December 23, 1954.

33. Quoted in Omer, "Defending a Religion Called Judaism," 348.

34. Kallen to Eliot, Letter, May 6, 1955.

35. Quoted in Schuchard, "Burbank with a Baedeker, Eliot with a Cigar," 19.

36. Quoted in Gilbert, *Redeeming Culture*, 92.

37. Kallen to Eliot, December 23, 1954.

38. Kallen, *Secularism Is the Will of God*, 95; emphasis in original.

39. Kallen, *Cultural Pluralism and the American Idea*, 87.

40. Kallen, 87.

41. Kallen, 87–88.

42. Herberg, *Protestant, Catholic, Jew*; Herberg, "Religion in a Secularized Society," 155.

43. Herberg, "Religion in a Secularized Society," 157.

44. Marsden, *Twilight of the American Enlightenment*, 131.

45. Herberg, "Religion in a Secularized Society," 158.

46. Kallen, *What I Believe and Why*, 148.

47. Kallen, "'Jew' and 'Judaist,'" 7.

48. Murrow, "Introduction."

49. "This I Believe," written by Horace Kallen, is part of the *This I Believe Essay Collection*, thisibelieve.org. Copyright © 2005–2018 by This I Believe, Inc. Used with permission.

50. MacLeish, *J. B.*

51. Kallen, *The Book of Job as a Greek Tragedy*, vii–xvi.

52. Frost, *A Masque of Reason*, xvi.

53. Omer, "Defending a Religion Called Judaism," 328. Omer also notes that the original 1918 version was probably the first work by Kallen that Eliot had ever read.

54. Kallen, "Retrospect and Prospect," 251.

55. Kallen to Wang, June 9, 1959.

56. Kallen, "Whither Israel," 132, 141, 143.

57. Kallen, *Utopians at Bay*, 290.

58. Kallen, *Humanisms.*

Epilogue

1. Kallen, *What I Believe and Why*, 181–86.

2. Winston, letter to Kaufman, March 18, 2017. He draws a parallel with Gayatri Chakravorty Spivak's notion of "strategic essentialism."

3. Kallen, *What I Believe and Why*, 184.

4. Baker, *Jew*, 104–10, 142–48; Greenberg, "'I'm Not White—I'm Jewish,'" 45, 50; see also Glenn and Sokoloff, *Boundaries of Jewish Identity*; Slavet, "Freud's Theory of Jewishness," 96–111.

5. Kallen, *What I Believe and Why*, 175; emphasis in original.

6. Kallen, 148.

7. Kallen, *Individualism*, 33–34.

8. Kallen, 110.

9. Kallen, "Humanisms."

10. Kallen, "This Is My Faith," 139, 145; emphasis in original.

11. Kallen, *Individualism*, 125–26.

12. Kallen, interview by John Irvin.

13. Kallen, "Hebraism and Modernity."

14. Kallen, interview by John Irvin.

15. Kallen, "Hebraism and Modernity."

16. See Weinfeld, "What Difference Does the Difference Make?"

17. Putnam, "God and the Philosophers," 182–83.

18. Kallen, *Art and Freedom*, 16; quoted in Putnam, 183.

19. Kallen, "How I Bet My Life," 189–201.

20. Alexander, *Civil Sphere*; Feldt, "New Futures, New Pasts," 855.

21. Trilling, *Sincerity and Authenticity*.

22. Taylor, "Politics of Recognition," 25–73.

23. Kallen, *Art and Freedom*, 963.

Bibliography

Abraham Cronbach Papers. Jacob Rader Marcus Center of the American Jewish Archives, Cincinnati.

Alexander, Jeffrey C. *The Civil Sphere.* Oxford: Oxford Univ. Press, 2006.

Alter, Robert. "Epitaph for a Jewish Magazine: Notes on the 'Menorah Journal.'" *Commentary* 39, no. 5 (1965): 51–55.

Anderson, Benedict. *Imagined Communities: Reflections on the Origin and Spread of Nationalism.* London: Verso, 1991.

"An Announcement." *Dial*, January 25, 1917.

"Anthropological Explanation of the Facial Aspect of the Jew." *American Israelite*, October 5, 1916.

Askowith, Hyman. "A Letter from the Menorah Journal." *American Jewish Chronicle*, February 22, 1918.

Baker, Cynthia M. *Jew.* New Brunswick, NJ: Rutgers Univ. Press, 2017.

Baldwin, J. Mark. *Darwin and the Humanities.* Baltimore: Review Publishing Company, 1909.

Bell, Daniel. *The Winding Passage: Essays and Sociological Journeys, 1960–1980.* Cambridge, MA: Abt Books, 1980.

Berkson, Isaac B. "A Community Theory of American Life: The Problem of Adjustment in the Light of Jewish Experience." *Menorah Journal*, December 1920, 311–21.

———. *Theories of Americanization: A Critical Study, with Special Reference to the Jewish Group.* New York: Teachers College, Columbia Univ., 1920.

Beuttler, Fred W. "Organizing an American Conscience: The Conference on Science, Philosophy and Religion, 1940–1968. (Volumes I–III)." ProQuest Dissertations Publishing, 1995. https://www.proquest.com/products-services/dissertations/.

Board of the Hebrew Union College Literary Society. Letter to Horace Kallen, January 6, 1915, manuscript collection 1, box 13, folder 1, Jacob Rader Marcus Center of the American Jewish Archives, Cincinnati.

Boas, Franz. Letter to Horace M. Kallen, November 20, 1933. RG 317, folder 629, Horace Kallen Papers, YIVO Institute for Jewish Research, New York.

Boni & Liveright. "Royalty Statement." June 30, 1924. RG 317, folder 59, Horace Kallen Papers, YIVO Institute for Jewish Research, New York.

———. "Royalty Statement." June 30, 1925, RG 317, folder 59, Horace Kallen Papers, YIVO Institute for Jewish Research, New York.

"Book Reviews." *Advocate of Peace through Justice* 86, no. 9/10 (October 1924): 574–75.

Bourne, Randolph. "The Jew and Trans-National America." *Menorah Journal*, December 1916.

———. "Trans-National America." *Atlantic Monthly*, July 1916.

Brandeis, Louis D. "Palestine and the Jewish Democracy." *Outlook*, January 5, 1916.

———. *The Jewish Problem: How to Solve It.* New York: Zionist Essays Publication Committee, 1915.

Britten, Clarence. Letter to Horace Kallen, December 28, 1917, manuscript collection 1, box 7, folder 15, Jacob Rader Marcus Center of the American Jewish Archives, Cincinnati.

Brown, Michael Gary. "All, All Alone: The Hebrew Press in America from 1914 to 1924." *American Jewish Historical Quarterly* 59, no. 2 (1969): 139–78.

Bush, Wendell T. "The Joint Meeting of the American and Western Philosophical Associations." *Journal of Philosophy, Psychology and Scientific Methods* 12, no. 4 (February 1915): 93–108. https://doi.org/10.2307/2013312.

Clayton, Bruce. *Forgotten Prophet: The Life of Randolph Bourne.* Baton Rouge: Louisiana State Univ. Press, 1984.

Cohen, Naomi W. "'The Maccabaean's' Message: A Study in American Zionism until World War I." *Jewish Social Studies* 18, no. 3 (1956): 163–78.

Covitt, Louis D. "The Anthropology of the Jew." *Monist* 26, no. 3 (July 1916): 366–96.

Croly, Herbert. Western Union Telegram to Horace M. Kallen. January 20, 1919, manuscript collection 1, box 7, folder 2, Jacob Rader Marcus Center of the American Jewish Archives, Cincinnati.

———. Letter to Horace Kallen. December 21, 1918, manuscript collection 1, box 7, folder 2, Jacob Rader Marcus Center of the American Jewish Archives, Cincinnati.

———. Letter to Horace M. Kallen. June 12, 1919, manuscript collection 1, box 7, folder 2, Jacob Rader Marcus Center of the American Jewish Archives, Cincinnati.

Cronbach, Abraham. "Psychoanalysis and Religion." *Journal of Religion* 2, no. 6 (November 1922): 588–99. https://doi.org/10.2307/1195526.

———. "The Psychoanalytic Study of Judaism." *Hebrew Union College Annual* 8/9 (January 1931): 605–740.

———. Letter to Horace Kallen. November 17, 1931, manuscript collection 1, box 51, folder 4, Jacob Rader Marcus Center of the American Jewish Archives, Cincinnati.

———. Letter to Horace Kallen. November 25, 1932, manuscript collection 1, box 51, folder 4, Jacob Rader Marcus Center of the American Jewish Archives, Cincinnati.

———. Letter to Horace Kallen. April 2, 1933, manuscript collection 1, box 51, folder 4, Jacob Rader Marcus Center of the American Jewish Archives, Cincinnati.

Cronbach, Abraham, Martin M. Weitz, and Hebrew Union College. *Religion and Its Social Setting: Together with Other Essays.* Cincinnati: Social Press, 1933.

Dalton, Kathleen. *Theodore Roosevelt: A Strenuous Life.* New York: Alfred A. Knopf, 2002.

Dardis, Tom. *Firebrand: The Life of Horace Liveright.* 1st ed. New York: Random House, 1995.

Darwin, Charles. *The Descent of Man, and Selection in Relation to Sex.* 2 vols. London: J. Murray, 1871.

Defries, Amelia. Letter to Horace Kallen. April 26, 1920, manuscript collection 1, box 7, folder 11, Jacob Rader Marcus Center of the American Jewish Archives, Cincinnati.

Defries, Amelia Dorothy. "Stephen Haweis as a Civic Artist." *American Magazine of Art* 8, no. 1 (1916): 13–18.

———. *The Interpreter Geddes: The Man and His Gospel.* New York: Boni & Liveright, 1928.

"Democracy versus the Melting Pot." *American Hebrew and Jewish Messenger*, March 5, 1915.

Dewey, John. "Individuality, Equality, Superiority." *New Republic*, December 13, 1922.

———. "The Principle of Nationality." *Menorah Journal*, October 1917.

———. *The Reflex Arc Concept in Psychology.* Chicago: Univ. of Chicago Press, 1896.

———. Letter to Horace Kallen. March 31, 1915, manuscript collection 1, box 7, folder 13, Jacob Rader Marcus Center of the American Jewish Archives, Cincinnati.

Diner, Hasia. *In the Almost Promised Land: American Jews and Blacks, 1915–1935.* Baltimore: Johns Hopkins Univ. Press, 1995.

"Domestic Notes: Happenings of Interest in American Jewry." *Jewish Exponent*, January 2, 1914.

Donlin, George. Letter to Horace Kallen. December 13, 1917, manuscript collection 1, box 7, folder 18, Jacob Rader Marcus Center of the American Jewish Archives, Cincinnati.

"Dr. Horace Kallen, Philosopher, Dies." *New York Times*, February 17, 1974.

Draper, John William. *History of the Conflict between Science and Religion.* New York: D. Appleton & Company, 1875.

"Editorial." *American Israelite*, February 25, 1915.

"Editorial." *American Jewish Chronicle*, December 28, 1917.

"Editorial: 'The Orchestration of Humanity.'" *American Hebrew and Jewish Messenger*, March 5, 1915.

"Editor's Note." *Menorah Journal*, February 1919, 51.

"Editor's Note." *Menorah Journal*, April 1919, 103.

"An Editorial Statement." *Menorah Journal*, January 1915.

Efron, John M. *Defenders of the Race: Jewish Doctors and Race Science in Fin-de-Siècle Europe.* New Haven, CT: Yale Univ. Press, 1994.

———. "Jewish Genetic Origins in the Context of Past Historical and Anthropological Inquiries." *Human Biology Open Access Pre-Prints*, Paper 42 (2013). http://digitalcommons.wayne.edu/humbiol_preprints/42.

———. *Medicine and the German Jews: A History.* New Haven, CT: Yale Univ. Press, 2001.

Efron, Noah J. *A Chosen Calling: Jews in Science in the Twentieth Century.* Baltimore: Johns Hopkins Univ. Press, 2014.

Egholm Feldt, Jakob. "New Futures, New Pasts: Horace M. Kallen and the Contribution of Jewishness to the Future." *European Review of History: Revue Européenne d'histoire* 23, no. 5/6 (November 2016): 847–62. https://doi.org/10.1080/13507486.2016.1203873.

———. *Transnationalism and the Jews: Culture, History, and Prophecy.* London : Rowman & Littlefield, 2016.

Egleston, Charles, ed. *The House of Boni & Liveright, 1917–1933: A Documentary Volume.* Detroit: Gale, 2004.

Eliot, Charles W. "The Jewish Contribution to Modern Social Ethics." *Menorah Journal*, June 1919.

———. "The Potency of the Jewish Race." *Menorah Journal*, June 1915, 141–44.

Eliot, George. *Daniel Deronda.* Project Gutenberg, 2010 [1876]. https://www.gutenberg.org/ebooks/7469.

Eliot, T. S. Letter to Horace M. Kallen. November 26, 1954, Horace M. Kallen research files, NS.02.15.01, box 2, folder 25, New School Archives and Special Collections, New York.

Ewell, Maryo Gard. "Arts Wisconsin." *Learning from the Past for a Creative Future* (blog), January 6, 2017. http://www.artswisconsin.org/learning-from-the-past-for-a-creative-future/.

Feuer, Lewis S. "Horace M. Kallen on War and Peace." *Modern Judaism* 4, no. 2 (May 1984): 201–13. https://doi.org/10.2307/1396462.

Fisch, Anna. Letter to Horace M. Kallen. September 1, 1942, RG 317, folder 58B, Horace Kallen Papers, YIVO Institute for Jewish Research, New York.

Fishberg, Maurice. "Assimilation: A Statement of Facts by a Scientist." *Menorah Journal*, February 1920, 25–37.

———. *The Jews: A Study of Race and Environment.* London: Walter Scott Publishing Company, 1911.

Francis, Mark. "The Reforming Spencerians: William James, Josiah Royce and John Dewey." In *Global Spencerism: The Communication and Appropriation of a British Evolutionist*, edited by Bernard Lightman, 103–22. Leiden, Netherlands: Brill, 2016.

Frank, Gelya. "Jews, Multiculturalism, and Boasian Anthropology." *American Anthropologist* 99 (1997): 731–45.

Free Synagogue. "Free Synagogue Presents the Book of Job in the Form of a Greek Tragedy as Restored by Horace Meyer Kallen." 1926. NS.02.15.01, box 1, folder 16, Horace M. Kallen research files, New School Archives and Special Collections, New York.

Fried, Benj. "Job and Leviathan: A Biblical Counter-Narrative for a Theology of Chaos." *CCAR Journal: The Reform Jewish Quarterly* 65, no. 3 (Summer 2017): 30–48.

Fried, Lewis. "Creating Hebraism, Confronting Hellenism: The Menorah Journal and Its Struggle for the Jewish Imagination." *American Jewish Archives Journal* 53 (2001): 147–74.

Frost, Robert. *A Masque of Reason*. New York: H. Holt, 1945.

Galton, Francis. "Photographic Composites." *Photographic News*, April 17, 1885, 234–45.

Gerstle, Gary. *American Crucible: Race and Nation in the Twentieth Century*. Princeton, NJ: Princeton Univ. Press, 2017.

———. "The Protean Character of American Liberalism." *American Historical Review* 99, no. 4 (1994): 1043–73.

Gilbert, James. *Redeeming Culture: American Religion in an Age of Science*. Chicago: Univ. of Chicago Press, 1997.

Gilman, Sander L. *Multiculturalism and the Jews*. London: Routledge, 2006.

———. *The Case of Sigmund Freud: Medicine and Identity at the Fin De Siècle*. Baltimore: Johns Hopkins Univ. Press, 1993.

Gilmer, Frank Walker. *Horace Liveright: Publisher of the Twenties*. New York: David Lewis, 1970.

Gleason, Philip. *Speaking of Diversity: Language and Ethnicity in Twentieth-Century America*. Baltimore: Johns Hopkins Univ. Press, 1992.

Glenn, Susan A., and Naomi B. Sokoloff, eds. *Boundaries of Jewish Identity*. Seattle: Univ. of Washington Press, 2010.

Goldberg, Chad Alan. *Modernity and the Jews in Western Social Thought*. Chicago: Univ. of Chicago Press, 2017.

Goldstein, Eric L. *The Price of Whiteness: Jews, Race, and American Identity*. Princeton, NJ: Princeton Univ. Press, 2006.

Goren, Arthur. *Dissenter in Zion: From the Writings of Judah L. Magnes*. Cambridge, MA: Harvard Univ. Press, 1982.

Grant, Madison. *The Passing of the Great Race: Or, the Racial Basis of European History*. New York: Charles Scribner's Sons, 1916.

Green, Chris. *The Social Life of Poetry: Appalachia, Race, and Radical Modernism.* Basingstoke, UK: Palgrave Macmillan, 2009.

Green, Christopher D. "Darwinian Theory, Functionalism, and the First American Psychological Revolution." *American Psychologist* 64, no. 2 (2009): 75–83.

Greenberg, Cheryl. "'I'm Not White—I'm Jewish': The Racial Politics of American Jews." In *Race, Color, Identity: Rethinking Discourses about "Jews" in the Twenty-First Century,* edited by Efraim Sicher, 35–55. New York: Berghahn Books, 2013.

Greene, Daniel. "A Chosen People in a Pluralist Nation: Horace Kallen and the Jewish-American Experience." *Religion and American Culture* 16, no. 2 (2006): 161–94.

———. *The Jewish Origins of Cultural Pluralism: The Menorah Association and American Diversity.* Bloomington: Indiana Univ. Press, 2011.

Haigh, A. E. *The Tragic Drama of the Greeks.* Oxford: Clarendon Press, 1896.

Hall, G. Stanley. "Yankee and Jew: An After-Dinner Address." *Menorah Journal,* April 1915, 87–90.

Hapgood, Norman. "The Jews and American Democracy." *Menorah Journal,* October 1916, 201–5.

Harcourt, Brace and Company. Letter to Horace M. Kallen. August 21, 1922, RG 317, folder 218, Horace Kallen Papers, YIVO Institute for Jewish Research, New York.

Harrison, Peter. *The Territories of Science and Religion.* Chicago: Univ. of Chicago Press, 2015.

Hart, Mitchell Bryan, ed. *Jews and Race: Writings on Identity and Difference, 1880–1940.* Waltham, MA: Brandeis Univ. Press, 2011.

———. *The Healthy Jew: The Symbiosis of Judaism and Modern Medicine.* Cambridge: Cambridge Univ. Press, 2007.

Hattam, Victoria. *In the Shadow of Race: Jews, Latinos, and Immigrant Politics in the United States.* Chicago: Univ. of Chicago Press, 2007.

Hedstrom, Matthew. *The Rise of Liberal Religion: Book Culture and American Spirituality in the Twentieth Century.* Oxford: Oxford Univ. Press, 2013.

Heinze, Andrew R. *Jews and the American Soul: Human Nature in the Twentieth Century.* Princeton, NJ: Princeton Univ. Press, 2004.

Herberg, Will. *Protestant, Catholic, Jew: An Essay in American Religious Sociology*. New York: Doubleday, 1955.

———. "Religion in a Secularized Society: The New Shape of Religion in America (Lecture I)." *Review of Religious Research* 3, no. 4 (April 1962): 145–58.

Herder, Dale Marvin. "Education for the Masses: The Haldeman-Julius Little Blue Books as Popular Culture during the Nineteen-Twenties." PhD diss., Michigan State University, 1975.

Higham, John. *Send These to Me: Jews and Other Immigrants in Urban America*. New York: Atheneum, 1975.

Himmelfarb, Gertrude. *The Jewish Odyssey of George Eliot*. New York: Encounter Books, 2009.

Hirschler, René. "A Basis for Jewish Consciousness." In *Jews and Diaspora Nationalism: Writings on Jewish Peoplehood in Europe and the United States*, edited by Simon Rabinovitch, 182–88. Waltham, MA: Brandeis Univ. Press, 2012.

"The Hobby Horse of Race." *American Hebrew and Jewish Messenger*, May 15, 1914.

Hollinger, David A. "Amalgamation and Hypodescent: The Question of Ethnoracial Mixture in the History of the United States." *American Historical Review* 108, no. 5 (December 2003): 1363–90. https://doi.org/10.1086/529971.

———. *Postethnic America: Beyond Multiculturalism*. New York: Basic Books, 1995.

———. *Science, Jews, and Secular Culture: Studies in Mid-Twentieth-Century American Intellectual History*. Princeton, NJ: Princeton Univ. Press, 1996.

———. "Why Are Jews Preeminent in Science and Scholarship? The Veblen Thesis Reconsidered." *Aleph*, no. 2 (2002): 145–63.

Holt, Edwin B. Letter to Horace Kallen. April 20, 1915, manuscript collection 1, box 13, folder 13, Jacob Rader Marcus Center of the American Jewish Archives, Cincinnati.

———. Letter to Horace Kallen. February 28, 1918, manuscript collection 1, box 13, folder 13, Jacob Rader Marcus Center of the American Jewish Archives, Cincinnati.

Hook, Sidney, and Milton R. Konvitz, eds. *Freedom and Experience: Essays Presented to Horace M. Kallen*. Ithaca, NY: Cornell Univ. Press, 1947.

Howsam, Leslie. *Old Books and New Histories: An Orientation to Studies in Book and Print Culture.* Toronto: Univ. of Toronto Press, 2006.

Hurwitz, Henry. "The Menorah Movement." *Menorah Journal*, January 1915, 50–55.

———. Letter to Horace Kallen. November 22, 1915, manuscript collection 1, box 14, folder 1, Jacob Rader Marcus Center of the American Jewish Archives, Cincinnati.

Hutchinson, John. "Ethnicity and Modern Nations." *Ethnic and Racial Studies* 23, no. 4 (January 2000): 651–69. https://doi.org/10.1080/01419870050033667.

Intercollegiate Menorah Association. *The Menorah Movement: For the Study and Advancement of Jewish Culture and Ideals.* Ann Arbor, MI: Intercollegiate Menorah Association, 1914.

"Is There a Jewish Race?" *Jewish Exponent*, January 28, 1910.

Jacobs, Joseph. "Mendelism and the Jews." *American Hebrew and Jewish Messenger*, November 24, 1911.

———. "The Jewish Type, and Galton's Composite Photographs." *Photographic News*, April 24, 1885, 234–45.

James, William. "Great Men, Great Thoughts, and the Environment." *Atlantic Monthly*, October 1880.

———. *The Varieties of Religious Experience.* New York: Modern Library, 1929.

———. *The Varieties of Religious Experience: A Study in Human Nature.* New York: Longmans, Green, and Company, 1902.

Jewett, Andrew. *Science, Democracy, and the American University: From the Civil War to the Cold War.* New York: Cambridge Univ. Press, 2012.

"The Jewish Race." *American Israelite*, July 11, 1912.

"The Jewish Race Problem." *American Hebrew and Jewish Messenger*, February 9, 1912.

"Jews a 'Recessive' Race Type." *American Hebrew and Jewish Messenger*, November 18, 1910.

"The Jews: A Study of Race and Environment." *American Hebrew and Jewish Messenger*, September 21, 1906.

Johnson, Martyn. Letter to Horace Kallen. December 3, 1917, manuscript collection 1, box 15, folder 6, Jacob Rader Marcus Center of the American Jewish Archives, Cincinnati.

———. Letter to Horace M. Kallen. December 11, 1917, manuscript collection 1, box 15, folder 6, Jacob Rader Marcus Center of the American Jewish Archives, Cincinnati.

Joost, Nicholas. *Scofield Thayer and the Dial: An Illustrated History*. Carbondale: Southern Illinois Univ. Press, 1964.

———. "The Dial in Transition: The End of the Browne Family's Control, 1913–1916." *Journal of the Illinois State Historical Society* 59, no. 3 (1966): 272–89.

Kallen, Horace M. "'Americanization' and the Cultural Prospect." In *Culture and Democracy in the United States*, 118–224. New York: Boni & Liveright, 1924.

———. *Art and Freedom: Volume 1*. 2 vols. New York: Duell, Sloan and Pearce, 1942.

———. *Art and Freedom: Volume 2*. 2 vols. New York: Duell, Sloan and Pearce, 1942.

———. "Can Judaism Survive in the United States?" *Menorah Journal*, December 1925, 544–59.

———. "Cosmic Systems and Philosophical Imagination." *Dial*, February 3, 1916.

———. *Creativity, Imagination, Logic: Meditations for the Eleventh Hour*. New York: Gordon and Breach, 1973.

———. *Cultural Pluralism and the American Idea: An Essay in Social Philosophy*. Edited by Stanley H. Chapman. Philadelphia: Univ. of Philadelphia Press, 1956.

———. *Culture and Democracy in the United States*. New York: Arno Press, 1970.

———. *Culture and Democracy in the United States*. New Brunswick, NJ: Transaction Publishers, 1998.

———. *Culture and Democracy in the United States: Studies in the Group Psychology of the American Peoples*. New York: Boni & Liveright, 1924.

———. "Democracy versus the Melting Pot." In *Culture and Democracy in the United States*, 59–117. New Brunswick, NJ: Transaction Publishers, 1998.

———. "Democracy versus the Melting Pot: A Study of American Nationality." *Nation*, February 18, 1915.

———. "Democracy versus the Melting Pot: A Study of American Nationality." *Nation*, February 25, 1915.

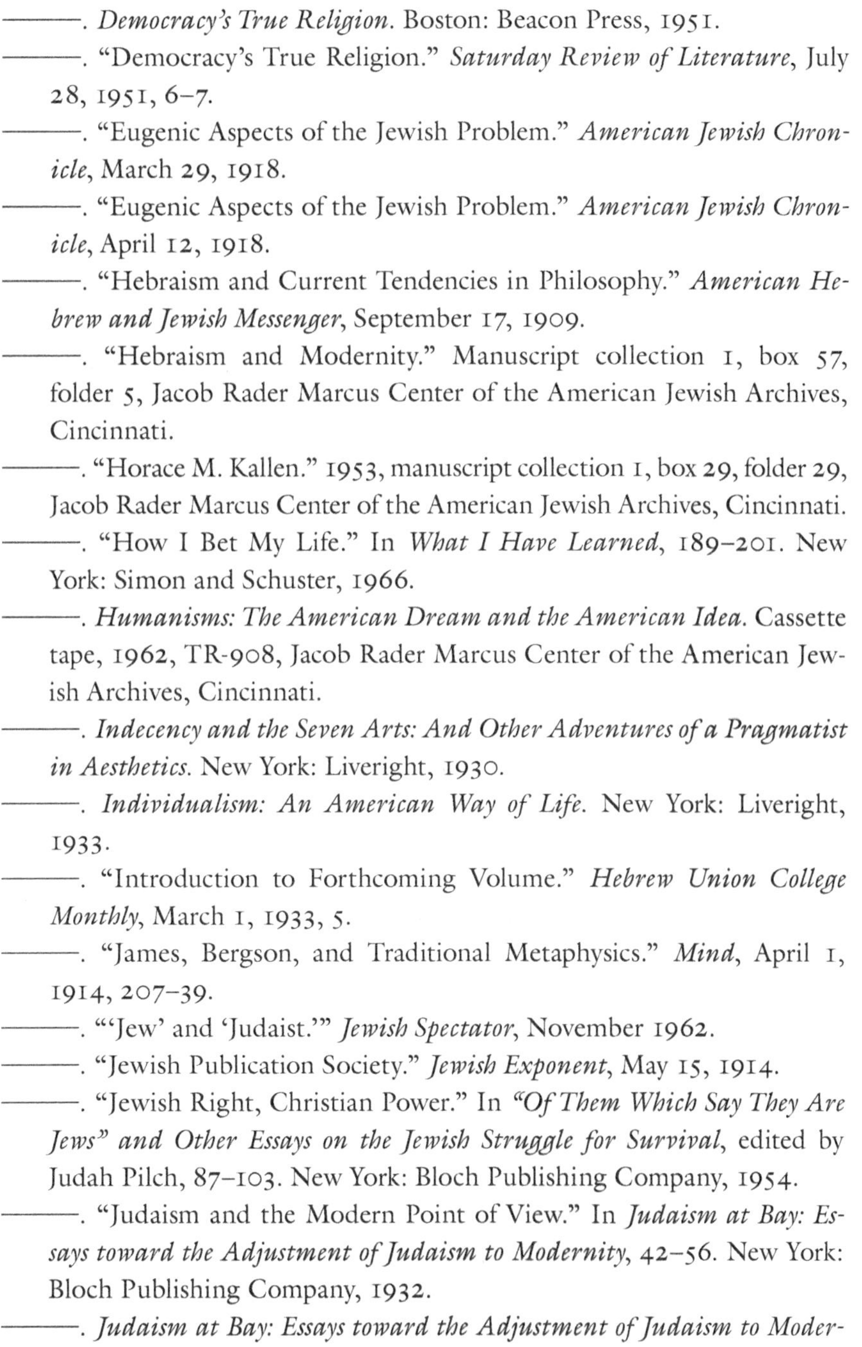

———. *Democracy's True Religion*. Boston: Beacon Press, 1951.

———. "Democracy's True Religion." *Saturday Review of Literature*, July 28, 1951, 6–7.

———. "Eugenic Aspects of the Jewish Problem." *American Jewish Chronicle*, March 29, 1918.

———. "Eugenic Aspects of the Jewish Problem." *American Jewish Chronicle*, April 12, 1918.

———. "Hebraism and Current Tendencies in Philosophy." *American Hebrew and Jewish Messenger*, September 17, 1909.

———. "Hebraism and Modernity." Manuscript collection 1, box 57, folder 5, Jacob Rader Marcus Center of the American Jewish Archives, Cincinnati.

———. "Horace M. Kallen." 1953, manuscript collection 1, box 29, folder 29, Jacob Rader Marcus Center of the American Jewish Archives, Cincinnati.

———. "How I Bet My Life." In *What I Have Learned*, 189–201. New York: Simon and Schuster, 1966.

———. *Humanisms: The American Dream and the American Idea*. Cassette tape, 1962, TR-908, Jacob Rader Marcus Center of the American Jewish Archives, Cincinnati.

———. *Indecency and the Seven Arts: And Other Adventures of a Pragmatist in Aesthetics*. New York: Liveright, 1930.

———. *Individualism: An American Way of Life*. New York: Liveright, 1933.

———. "Introduction to Forthcoming Volume." *Hebrew Union College Monthly*, March 1, 1933, 5.

———. "James, Bergson, and Traditional Metaphysics." *Mind*, April 1, 1914, 207–39.

———. "'Jew' and 'Judaist.'" *Jewish Spectator*, November 1962.

———. "Jewish Publication Society." *Jewish Exponent*, May 15, 1914.

———. "Jewish Right, Christian Power." In *"Of Them Which Say They Are Jews" and Other Essays on the Jewish Struggle for Survival*, edited by Judah Pilch, 87–103. New York: Bloch Publishing Company, 1954.

———. "Judaism and the Modern Point of View." In *Judaism at Bay: Essays toward the Adjustment of Judaism to Modernity*, 42–56. New York: Bloch Publishing Company, 1932.

———. *Judaism at Bay: Essays toward the Adjustment of Judaism to Modernity*. New York: Bloch Publishing Company, 1932.

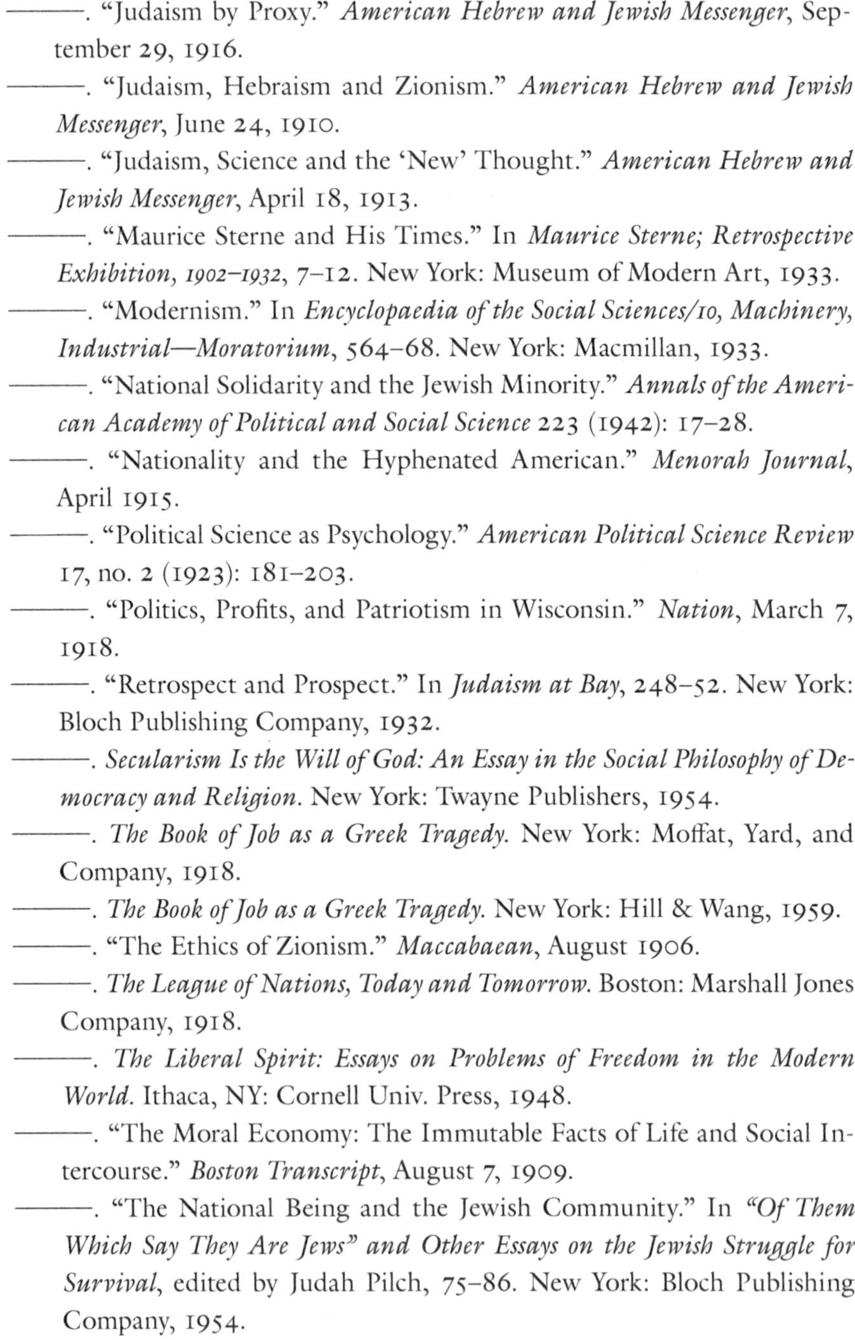

———. "Judaism by Proxy." *American Hebrew and Jewish Messenger*, September 29, 1916.

———. "Judaism, Hebraism and Zionism." *American Hebrew and Jewish Messenger*, June 24, 1910.

———. "Judaism, Science and the 'New' Thought." *American Hebrew and Jewish Messenger*, April 18, 1913.

———. "Maurice Sterne and His Times." In *Maurice Sterne; Retrospective Exhibition, 1902–1932*, 7–12. New York: Museum of Modern Art, 1933.

———. "Modernism." In *Encyclopaedia of the Social Sciences/10, Machinery, Industrial—Moratorium*, 564–68. New York: Macmillan, 1933.

———. "National Solidarity and the Jewish Minority." *Annals of the American Academy of Political and Social Science* 223 (1942): 17–28.

———. "Nationality and the Hyphenated American." *Menorah Journal*, April 1915.

———. "Political Science as Psychology." *American Political Science Review* 17, no. 2 (1923): 181–203.

———. "Politics, Profits, and Patriotism in Wisconsin." *Nation*, March 7, 1918.

———. "Retrospect and Prospect." In *Judaism at Bay*, 248–52. New York: Bloch Publishing Company, 1932.

———. *Secularism Is the Will of God: An Essay in the Social Philosophy of Democracy and Religion*. New York: Twayne Publishers, 1954.

———. *The Book of Job as a Greek Tragedy*. New York: Moffat, Yard, and Company, 1918.

———. *The Book of Job as a Greek Tragedy*. New York: Hill & Wang, 1959.

———. "The Ethics of Zionism." *Maccabaean*, August 1906.

———. *The League of Nations, Today and Tomorrow*. Boston: Marshall Jones Company, 1918.

———. *The Liberal Spirit: Essays on Problems of Freedom in the Modern World*. Ithaca, NY: Cornell Univ. Press, 1948.

———. "The Moral Economy: The Immutable Facts of Life and Social Intercourse." *Boston Transcript*, August 7, 1909.

———. "The National Being and the Jewish Community." In *"Of Them Which Say They Are Jews" and Other Essays on the Jewish Struggle for Survival*, edited by Judah Pilch, 75–86. New York: Bloch Publishing Company, 1954.

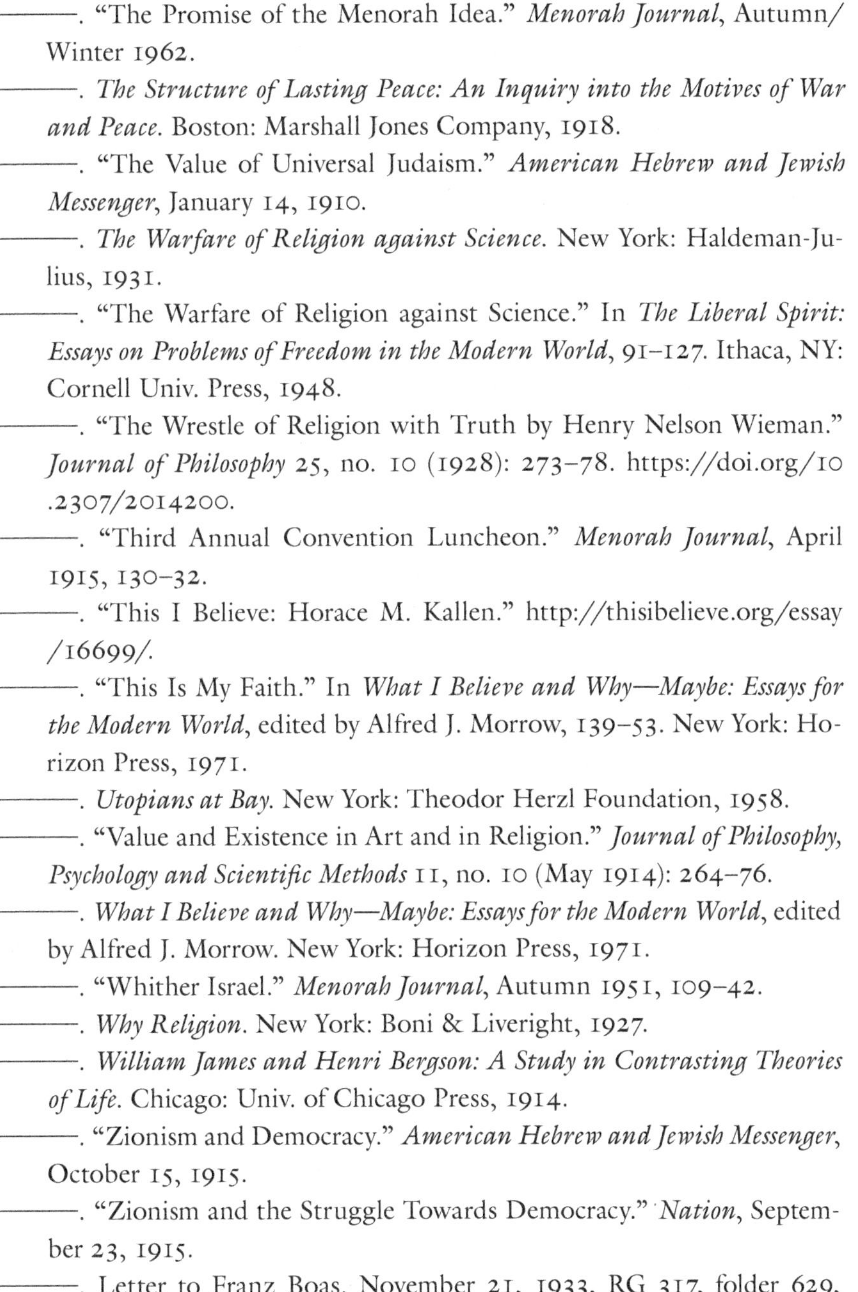

———. "The Promise of the Menorah Idea." *Menorah Journal*, Autumn/Winter 1962.

———. *The Structure of Lasting Peace: An Inquiry into the Motives of War and Peace*. Boston: Marshall Jones Company, 1918.

———. "The Value of Universal Judaism." *American Hebrew and Jewish Messenger*, January 14, 1910.

———. *The Warfare of Religion against Science*. New York: Haldeman-Julius, 1931.

———. "The Warfare of Religion against Science." In *The Liberal Spirit: Essays on Problems of Freedom in the Modern World*, 91–127. Ithaca, NY: Cornell Univ. Press, 1948.

———. "The Wrestle of Religion with Truth by Henry Nelson Wieman." *Journal of Philosophy* 25, no. 10 (1928): 273–78. https://doi.org/10.2307/2014200.

———. "Third Annual Convention Luncheon." *Menorah Journal*, April 1915, 130–32.

———. "This I Believe: Horace M. Kallen." http://thisibelieve.org/essay/16699/.

———. "This Is My Faith." In *What I Believe and Why—Maybe: Essays for the Modern World*, edited by Alfred J. Morrow, 139–53. New York: Horizon Press, 1971.

———. *Utopians at Bay*. New York: Theodor Herzl Foundation, 1958.

———. "Value and Existence in Art and in Religion." *Journal of Philosophy, Psychology and Scientific Methods* 11, no. 10 (May 1914): 264–76.

———. *What I Believe and Why—Maybe: Essays for the Modern World*, edited by Alfred J. Morrow. New York: Horizon Press, 1971.

———. "Whither Israel." *Menorah Journal*, Autumn 1951, 109–42.

———. *Why Religion*. New York: Boni & Liveright, 1927.

———. *William James and Henri Bergson: A Study in Contrasting Theories of Life*. Chicago: Univ. of Chicago Press, 1914.

———. "Zionism and Democracy." *American Hebrew and Jewish Messenger*, October 15, 1915.

———. "Zionism and the Struggle Towards Democracy." *Nation*, September 23, 1915.

———. Letter to Franz Boas. November 21, 1933, RG 317, folder 629, Horace Kallen Papers, YIVO Institute for Jewish Research, New York.

———. Letter to Pierre Loving. January 15, 1936, RG 317, folder 198, Horace Kallen Papers, YIVO Institute for Jewish Research, New York.
———. Letter to Anna Fisch. September 14, 1942, RG 317, folder 58B, Horace Kallen Papers, YIVO Institute for Jewish Research, New York.
———. Letter to Franklin D. Roosevelt. March 1, 1945, RG 317, folder 996, Horace Kallen Papers, YIVO Institute for Jewish Research, New York.
———. Letter to T. S. Eliot. May 6, 1955, NS.02.15.01, box 2, folder 25, Horace M. Kallen research files, New School Archives and Special Collections, New York.
———. Interview by John Irving. Cassette tape, n.d., TR-922 and TR-923, Jacob Rader Marcus Center of the American Jewish Archives, Cincinnati.
———. Letter to Henry Hurwitz. October 27, 1913, manuscript collection 2, box 23, folder 1, Jacob Rader Marcus Center of the American Jewish Archives, Cincinnati.
———. Letter to Henry Hurwitz. 1915, manuscript collection 2, box 23, folder 1, Jacob Rader Marcus Center of the American Jewish Archives, Cincinnati.
———. Letter to Julian Mack. January 19, 1915, manuscript collection 1, box 20, folder 10, Jacob Rader Marcus Center of the American Jewish Archives, Cincinnati.
———. Letter to Henry Hurwitz. July 26, 1916, manuscript collection 1, box 14, folder 1, Jacob Rader Marcus Center of the American Jewish Archives, Cincinnati.
———. Letter to Henry Hurwitz. March 2, 1917, manuscript collection 1, box 14, folder 1, Jacob Rader Marcus Center of the American Jewish Archives, Cincinnati.
———. Letter to Martyn Johnson. December 13, 1917, manuscript collection 1, box 15, folder 6, Jacob Rader Marcus Center of the American Jewish Archives, Cincinnati.
———. Letter to George Donlin. January 11, 1918, manuscript collection 1, box 7, folder 18, Jacob Rader Marcus Center of the American Jewish Archives, Cincinnati.
———. Letter to Martyn Johnson. January 24, 1918, manuscript collection 1, box 15, folder 6, Jacob Rader Marcus Center of the American Jewish Archives, Cincinnati.

———. Letter to Jacob Billikopf. March 5, 1918, manuscript collection 13, box 13, folder 12, Jacob Rader Marcus Center of the American Jewish Archives, Cincinnati.

———. Letter to George Donlin. March 18, 1918, manuscript collection 1, box 7, folder 18, Jacob Rader Marcus Center of the American Jewish Archives, Cincinnati.

———. Letter to Edwin Holt. April 9, 1918, manuscript collection 1, box 13, folder 13, Jacob Rader Marcus Center of the American Jewish Archives, Cincinnati.

———. Letter to George Donlin. December 2, 1918, manuscript collection 1, box 7, folder 18, Jacob Rader Marcus Center of the American Jewish Archives, Cincinnati.

———. Letter to Rachel Jastrow. February 28, 1919, manuscript collection 1, box 14, folder 20, Jacob Rader Marcus Center of the American Jewish Archives, Cincinnati.

———. Letter to Amelia Defries. June 8, 1920, manuscript collection 1, box 7, folder 11, Jacob Rader Marcus Center of the American Jewish Archives, Cincinnati.

———. Letter to B. W. Huebsch. October 28, 1922, RG 317, folder 722, Horace Kallen Papers, YIVO Institute for Jewish Research, New York.

———. Letter to Lincoln MacVeagh. October 15, 1923, RG 317, folder 221, Horace Kallen Papers, YIVO Institute for Jewish Research, New York.

———. Letter to Manuel Komroff. December 11, 1923, RG 317, folder 59, Horace Kallen Papers, YIVO Institute for Jewish Research, New York.

———. Letter to Abraham Cronbach. December 22, 1927, manuscript collection 9, box 2, folder 27, Jacob Rader Marcus Center of the American Jewish Archives, Cincinnati.

———. Letter to Abraham Cronbach. January 4, 1928, manuscript collection 9, box 2, folder 27, Jacob Rader Marcus Center of the American Jewish Archives, Cincinnati.

———. Letter to Martin Weitz. June 3, 1932, manuscript collection 1, box 51, folder 4, Jacob Rader Marcus Center of the American Jewish Archives, Cincinnati.

———. Letter to Van Meter Ames. April 27, 1943, manuscript collection 1, box 1, folder 15, Jacob Rader Marcus Center of the American Jewish Archives, Cincinnati.

———. Letter to T. S. Eliot. December 23, 1954, manuscript collection 1, box 8, folder 26, Jacob Rader Marcus Center of the American Jewish Archives, Cincinnati.

———. Letter to Arthur Wang. June 9, 1959, manuscript collection 1, box 13, folder 7, Jacob Rader Marcus Center of the American Jewish Archives, Cincinnati.

———. Untitled. Horace M. Kallen research files, NS.02.15.01, box 1, folder 18, New School Archives and Special Collections, New York.

Katznelson, Ira. *Fear Itself: The New Deal and the Origins of Our Time.* New York: Liveright, 2014.

Kaufman, Matthew. "Horace M. Kallen's Use of Evolutionary Theory in Support of American Jews and Democracy." *Zygon: Journal of Religion and Science* 52, no. 4 (December 2017): 922–42.

Keith, Bruce. "The Foundations of an American Discipline: Edward A. Ross at the University of Nebraska, 1901–1906." *Mid-American Review of Sociology* 13, no. 2 (1988): 43–56.

Klautke, Egbert. *The Mind of the Nation: Völkerpsychologie in Germany, 1851–1955*. New York: Berghahn Books, 2013.

Kohler, Kaufmann. "Third Annual Convention Luncheon." *Menorah Journal*, April 1915, 128–29.

Komroff, Manuel. Letter to Horace M. Kallen. November 10, 1923, RG 317, folder 59, Horace Kallen Papers, YIVO Institute for Jewish Research, New York.

Konvitz, Milton R. "Horace M. Kallen." In *The "Other" New York Intellectuals*, edited by Carole S. Kessner, 144–59. New York: NYU Press, 1994.

———. "In Praise of Hyphenation and Orchestration." In *The Legacy of Horace M. Kallen*, 15–35. Rutherford, NJ: Fairleigh Dickinson Univ. Press, 1987.

Korelitz, Seth. "The Menorah Idea: From Religion to Culture, from Race to Ethnicity." *American Jewish History* 85 (1997): 75–100.

Kotzin, Daniel P. *Judah L. Magnes: An American Jewish Nonconformist.* Vol 1. Syracuse, NY: Syracuse Univ. Press, 2010.

Kroeber, Alfred L. "Are the Jews a Race?" *Menorah Journal*, December 1917, 290–94.

Krupnick, Mark. "The Menorah Journal Group and the Origins of Modern Jewish-American Radicalism." *Studies in American Jewish Literature* 5, no. 2 (1979): 56–67.

Larrimore, Mark. *The Book of Job: A Biography*. Princeton, NJ: Princeton Univ. Press, 2013.

Latham, H. S. Letter to Herbert Croly. October 23, 1922, RG 317, folder 269, Horace Kallen Papers, YIVO Institute for Jewish Research, New York.

Leonard, Miriam. *Socrates and the Jews: Hellenism and Hebraism from Moses Mendelssohn to Sigmund Freud*. Chicago: Univ. of Chicago Press, 2012.

Liebman, Joshua Loth. *Peace of Mind*. New York: Simon & Schuster, 1946.

Lightman, Bernard. "Spencer's American Disciples: Fiske, Youmans, and the Appropriation of the System." In *Global Spencerism: The Communication and Appropriation of a British Evolutionist*, edited by Bernard Lightman, 123–48. Leiden, Netherlands: Brill, 2016.

Lippmann, Walter. "The Mental Age of Americans." *New Republic*, October 25, 1922.

Lipsky, Abram. "Are the Jews a Pure Race?" *American Hebrew and Jewish Messenger*, July 12, 1912.

Liveright, Horace. Letter to Horace M. Kallen. April 5, 1924, RG 317, folder 59, Horace Kallen Papers, YIVO Institute for Jewish Research, New York.

———. Letter to Horace M. Kallen. June 18, 1930, RG 317, folder 268, Horace Kallen Papers, YIVO Institute for Jewish Research, New York.

Luker, Ralph E. "Wieman, Henry Nelson." *American National Biography Online*. http://www.anb.org/articles/08/08-01908.html.

MacLeish, Archibald. *J. B.: A Play in Verse*. Boston: Houghton Mifflin, 1958.

Macpherson, Hector. *Herbert Spencer: The Man and His Work*. London: Chapman and Hall, 1900.

Macrae, John. Letter to Horace M. Kallen. August 4, 1922, RG 317, folder 160, Horace Kallen Papers, YIVO Institute for Jewish Research, New York.

Madison, Charles A. *Jewish Publishing in America: The Impact of Jewish Writing on American Culture*. New York: Sanhedrin Press, 1976.

Marsden, George M. *The Twilight of the American Enlightenment: The 1950s and the Crisis of Liberal Belief*. New York: Basic Books, 2014.

Mason, Alpheus T. *Brandeis: A Free Man's Life*. New York: Viking, 1956.

Matthews, Brander. "Making America a Racial Crazy-Quilt." *Literary Digest International Book Review*, August 1924.

Matthews, Fred. *Quest for an American Sociology: Robert E. Park and the Chicago School.* Montreal: McGill-Queen's Univ. Press, 1977.

Meador, Keith G. "'My Own Salvation': The Christian Century and Psychology's Secularizing of American Protestantism." In *The Secular Revolution: Power, Interests, and Conflict in the Secularization of American Public Life*, edited by Christian Smith, 269–309. Berkeley: Univ. of California Press, 2003.

Meyer, Michael A. *Response to Modernity: A History of the Reform Movement in Judaism.* New York: Oxford Univ. Press, 1988.

Montefiore, Claude G. "Book Reviews." *Harvard Theological Review* 12, no. 2 (April 1919): 219–24.

———. *Liberal Judaism and Hellenism.* London: Macmillan, 1918.

Moore, James R. *The Post-Darwinian Controversies: A Study of the Protestant Struggle to Come to Terms with Darwin in Great Britain and America 1870–1900.* Cambridge: Cambridge Univ. Press, 1979.

Morris-Reich, Amos. *The Quest for Jewish Assimilation in Modern Social Science.* London: Routledge, 2008.

Munro, W. B., and A. C. Hanford, eds. "Book Reviews." *American Political Science Review* 19, no. 2 (May 1925): 395–99.

Murray, Gilbert. "Job as a Greek Tragedy." *Menorah Journal*, April 1919, 93–96.

Murrow, Edward R. "Introduction to the Original This I Believe." http://thisibelieve.org/essay/16844/.

Musher, Sharon Ann. *Democratic Art: The New Deal's Influence on American Culture.* Chicago: Univ. of Chicago Press, 2015.

Myers, Charles S. "Is There a Jewish Race?" *American Hebrew and Jewish Messenger*, August 4, 1911.

"The 'Nation's' Jubilee." *Nation*, July 8, 1915.

"No Jewish Race." *American Israelite*, March 27, 1913.

O'Brien, John. "Book Review." *Journal of Social Forces* 2, no. 5 (November 1924): 781–82.

Office of Public Relations, HUC-JIR. Letter to Horace Kallen. March 15, 1965, manuscript collection 1, box 13, folder 1, Jacob Rader Marcus Center of the American Jewish Archives, Cincinnati.

Oja, Carol J. "Gershwin and American Modernists of the 1920s." *Musical Quarterly* 78, no. 4 (Winter 1994): 646–68.

Omer, Ranen. "'It Is I Who Have Been Defending a Religion Called Judaism': The T. S. Eliot and Horace M. Kallen Correspondence." *Texas Studies in Literature and Language* 39, no. 4 (1997): 321–56.

Omer-Sherman, Ranen. "Rethinking Eliot, Jewish Identity, and Cultural Pluralism." *Modernism/Modernity* 10, no. 3 (2003): 439–45.

———. "'Thy People Are My People': Emma Lazarus, Daniel Deronda, and the Ambivalence of Jewish Modernity." *Journal of Modern Jewish Studies* 1, no. 1 (2002): 49–72. https://doi.org/10.1080/1472588011 0120433.

"The Outlook's Opinion." *Outlook*, January 5, 1916.

Palmer, W. P. *Emanuel Haldeman-Julius and the Education of the Poor of America*. Distributed by ERIC Clearinghouse, 2006. https://eric.ed .gov/?id=ED500899.

Paul, Diane. *Controlling Human Heredity: 1865 to the Present*. Atlantic Highlands, NJ: Humanities Press, 1995.

Paul, Diane B. "Darwin, Social Darwinism and Eugenics." In *The Cambridge Companion to Darwin*, edited by Jonathan Hodge and Gregory Radick, 214–39. Cambridge: Cambridge Univ. Press, 2003.

Pearson, Karl. Letter to Horace Kallen. January 6, 1908, manuscript collection 1, box 24, folder 23, Jacob Rader Marcus Center of the American Jewish Archives, Cincinnati.

Perloff, Marjorie. "A Response to Ronald Schuchard." *Modernism/Modernity* 10, no. 1 (January 2003): 51–56.

Perry, Ralph Barton. *The Moral Economy*. New York: Charles Scribner's Sons, 1909.

"Persons Talked about." *American Hebrew and Jewish Messenger*, August 4, 1911.

Pianko, Noam. "'The True Liberalism of Zionism': Horace Kallen, Jewish Nationalism, and the Limits of American Pluralism." *American Jewish History* 94, no. 4 (December 2008): 299–329.

———. *Zionism and the Roads Not Taken*. Bloomington: Indiana Univ. Press, 2010.

Pinsker, Leon. *Auto-Emancipation*. New York: Maccabaean, 1906. //catalog .hathitrust.org/Record/100537418.

Pollack, Howard. *George Gershwin: His Life and Work*. Berkeley: Univ. of California Press, 2007.

———. "The Politics of Recognition." In *Multiculturalism : Examining the Politics of Recognition*, edited by Amy Gutmann, 25–73. Princeton, NJ: Princeton Univ. Press, 1994.

Putnam, Hilary. "God and the Philosophers." *Midwest Studies in Philosophy* 21, no. 1 (1997): 175–87. https://doi.org/10.1111/j.1475-4975.1997.tb00522.x.

"The Question of Race." *Jewish Exponent*, February 4, 1910.

"Race and Environment." *American Hebrew and Jewish Messenger*, October 27, 1911.

Radin, Max. "A Mistaken Hypothesis." *Menorah Journal*, April 1919, 97–103.

Raisin, Max. "On 'Universal Judaism.'" *American Hebrew and Jewish Messenger*, February 11, 1910.

Reichler, Rabbi Max. *Jewish Eugenics: A Paper Read before the New York Board of Jewish Ministers.* New York: Bloch Publishing Company, 1916.

Reisch, George. *How The Cold War Transformed Philosophy of Science: To the Icy Slopes of Logic.* Cambridge: Cambridge Univ. Press, 2005.

Ripley, William Z. *The Races of Europe: A Sociological Study.* London: Kegan Paul, Trench, Trubner & Company, 1899.

Roosevelt, Nicholas. "Professor Kallen Proposes to Balkanize America: A Democracy of Nationalities to Solve Our Racial Problems." *New York Times*, April 20, 1924.

Rorty, Richard. *Objectivity, Relativism, and Truth: Philosophical Papers.* Vol. 1. Cambridge: Cambridge Univ. Press, 1999.

Rosen, Christine. *Preaching Eugenics: Religious Leaders and the American Eugenics Movement.* Oxford: Oxford Univ. Press, 2004.

Ross, Edward Alsworth. *The Old World in the New: The Significance of Past and Present Immigration to the American People.* New York: Century Company, 1914.

Russak, Ben. Letter to Horace M. Kallen. July 2, 1937, RG 317, folder 65, Horace Kallen Papers, YIVO Institute for Jewish Research, New York.

———. Letter to Horace M. Kallen. September 4, 1937, RG 317, folder 65, Horace Kallen Papers, YIVO Institute for Jewish Research, New York.

Russell, Bertrand. "Americanization." *Dial*, August 1924.

———. *New Hopes for a Changing World.* New York: Simon & Schuster, 1951.

Rutkoff, Peter M., and William B. Scott. *New School: A History of the New School for Social Research.* New York: Free Press, 1986.

Santayana, George, and William G. Holzberger. *The Letters of George Santayana: Volume 4*. 8 vols. Cambridge, MA: MIT Press, 2003.

Santon, E. F. Letter to Horace M. Kallen. September 30, 1922, RG 317, folder 160, Horace Kallen Papers, YIVO Institute for Jewish Research, New York.

Sarna, Jonathan. "The American Jewish Press." In *The Oxford Handbook of Religion and the American News Media*, edited by Diane Winston, 538–48. New York: Oxford Univ. Press, 2012.

———. "Two Ambitious Goals: Jewish Publishing in the United States." In *Print in Motion: The Expansion of Publishing and Reading in the United States, 1880–1940*, edited by Carl F. Kaestle and Janice A. Radway, 376–91. Chapel Hill: Univ. of North Carolina Press, 2009.

Schmidt, Nathaniel. *The Messages of the Poets: The Books of Job and Canticles and Some Minor Poems in the Old Testament, with Introductions, Metrical Translations, and Paraphrases*. Vol. 7. New York: Charles Scribner's Sons, 1911.

———. Letter to Horace Kallen. October 25, 1911, manuscript collection 1, box 27, folder 1, Jacob Rader Marcus Center of the American Jewish Archives, Cincinnati.

Schmidt, Sarah. "Horace M. Kallen: The Zionist Chapter." In *The Legacy of Horace M. Kallen*, edited by Milton R. Konvitz, 76–89. Rutherford, NJ : Fairleigh Dickinson Univ. Press, 1987.

———. "The Zionist Conversion of Louis D. Brandeis." *Jewish Social Studies* 37, no. 1 (Winter 1975): 18–34.

Schmidt, Sarah L. "Horace M. Kallen and the 'Americanization' of Zionism—In Memoriam." *American Jewish Archives Journal* 28, no. 1 (1976): 59–73.

———. *Horace M. Kallen: Prophet of American Zionism*. Brooklyn: Carlson Publishing, 1995.

Schoenbach, Lisi. *Pragmatic Modernism*. Oxford: Oxford Univ. Press, 2012.

Schuchard, Ronald. "Burbank with a Baedeker, Eliot with a Cigar: American Intellectuals, Anti-Semitism, and the Idea of Culture." *Modernism/Modernity* 10, no. 1 (January 2003): 1–26.

Schulman, Samuel. "A Last Word on the Rabbinical Conference." *American Hebrew and Jewish Messenger*, February 25, 1910.

———. "Why American Jews Consider Zionism Undesirable." *Outlook*, January 5, 1916.

Shore, Marlene. *The Science of Social Redemption: McGill, the Chicago School, and the Origins of Social Research in Canada.* Toronto: Univ. of Toronto Press, 1987.

Silver, Abba Hillel. "Why Do the Heathen Rage?" In *Therefore Choose Life: Selected Sermons, Addresses, and Writings of Abba Hillel Silver*, edited by Herbert Weiner, 1:364–87. Cleveland: World Publishing, 1967.

Simon, Leon. "Religion and Nationality." *Menorah Journal*, June 1919, 154, 226–33.

Simpson, George Gaylord. "The Baldwin Effect." *Evolution*, no. 7 (June 1953): 110–17.

Slavet, Eliza. "Freud's Theory of Jewishness: For Better and for Worse." In *The Jewish World of Sigmund Freud: Essays on Cultural Roots and the Problem of Religious Identity*, edited by Arnold D. Richards, 96–111. Jefferson, NC: McFarland, 2010.

Sluga, Glenda. *The Nation, Psychology, and International Politics, 1870–1919.* Basingstoke, UK: Palgrave Macmillan, 2006.

Smertenko, Johan J. "A Course Charted." *Nation*, August 6, 1924.

Smith, Anthony D. *The Ethnic Origins of Nations.* Oxford: Basil Blackwell, 1987.

Sollors, Werner. "A Critique of Pure Pluralism." In *Reconstructing American Literary History*, edited by Sacvan Bercovitch, 250–79. Cambridge, MA: Harvard Univ. Press, 1986.

———. *Beyond Ethnicity: Consent and Descent in American Culture.* Oxford: Oxford Univ. Press, 1986.

———, ed. *The Invention of Ethnicity.* New York: Oxford Univ. Press, 1989.

———, ed. *Theories of Ethnicity: A Classical Reader.* New York: NYU Press, 1996.

Soltes, Mordecai. "The Yiddish Press: An Americanizing Agency." In *American Jewish Yearbook*, 26:165–372. Philadelphia: Jewish Publication Society of America, 1924.

Spencer, Herbert. *The Principles of Psychology.* London: Longmans, Green, and Company, 1855.

Sulloway, Frank J. Freud, *Biologist of the Mind: Beyond the Psychoanalytic Legend.* New York: Basic Books, 1979.

Taylor, Charles. *A Secular Age.* Cambridge, MA: Harvard Univ. Press, 2007.

"There Is No Jewish Race!" *Maccabaean*, 1910.

"Three American Philosophers Exploring Rome in Motor Car." Manuscript collection 1, box 62, folder 7, Jacob Rader Marcus Center of the American Jewish Archives, Cincinnati.

Toch, Ernst. Letter to Ben Russak. July 17, 1937, RG 317, folder 65, Horace Kallen Papers, YIVO Institute for Jewish Research, New York.

"To Stage 'Book of Job.'" *New York Times*, December 24, 1913.

Toll, William. "Ethnicity and Freedom in the Philosophy of Horace M. Kallen." In *The Jews of North America*, edited by Moses Rischin, 153–68. Detroit: Wayne State Univ. Press, 1987.

———. "Horace M. Kallen: Pluralism and American Jewish Identity." *American Jewish History* 85, no. 1 (March 1997): 57–74.

Trilling, Lionel. *Sincerity and Authenticity.* Oxford: Oxford Univ. Press, 1974.

Turner, Jonathan H. "Herbert Spencer's Sociological Legacy." In *Herbert Spencer: Legacies*, edited by Mark Francis and Michael Taylor, 60–88. London: Routledge, 2015.

"Unity—April 2, 1934." Manuscript collection 1, box 77, folder 5, Jacob Rader Marcus Center of the American Jewish Archives, Cincinnati.

US State Department. "Milestones: 1921–1936—Office of the Historian." https://history.state.gov/milestones/1921-1936/immigration-act.

Veblen, Thorstein. "The Intellectual Preeminence of Jews in Modern Europe." *Political Science Quarterly*, no. 29 (1919): 33–42.

Vizetelly, Frank H. "The American Hebrew." http://www.jewishencyclopedia.com/articles/1387-american-hebrew-the.

Walker, Stuart. "The Book of Job on the Stage." *Menorah Journal*, April 1919, 104–8.

Weinberg, Julius. *Edward Alsworth Ross and the Sociology of Progressivism.* Madison: State Historical Society of Wisconsin, 1972.

Weindling, Paul. "The Evolution of Jewish Identity: Ignaz Zollschan between Jewish and Aryan Race Theories, 1910–1945." In *Jewish Tradition and the Challenge of Darwinism*, edited by Geoffrey Cantor and Marc Swetlitz, 116–36. Chicago: Univ. of Chicago Press, 2006.

Weinfeld, David. "What Difference Does the Difference Make? Horace Kallen, Alain Locke, and the Development of Cultural Pluralism in America." PhD diss., New York University, 2014.

Weitz, Martin. Letter to Horace Kallen. June 14, 1932, manuscript collection 1, box 51, folder 4, Jacob Rader Marcus Center of the American Jewish Archives, Cincinnati.

———. Letter to Horace Kallen. April 3, 1933, manuscript collection 1, box 51, folder 4, Jacob Rader Marcus Center of the American Jewish Archives, Cincinnati.

Westbrook, Robert B. *John Dewey and American Democracy.* Ithaca, NY: Cornell Univ. Press, 1991.

"What Is the Menorah Movement?" *Menorah Journal* 2 (1916): v–viii.

Wheelock, Ward. Letter to Horace Kallen. April 14, 1953, manuscript collection 1, box 29, folder 29, Jacob Rader Marcus Center of the American Jewish Archives, Cincinnati.

White, Andrew Dickson. *A History of the Warfare of Science with Theology in Christendom.* New York: D. Appleton & Company, 1896.

Wieman, Henry Nelson. *The Wrestle of Religion with Truth.* New York: Macmillan, 1927.

Wilson, Woodrow. Letter to Horace Kallen. September 30, 1918, manuscript collection 1, box 31, folder 16, Jacob Rader Marcus Center of the American Jewish Archives, Cincinnati.

Winston, Andrew S. Letter to Matthew Kaufman. March 18, 2017.

Wisconsin Dramatic Society. "The Rise of the Curtain." *Play-Book*, April 1913.

Wolfson, Harry. Letter to Horace Kallen. March 17, 1918, manuscript collection 1, box 32, folder 4, Jacob Rader Marcus Center of the American Jewish Archives, Cincinnati.

Wolin, Ross. *The Rhetorical Imagination of Kenneth Burke.* Columbia: Univ. of South Carolina Press, 2001.

Wundt, Wilhelm. *Elemente Der Völkerpsychologie.* Leipzig: Kröner, 1912.

Young, Robert J. C. *Colonial Desire: Hybridity in Theory, Culture and Race.* London: Routledge, 2005. http://kcl.eblib.com/patron/FullRecord.aspx?p=237245.

Zimmern, Alfred E. "Nationality in the Modern World." *Menorah Journal*, August 1918, 205–13.

◆ ◆ ◆

Index

Matthew J. Kaufman received a PhD in Humanities from York University in Toronto and is a Reconstructionist rabbi. He has served Reconstructionist, Reform, and Conservative Jewish communities in the United States and Canada for over twenty years.